A Life Well Lived

The official autobiography
of
Richard Digance

This book is dedicated to the many people I met along the way, those who made my dreams come true and some who turned out to be a nightmare. It's all a part of life's great tapestry.

With love and affection to my two daughters, Polly and Rosie, my grandchildren Izzy and Ellie and son-in-law David

You are about to read the life story of a man who committed his life to entertainment.

Richard Digance is a BAFTA Nominated entertainer and musician, a Gold Award recipient from The British Academy of Composers and Songwriters and an award-winning composer of radio documentaries. He's also a published author and second-rate artist.

That's the official description out of the way so now you are invited to sit back and read his real story at your leisure. It's a life that began in the most unexciting of fashions in the East End of London, a life that changed a rubbish schoolkid who never did his homework into a wordsmith and composer with numerous awards to show for his desire to find a better, more fulfilling life.

Once Upon a time
In the East End side of London
A man set out to climb
The biggest mountain in the world
They say he had a dream
That someday he'd be someone
One day he had a dream
And they say that dreams come true

There's a man I used to know
Who lived on the edge of nowhere
There's a man I used to know
But he's not there anymore
He was never teacher's pet
They said he must try harder
Try harder to turn up
And to stay awake in school

But there were better things to do
Like absolutely nothing
So that's exactly what he did
And he did nothing really well
Jobs we hard to find
Because he wasn't really looking
He never looked behind him
There wasn't much to see
But from that dead end street
He climbed that biggest mountain

Contents

The Introduction

Hello, so here we go with what I consider to be a life well lived. I've been around a long time, a very long time thankfully, so there's lots to write about and share with you. So, welcome to my life, a life very well lived. What I've done over the years can be stated in this book as factual or as a near as dammit estimation. Roll both those things together and it is clear how much of my life has been taken up with performance and writing in an industry I have loved so much. In actual fact, I have worked within not one but two industries, show-business and music. I'll try to break it all down and show you what I mean and I think you'll see a remarkable difference between the two.

The next couple of pages are utterly boring and written to get my brain into gear. Unless you are one for facts and figures I suggest you don't waste your time reading this, but move straight on to Chapter One.

Fact; 55 years of performance and storytelling in 21 countries around the world. Can I name the countries?

Great Britain, The United States of America, Australia, Canada, Germany, The Falkland Islands, Indonesia, Belgium, France, Norway, Sweden, Morocco, Austria, Thailand, Hong Kong, Belize, Ascension Island, Cyprus, The United Emirates, Switzerland and Spain.

Fact; 42 albums recorded, comprising of nearly 500 self-written songs since 1968. Can I list the albums? I very much doubt it but I'll have a go.

1. Pisces
2. Homework
3. England's Green & Pleasant Land
4. How The West Was Lost
5. Treading The Boards
6. In Concert, Transatlantic
7. Commercial Road
8. Live at The Queen Elizabeth Hall
9. A Digance Indulgence
10. Live at the Fairfield Halls
11. Water Under The Bridge
12. Drag Queen Blues -American release on Mercury
13. In Conversation
14. In More Conversation
15. Guitar Tunes
16. Latest
17. Richard Digance-Serious Songs
18. Richard Digance – Funny Songs
19. Richard Digance Anthology
20. Finishing Tape
21. Back On Song
22. Compilation
23. The New Richard Digance
24. A Varied Selection
25. This Is Great Britain
26. Searching
27. 45rpm
28. Golden Anniversary
29. Toast of Christmas Past

Yay, against the odds I did it.

Fact; 2,700 published songs and soundtracks used for live shows, albums, documentaries, TV and radio appearances for over half a Century. No, I'm not going to name them but still a fact that led to my BAFTA Nomination and my Gold Award from The British Academy of Composers and Songwriters in 2003, something I am remarkably proud of.

Accurate estimation; nearly 5,000 shows comprising of some 60,000 songs sung, not all different of course and many not in tune.

Accurate estimation; 750,000 miles to shows and the same to return home, totalling one and a half million miles on the road, to say nothing of air miles or leagues of ocean covered through my work as a cruise entertainer.

Accurate estimation; Including big festivals, theatres, cruises and anywhere else that would book me, I have performed to well over 6 million people, to say nothing of the 3 million I performed to as a support act to some of the biggest names in the music and show business industries. As a corporate entertainer I have performed for over 70 companies at conferences and business gatherings.

Fact; 11 years of my own TV Specials with an average of 5.20 million viewers per show. Mind you, there were only 3 channels then and not 650, but in my defence people still had the option to switch over.

Fact; Over 500 published poems, but that's a rough estimation as I wouldn't know how to count them, let alone list them all in rhyme.

Fact; I have played guitar with Status Quo, The Moody Blues, Suzie Quatro, Juan Martin, Elkie Brooks, Brian May of Queen and numerous solo performers on my London Weekend TV series of specials.

Accurate estimation; If you roll all the recording hours into one, then I reckon I have spent nearly five years of my life in a recording studio, to say nothing of the countless hours in TV studios, including approaching 200 appearances on Channel 4s Countdown, one of only two guests to have appeared with all the different presenters of the programme since it began.

Fact; I have ghost-written autobiographies for four household-name celebrities including much-loved football pundit and close friend Chris Kamara and more after-dinner speeches than I care to recall, though special mention should be given to George Best.

Fact; I have written celebration rhymes for nearly 100 published greetings cards for Carte Blanche Greetings Cards and for Clintons Cards.

Fact; My Animal Alphabet books are used around the world as English Teaching Aids as follows;

Fearon Teacher Aids Series, Grades 4-6, Illinois, USA

Canadian Ministry of Education-The British Columbia Foundation Skills Assessment, Vancouver Canada

Oxford University Press Anthology of Verse, book 5

The New Comprehensive Strategies 1-5, Book 3, The West Indies

People For The Ethical Treatment of Animals (PETA) Foundation, London

The Animal Alphabet, BBC series

Western Australia Learning Aids

New Language For Learners, Form 1, Swaziland

April 2015- The English Genie Course, book 6, India

Fact; 24 books published.

1. Animal Alphabet
2. Another Animal Alphabet
3. The Richard Digance Songbook
4. Backwater
5. Run Out In The Country
6. Wealth of Comedy
7. Today Chardock Tomorrow The World
8. A History of Aston Villa
9. My Poems
10. Remembers and Rhymes
11. Richard Digance Rhymes
12. How To Get Rich On a Fiver
13. My Thoughts
14. My Words
15. 365 Daily Rhymes
16. The Complete Works
17. Father Christmas's Journey
18. My 100 Strangest Shows
19. Murder Mystery
20. Football Is About To Burst
21. Four Months Lost
22. You Should Have Been There
23. The Gig
24. A Life Well Lived

Accurate estimation; I think I have sold approximately 140 paintings through my exhibitions around Britain and I managed to hide the numbers underneath the paint.
Fact; In 2000 I made my one and only film appearance, as a London taxi driver, in One Step Beyond, directed by Clare Gilbert.
Fact; TV and radio ads and jingles too numerous to list I'm afraid but I would guess at a few hundred.
Fact; I composed and recorded for Bill Bryson's audio book adaption of The Road To Little Dribbling, 4 songs and 38 soundtrack instrumentals.

So just maybe, and I admit I'm not sure myself, I had some sort of rough idea of what I was doing. Yet there was no hint of this happening when I left school with just 4 'O' levels and no idea what I was going to do for a job. In all fairness to me I did warn you that those lists would be boring. Please allow me now to tell you the unabridged story of my private life and my life entertaining and hopefully you will find it far more entertaining than previous pages. Hey, if you've got it, flaunt it.

Let me also tell you it's the one job you really can't cheat at. You're either up for the challenge and the sacrifices you have to make in your life or you get out and do something less demanding, something simpler with a regular wage going into your bank. I've never met a musician in my life who had an easy run without hurdles to fall over, not a single one. It all depended upon how many times you were prepared to run around the running track as the hurdles got ever higher. It went with the apprenticeship, even though so many fell at the first fence. Musicians have suffered more bruises than a professional boxer, yet they still get up and want more. A musician, yes, but I could never have been a professional boxer, count me out, boom boom.

I must admit I didn't do too well when it all began either. I had no money and a modicum of talent, yet I had tons of desire, along with a few extra tons of hope thrown in for good measure.

This is a testament that if you keep at it things may turn out in your favour, even in your darkest moments, against all the odds. It seems to have worked for me. When people tell you to grow up and get a proper job, when members of your family think you've gone completely round the twist, that's when you keep going, feeling the pain as you continue to bash your head against a brick wall. That is also part of the apprenticeship along with the bruises. I remember a friend of mine telling his Dad he wanted to be a musician when he grew up and his Dad told him that he couldn't do both.

Some would argue, judging by recent events, it was a wrong choice for me. Maybe, but it wasn't my fault that a caring bunch of politicians refused to help the music industry an inch, telling us all to stop feeling sorry for ourselves and find work elsewhere. Well, well, well, all I can say is what goes around come around Mr Cummings and Mr Hancock. There are situations vacant but not for those whose brains encounter vacant situations.

I'm proud to be in a creative industry regardless of what others may think about me. When I set out over half a century ago I was told it wasn't really a proper job and to be told the same thing again so many years later shouldn't have surprised me in the least. Maybe I took it better from my Dad. In actual fact, it didn't surprise me but it hurt. All my life I have tried to bring pleasure to people and I wasn't up for taking that kind of verbal from those types who seem to delight in bringing displeasure and hardship while they check their Stock Exchange portfolios.

Who do you turn to when nights are ever colder?
Who do you turn to, to lean upon their shoulder?
When the darkest clouds are rolling in
And you're at your lowest ever
Look all around they will be thin on the ground
But friends they are forever

Who do you turn to at a time when you're in danger?
Who do you turn to as the days get ever stranger?
A friend in need is a friend indeed
No matter what the weather
When things go wrong and most have gone
Friends they are forever

Music has been my life since I was seventeen and a half years old. When my fifty-year plus musical journey began in 1967 the Number One hit song was Release Me by Engelbert Humperdinck, obviously not the bloke's real name and a record I never bought. That decade ended with Cat Stevens, as he was known then, at the top of the charts with I'm Gonna get me a Gun, a boast that I don't think ever materialised, thankfully. Harold Wilson was our pipe-smoking Prime Minister, the only one I can recall with a northern accent, nice one Harold. Sandie Shaw, a good old East End girl from Dagenham, won The Eurovision Song contest for the United Kingdom with Puppet

On a String without wearing shoes and the first BBC local radio station opened in Leicester. Jeremy Thorpe became trilby-bearing leader of The Liberal Party and homosexuality was decriminalised, good news for Jeremy Thorpe as it turned out, confirmed by some excellent acting by Hugh Grant, something I never expected to mention in a book about my life. I can't even admit to being much of a fan but there again I doubt if he'd get off on my music.

As my daughter Rosie puts it, every single brick of our house represents a hundred miles of midnight motorway, and she's absolutely right. I often look at the place and wonder how a few songs and a strummed guitar gave me my safe haven to live a life of relative ease in the beautiful tranquillity of the English countryside. Yes, it has an outside lounge, but hey, things will improve when I have a get back on stage once again after the bacterial blip.

That seems to be the image of early life in the East End of London, tin baths in front of the fire on a Sunday night in winter and all that stuff, but it wasn't true in my case, I rarely had a bath. My upbringing was both safe and comfortable, apart from the times I shared a bath with my brother and to be honest that didn't feel comfortable in any way and four legs got in the way of my little rubber frogmen.

The world I was born into was a world a million miles from what we live in today. I sense right now that Great Britain is more divided than it has ever been and none of us know if a social repair kit will do the job.

This is Great Britain the Britain I knew
This is Great Britain the place where I grew
This is Great Britain when Britain was great
We'll be great again we just don't know the date

The musical world that I actively entered into in my late teens was a strange world too. Until firstly Rock and Roll in the 50s and then The Beatles and The Rolling Stones arrived in the 60s, we were all forced to listen to all the drab singers our parents loved with melting hearts and they were all as boring as hell. Most of the males wore bow ties and frilly shirts, singing dreary romantic ballads that made the ladies cry, whilst most of the females wore frilly dresses and also sang dreary romantic ballads but with much higher voices and more vibrato than their male counterparts. I seem to remember it felt like being at a wedding reception until the new upbeat forms of music came along and rescued us.

As far as I was concerned the time had come for the 60s musical revolt to begin and I'm so pleased I just happened to be around at the time to see and hear it all, even to play a very small particle part in it myself towards the end of the decade. If I were ever able to return to a certain part of my life it would be the 60s, at least I'd get my hair back and be able to afford a VW camper van.

The major problem for me was the revolution, in my case, took an unexpected route away from the obvious, from being a mod to an apprentice hippie. I watched the television music show Ready Steady Go every Friday night, presented by Keith Fordyce and Cathy McGowen who looked very much like Claudia Winkleman, and I became mildly fascinated by a denim-clad, oddball singer by the name of Donovan. He looked vulnerable and as skint as an American hobo hitching a ride on the railroad. He didn't really fit into the modern pop format of the show, or life in general it would seem, and yet in a funny kind of a way he did. He made me curious even though I wasn't sure about what exactly. He looked both vulnerable and innocent but his words were more meaningful than most songs I had ever heard before.

He sat on a stool strumming an acoustic guitar and playing a mouthorgan whilst a confused studio audience tried to dance along to his music like they did to the bands he was wedged between. I remember giggling as I watched trendy youngsters, or so they thought, trying to dance to Catch The Wind and Jennifer Juniper. I never realised something strange was about to happen with regards to my personal musical tastes, something that would mould the rest of my life. I've never cited Donovan as an inspiration, probably because I didn't realise he was until I started writing this book, but just maybe he was as I think back. I met him a few times, he did my radio show on Capital Radio and we were chalet neighbours a few years back at a festival at Butlins in Skegness. I'm annoyed I didn't thank him for such inspiration but, as I say, it's a very recent realisation.

He wasn't Glasgow-born Donovan Leitch to me, more plain and simple Donovan who rode his freedom sledge along the astral highway of desire or however such types described themselves back then. I was watching a folksinger at a time when I had not the slightest idea what a folksinger was. I was going to be a folksinger myself one day and I had no idea about that either. It would be a few years coming and it would manifest in Glasgow where, as I mentioned, Donovan was born so maybe, just maybe, it was feat written in the stars with dodgy spelling in my case.

Maybe I had secretly wanted his lifestyle as a wandering minstrel in the shadows of Woody Guthrie. James Dean may well have been the rebel without a cause but at this time I was more a rebel without a clue, not much of a clue of what I wanted to do or who I wanted to be. The answer, my friend, was blowing in the wind to quote the masterful Bob Dylan. Something definitely was blowing in the wind but I had no idea at the time it would develop into a hurricane and change my life forever.

I've travelled many a mile
From Cornwall up to Carlisle
I've seen all England can show me
But still very few know me
Sometimes I want to get home
Spend a few hours on my own
With you, yes with you
You're the best friend that I ever knew

It's a long winding road I chose
Where it leads me god only knows
This is my own King's shilling
As each dream I had I'm fulfilling
Sometimes when my eyes are sore
I wonder what's it all for
So do you, yes so do you.
But it's dreams that help me get through

I still hear my father's voice
Who disagreed with my choice
A proper job he suggested
My long hair and guitar he detested
But now I leave it behind
His moaning is far from my mind
That's sad, oh so sad
That distant echo of Dad

Chapter 1 - The Beginning

To begin my lonesome travels as a musician on the road I need to return to the 1960s and I bet you wish you'd been with me during those wonderful days of liberation, free love, a time when the whole world seemed to smell of something rather strange. Everyone called each other man, despite which sex they were and people had very thin legs and long hair. Denim became the order of the day, so much so they even brought out an after-shave lotion of the same name, a complete waste of time as those who wore denim never ever bothered to wear some sexy after-shave lotion. Some of us didn't even bother to shave. Oh well, at least it made a nice change from the various bits and pieces of Old Spice.

To become more familiar with the aspiring British folk scene I had to venture to the other side of London from where I lived. There were a few bastions of folk music in the East End, one or two but not that many, but the other side of the city was far more vibrant, and therefore more compelling to a new folk music fan. It meant taking a tube-train from East Ham station and travelling for over an hour to the west side of London. Walking to the station with my long hair and duffle coat made me feel like a trespasser in my home area, yet when I got off the train at the other end I felt a sense of belonging, a sense of freedom and self-expression. It was like walking into The Woodstock festival in my head. One day I promised myself that I would move out that way, to the other side of London where it was all happening. I did for a while, renting a flat in Fawe Park Road, Putney, and I hated it. Nobody spoke to one another, unlike the East End, so I didn't stay there long. Nice houses where people went about their lives in silence, dismissing all around them.

One such tube journey took me to a small coffee house in Old Brompton Road called The Troubadour. I was a young, rebel teenager eager to find myself and I'd found the very place that would help me. Hang on, I have an idea. Take my hand and I will take you back over half a century. Let's go to The Troubadour together.

I'm about to take you in there too, by my side, so we start by giving you the visual image of a small coffee house, a very small coffee house with lots of vintage coffee pots hanging from the ceiling like Christmas decorations. We enter in and walk diagonally across to a small flight of stairs in the right-hand corner that led down to the cellar. Before I take you down the steep stairs that turn back on themselves, let me tell you about this iconic place.

The rebellious periodical Private Eye was first produced and sold there as a kind of underground magazine. It's also where the Ban The Bomb movement was founded before it expanded into the CND, the Campaign For Nuclear Disarmament. It has a CV as long as your arm, this tiny coffee shop that you could walk past without even knowing it was there. So, we have walked through small tables of bohemian types, sitting at tables, plotting and planning, possibly the things I've mentioned, or possibly not. We don't hang around on the ground floor though as the action we are seeking is down that rickety staircase, in the cellar below. They may all be in deep discussion about various important and rebellious issues but that's not why we're here, so it matters not.

Two old boys are sat in the corner playing chess whilst smoking roll-ups, oh how times changed. They are harmless enough, engrossed, and certainly not politically incorrect as they would be in these modern times. They were simply minding their own business in a manner that would now constitute a two thousand pound fine.

The cellar is small and musty with a capacity of no more than fifty or sixty sardines or forty or fifty people. To our right is a small area that serves coffee and we turn to our left and see a tiny stage protruding from a couple of alcoves where they probably stored wine, years before, as they were directly below a trapdoor in the pavement above. One such alcove is no bigger than four feet by five feet, probably the smallest dressing-room in the whole world, and sitting in there, waiting to go on stage, is one certain Bob Dylan. Yes, the one and only Bob Dylan no less. My real inspiration way above others I have and will mention in my story of life. There was no pa system necessary because the place was far too small and yet, even so, the tiny place smacked of great importance at the time and was well worth the train journey across London.

Just to digress for a moment, turning right as you leave The Troubadour, down to the traffic lights and turning left, you end up outside Earls Court where Dylan would play to thousands in later years. Although I never saw it myself, rumour has it that Led Zeppelin trotted off to the coffee house after doing a huge Earls Court gig so they could have a bluesy jam session to end their wonderful evening. That epitomises and confirms the reputation that The Troubadour had. I would have loved to have watched Jimmy Page play his guitar so close to me.

Back to our own trip. Bob Dylan did his first ever London gig at The Troubadour coffee house. Martin Windsor and Redd Sullivan ran the folk club there and they both went on before the main act and, boy, did they have some lungs on them. Martin, who always wore a blue double-breasted suit, strange attire for a folkie, looking more like an undertaker or accountant than a singer, and he played a huge acoustic guitar with great gusto whilst Redd just stood beside him and sang very loudly, often with his finger in his ear or with his hands in his pockets. Martin looked like an old Richard Thompson and Redd looked like an old Art Garfunkel.

We take our seats about two rows back and Redd Sullivan introduces, all the way from America, Bob Dylan. My heart pounds. Your heart pounds too. Can you believe this is really happening?

He didn't look up as he unscrewed himself out of the tiny dressing room and sat on the stage. There are various photos around that were apparently taken during this gig, but they show him standing up. He was seated on a glorified milking stool let me tell you. He wore a pale green tee-shirt underneath an unbuttoned dark denim shirt. I still remember how small Bob Dylan was, quite a diminutive chap and yet he was close enough to reach out and touch, not that he would have been that impressed as he was untouchable. He had very long fingernails in comparison to the size of the rest of his body and they were soon at work as he began to play.

Without any kind of introduction, just a nod, he begins his set with Boots Of Spanish Leather and A Man Of Constant Sorrow, a set that ends with his rendition of the aforementioned Blowin' In The Wind, a song that became a huge worldwide hit for Peter, Paul and Mary. He didn't say much at all other than a rambling tribute to Woody Guthrie, enthralling stuff for me and the rest of the tiny audience. We'd all heard of Guthrie but none of us knew that much about him, other than that he sometimes sang with Ramblin' Jack Elliott who, coincidentally, also appeared at The Troubadour a few years later.

The point I wish to make about that night at The Troubadour was that I went on my own, but can you imagine if you had been there? I indeed hope you have imagined. Wouldn't you have just loved sitting no more than three feet away from the mighty Bob Dylan as he sang out those magical words he strung together? Of course you would, what an experience. I would loved to have shared that moment with someone, but I never did.

I visited The Troubadour many times in the few years that followed. I saw Sonja Kristina do a great solo gig there before she fronted Curved Air and there were others who played there who I sadly missed out on and amongst those performers I never saw were Paul Simon, Jimi Hendrix and Elvis Costello. Oh yes, I missed out on a few but at least we saw Bob Dylan didn't we?

I continued to make trips to Old Brompton Road as often as I could muster the train fare and I eventually got to know a few other folkies who frequented the place with certain regularity.

One in particular was Linda Peters, a beautiful singer who performed with Paul McNeill. Ironically, they released a single of the Dylan song 'You Aint Going Nowhere' and, despite my shyness, I would chat with Linda as she was such a beautiful person and singer. She later married Richard Thompson and the rest, as they say, is history, or geography if you wish to change the subject. I saw Linda perform a year or so before I heard the remarkable Sandy Denny for the first time.

Another ironic fact is that Sandy worked as a nurse in the very same Old Brompton Road, just down the road from The Troubadour. I never saw the great woman there, she who single-handedly created the electric folk/rock movement on her own, but I did see her play for the first time at The Prince of Wales pub, at a club run by Rod Hamilton, also just down the road from The Troubadour, across the railway bridge and on the right. I wouldn't mind betting you would have liked to have been by my side at Rod's club too? Watching Sandy Denny perform was spine-chilling. Yes, she loved life a little more than she should have, but there's nothing wrong with that.

A short time ago, before the first lockdown, I met up with Sandy's daughter Georgia Rose, over from Australia, and she loved hearing stories about her Mum.

I performed at The Troubadour myself just the once, on a Wednesday night gathering fronted by guitarist Gordon Giltrap and it would be fair to say that I died on my backside. Yes, I went down like a French kiss at a family re-union and I'm more than pleased you weren't by my side to watch me shrink into a further, deeper oblivion without even trying on that particular occasion. I doubt if the 6 or 7 people in the audience remember it and I'm grateful for that.

The venue is still there, despite the financial crashes of 2020. It still has plenty to boast as both Adele and Ed Sheeran have apparently played there in more recent times. I hope that's true. It has a magical legacy that will live on forever, this insignificant little coffee shop in the Brompton Road. Maybe the occasional Al Stewart lyric springs to mind, maybe not, it isn't that important but you would know what I mean if you'd heard Al's Bedsitter Images album.

As I mentioned, Bob Dylan went on to play at Earls Court to massive crowds and I so wanted to see him again but I couldn't get a ticket and so I took a train up to Newcastle City Hall, a birthday present from my Mum, and I have to say I much preferred that night at The Troubadour where I have just taken you. That was special, although he didn't speak much on that night in Newcastle either. He strummed an electric guitar much to the total confusion and annoyance of the audience, none of whom were that impressed, me included. Bob Dylan's fingers weren't built for an electric guitar. He later did gigs just sitting at a piano, equally strange.

It's almost time to take you somewhere else where I would have enjoyed your company and leave Bob Dylan to his decades of brilliant songwriting that would follow, but this just had to be the very first recall as he was such an inspiration to me. His Freewheelin' album especially changed the direction of my life completely and helped me carve my early beginnings as a musician in my infancy, so the fact that you and I went to see him at that tiny venue in Old Brompton Road takes top billing as far as I'm concerned. Donovan or Dylan? Does it really matter? Chalk an d cheese maybe, it doesn't really matter because I was inspired by both just the same. They both played acoustic guitars and huffed and puffed at mouth organs and had a ridiculous dress-sense that I would soon adopt, thus looking equally ridiculous to my friends.

As a final thought, I was remembering just now how I ever came to hear about Bob Dylan in the first place, this mod of the 60s into the Beatles and The Rolling Stones. Well, my brother Leonard, who I haven't seen for over half a century due to him moving to Vancouver, Canada, was an art student at Goldsmiths College in London and he got into weird music through having weird friends. Hey, he was at art college after all. I really don't remember too much about him but he smoked copious number of Bristol cigarettes.

Take a tip take a Bristol
Today's cigarette is a Bristol
They have a taste you'll never forget
Bristol is today's cigarette

One day he brought a Dylan album home along with a jazz album by Andre Previn and J.J.Johnson and a girlfriend hanging on is arm called Chris Harman who spoke funny because she came from Scunthorpe, and I started to play the albums when the rest of my family were out of the house. I became transfixed and my interest in folk music had secretly begun. I wasn't that interested in the jazz stuff, never have been, it's just other music played with the wrong chords and notes.

A few decades ago now a book publisher, Robson Books, invited me to write my autobiography 'A Wealth of Comedy.' Content-wise they were more interested in my career in entertainment and the famous people I knew rather than my actual life and so I vowed, one day, I would write the story of my real life as opposed to my work, and you are about to read the result because that day has finally arrived.

I have read so many autobiographies by those who were blessed, like myself, with working in the television and entertainment industries and it does seem to be an excuse for giant name-dropping. I seem to remember within the pages of A Wealth of Comedy I was the only person I hadn't heard of. It was thinking back on that book that the realisation struck me that my story has to include both the famous and the not so famous, of course it does.

I've been in the entertainment industry for most of my life and so I've had the famous and the not so famous as workmates. It doesn't mean I got on well with them all, just like you probably didn't get on with everyone you worked with, but they were there and so they need to be mentioned at times. Obviously, some people that affected your life have to be included, as they are in here on numerous occasions, but it doesn't need to be a roll call of the famous on every page, I've tried really hard to be aware of that.

My intention is to make this book a happy compromise with no mention of how I nearly met Elvis, which I didn't by the way, although I did once tune Roy Orbison's guitar, fact. Yes, I met Roy Orbison when I shared the bill with him at The London Palladium and I visited Sun Studios where he began as a session singer in Memphis. Phew, I only met the legend that was Roy Orbison. He left us way back in 1988 but he never died.

I had a life way before I turned to the entertainment industry. I was born like you, I went to school like you and made a bundle of mistakes along the way, probably like you too. I had failed romances like you obviously did and numerous disputes with parents I rebelled against. We're all similar in so many ways. Maybe where we differ is I've had the same job for over half a century. No celebratory gold watch to show for it but tons of stories to share with you instead. I didn't have any qualifications to get another job anyway.

As I wondered how to piece the book together in a different and hopefully far more interesting way, how to embrace each period of my life, I realised it would be best to tell you of the different stages in my life relating to where I lived at any given time. Well it made sense when I came up with the idea.

I haven't exactly travelled around like some wandering desert nomad but I've certainly moved a few times, just the same as everyone else I suppose, although not always by choice, and each new address that comes to mind produces different events and stories to share with you. By referring to such addresses it helps me to keep events in some kind of chronological order, he said knowing the chances were slim. I thought it would be a far more unique way of telling my story too, from the East End of London at the starting line to the beautiful Wiltshire countryside I see each morning as I continue my journey through the latter laps of my life.

During my early years I spent most of my time in and around London, my place of birth so hardly surprising, so much so that I could take you on a journey around a Monopoly Board and have a story to coincide with every single property and railway station. It would be an interesting trip until we reach the Income Tax square and then I'm off. Hey what a great idea, I'm going to give it a try. I probably won't get them all as I doubt if I'll remember all the streets on the board but I won't cheat and look them up. Here goes;

Whitechapel Road was my route from home into London and where The Elephant Man, the subject matter of one of my documentaries, was displayed in a shop window as a weird circus freak, poor man.

Old Kent Road was my gran Mary's favourite song and one she played on the piano after the war. It was also the home of The Copper Kettle Folk Club run by Cliff Aungier who, quite wisely, never booked me.

Euston Road housed the studios of Capital Radio where I worked for nearly five years.

Pentonville Road, pass I've never been to prison, not yet anyway.

Angel Islington was where I played a gig in London's oldest music hall theatre.

Those purple things have got me stumped. Pall Mall, well I remember smoking them for a while. Marlborough Street I have no idea where it is but I smoked them as well and the same can be said for Northumberland Avenue. Shame Northumberland Avenue ruined a coloured set of cigarettes but hey ho.

Vine Street? I did a Christmas concert at Vine Street police-station, had a few drinks and was thus given a police escort back to Essex, blue flashing lights included as I illegally weaved my way along the road with bleary eyes. Bow Street, another police zone, I have no personals to declare other than it's where Sir Robert Peel created a police force, thus why they were once known as bobbies. As a child I remember coppers didn't used to shave their heads and carry endless items on their belts like radios and microwave ovens. Coppers pedalled bicycles, carried truncheons, and clipped you round the ear if you threw a hand-grenade at them. None of this modern nonsense. It was a time when all coppers were older than me too. Nowadays some of them look as though their Mums got them ready for work.

Trafalgar Square I did a concert for Shelter with Irish songwriter Paul Brady, whilst Fleet Street printed The Melody Maker, the music paper I so longed to see my name in when I started out. Over halfway round so bear with me. The Strand was my inspiration for one of my songs about the flower-seller Rosemary MacLaren, the original My Fair Lady. Piccadilly was where I recorded my early shows for The BBC, Leicester Square was where I went and watched the preview of my one and only film appearance and where Capital Radio moved its studios to, and Coventry Street I'd never even heard of until it appeared on the Monopoly board.

Sharp right at Go To Jail and we're in Bond Street where I worked for Chappell's Music, Regent Street, the home of my agents International Artists and Oxford Street was where I bought my guitar strings at a shop called John Alvey Turner, used and recommended to me by master guitarist John Renbourn.

Park Lane and Mayfair were way above my station I'm afraid, but hey that wasn't a bad attempt. I passed Go many times but I rarely collected two-hundred pounds in those early days, but I didn't collect parking tickets either. This was all long before someone came up with that stupid idea. We parked where we wanted for as long as we wanted and no messing. So much easier I'm sure you agree?

It's easy for you to Google and read of my awards and achievements in music and television and you are more than welcome to do so, but I wanted to be far more personal than that, so this is a story of a kid who didn't do very well at school, didn't do very well at college either, and yet managed to build a life in the entertainment world, doing exactly what he wanted to do. A teenager who ran back to Mum and Dad with his tail between his legs as yet another dream turned into a tragic nightmare of dark failure.

As already mentioned, the book begins, as did I, in the East End of London, the friendly old-style East End of London, and each chapter will take me to another house move and more events that spring to mind. I have totally loved sending my brain backwards, it isn't hard these days, to re-live moments that are now long gone and I hope you enjoy reading this book as much as I have enjoyed writing about them.

We have all had more time on our hands than ever we expected during the lockdowns of 2020 and 2021 and we all know, with such an uncertain future ahead of us, we can delve into the distant past to find solace, when times were certainly not as complicated as they are today in this forbidding modern world. It's corny for sure but the world was indeed an entirely different place in 1949, the year I was born, far different to the crazy world we all try to understand and survive in today.

Unfortunately for me, 1949 was a hell of a long time ago. I share the year of my birth with the amazingly beautiful Meryl Streep, a kind lady who sent me autographed stuff when I was raising money for a medical centre in Lyme Regis where she filmed French Lieutenant's Woman, the heart-throb actor Richard Gere and brilliant songwriter Billy Joel and so I share all my incredible attributes with those three, yes, we all have feet with toes on the end and there, sadly, the similarities end.

The most peculiar change since then is that beef was the cheap meat that most families could afford and the real occasional luxury was chicken. Blimey, nowadays if it wasn't for wedding receptions and barbecues the country would be overrun with the damn things, millions of them crossing the road for reasons we've never worked out, but that wasn't always the case. The big movie of the year was The Third Man, the story of Harry Lime starring Michael Rennie and the best-selling book was George Orwell's 1984. Ah, Michael Rennie, I never thanked him for sorting out my bouts of indigestion and so it's time I did, thanks Mick.

I lived through the post-war austerity and hardship that the whole nation endured, The Beatles and the flower-powering swinging 60s and way beyond into the world of holidays abroad, mobile phones and computers, yes back to the days when we actually wrote letters and had friends as opposed to faceless names on social media. To own your very own fountain pen, a Parker, was something very special as opposed to nowadays when actually finding a fountain pen would be something equally special. Incidentally, I still write my songs and poems with a fountain pen, it makes me feel literary. Back in those distant days people collected stamps as opposed to emails.

Oh yes, there have certainly been some changes since the day I entered the world and I am about to prove the point further through the pages that follow. Sit back as we travel further back to the days that Doctor Who may not even remember with much clarity and then forward to my world today. To many of you it will be nothing more than a history lesson, but just remember that all things mentioned were, at some point in my life, current affairs. Just eight lines of a song can describe how different the country was back in the 1950s. We were still waiting for someone to run a mile in under four minutes, cricketers wore caps and not crash- helmets and racing drivers wore white overalls and gloves as they sat upright in their dynamic cars. I didn't know what golf was and people read comics.

I remember all my adolescent days
And that's going back a few years now
The Eagle, Black Jacks, Everlasting Strips
Things I read like Biggles
and newspapers round my chips
National Health orange juice
Birthday ten-bob notes
Idiot mittens with string around our throats

Oh yes, comics and magazines were a major part of all of our lives. It's strange how comic titles move you through adolescence. My first was The Tiger, in which I followed the football career of Roy Race, Roy Of The Rovers and his team Melchester in their red and yellow shirts and blue shorts. As I grew older I moved to The Victor and New Hotspur, far more grown-up written content, before the football magazines came along. I had Charles Buchan's Football Monthly and Soccer Star until I caught my first fish and thus subscribed to Angling Times. My brother had The Eagle which featured Dan Dare and all that space stuff and my sister had Sunny Stories. My Mum had

Woman's Own and Woman's Realm and my Dad didn't read anything, preferring to sleep in the armchair or moan about all people not born in West Ham in general and Mortlake Road in particular.

I was born at a very early age on 24th February, 1949 at Howards Road Hospital, Plaistow in the East End of London. You'd think it would be an annual national holiday, a day of great commemoration, but apparently not. It would be the beginning of a life well-lived for sure, although I would never have put money on it being so when I was taken from the hospital to our family home in Denbigh Road, East Ham, a couple of hundred yards from Upton Park, the old ground of West Ham United. It was actually my grandparents' house as Mum, Doris, and Dad's, Len's, place in Canning Town had been flattened by some most unreasonable German bombers five years previously. I was conceived in Mortlake Road, next to West Ham Speedway Stadium, a landmark that no longer exists, a bit of a shame as it seated more spectators than Wembley Stadium would you believe. Yes, 120,000 people went there every single week.

Speedway used to be massive after the war, as did stock-car racing, and both happened at West Ham Stadium, now a housing estate, usually on a Tuesday evening. A Tuesday? Yes, the day of the week when very little happens, well it definitely used to happen back then with tens of thousands walking to the stadium to watch heart-stopping action that even had its very own smell as soon as they started up their engines, an oily aroma I still smell in my nostrils as I think about it. My hearing isn't quite what it used to be and I blame the speedway bikes as much as loud pa systems I have used over the years.

After the war ended, my parents applied for re-housing due to the bomb damage and I was only a year old when we moved from Denbigh Road to a brand-new council flat, 39 Blaney Crescent, also in East Ham. Yes, red tape was as prevalent then as it is today, five years to be given somewhere of their own to rent and live.

We lived in the bottom flat and so we had a garden, which was just as well because my sister had a tortoise, Tony, that loved dandelions. One day, he ran away, he'll be yards away by now. The garden was slightly bigger than a postage stamp, but it was a garden just the same, even though it was hard to stretch out on a blanket and we definitely didn't have a flowerbed in the shape of The Queen's head. Yes, the garden was so small that we couldn't sit outdoors if we had visitors. If we'd wanted to grow vegetables in that garden then a pea would have filled the vegetable patch. But hey, we had the luxury of a garden, unlike most of our very envious neighbours. It was almost like living in the countryside with the freedom it afforded us.

At my time of birth my Mum worked as a sales assistant at Marks & Spencer before turning her hand to being a butcher's assistant in an area by the River Thames known as Silvertown, where everyone seemed to work for Tale & Lyle sugar or British Standard Telephone and Cables, not sure what they did but it sounds like something technical. The butcher's shop was owned by Alf and Rita Jinks and when I was old enough to go, but not old enough to stay at home and play with my mates while my parents went to work, I went with Mum and kicked a tennis ball around on the wasteland outside the shop for hours. In just one day on that bombsite I could easily play a dozen cup-finals that all featured West Ham United and Manchester United strangely enough. West Ham always won, often by ten or twelve superb goals. I used to be so many Manchester United players who were sadly lost in the Munich air disaster, hardly surprising as Roger Byrne was captain of England and Duncan Edwards was the greatest footballer on the planet. That was a great team, Bobby Charlton struggled to get regular games they were so good.

My Dad was an ambulance driver, serving with what was then Essex County Council, based in Ripple Road, Barking, now considered to be a part of Greater London. Barking was a posh place with detached houses, no idea what it's like these days as I haven't been there for years. My mates and I often cycled to Barking Abbey as we were told, and indeed believed, that the Three Musketeers were buried there under three gravestones in a row. We didn't know the trio weren't even real.

Mum and Dad both changed occupations a few times through my childhood, Dad ending up at Ford Motor Company as a lorry driver and Mum moved on to Bards Sweet Factory in Romford Road, Manor Park. Oh and they both smoked Golden Virginia roll-ups which meant I had a surfeit of empty tobacco tins to play with as opposed to Lego or Bako.

To emphasise how much the world has changed we never had a television until I was 9 years old and sometimes, when we finally owned one, we lost the picture if a gust of wind moved the aerial. Mind you, there were only two channels, BBC and ITV. Adverts began on the telly in 1954, the first being a toothpaste ad and then another for hot chocolate if my memory serves me correctly. Toothpaste didn't come in tubes then but in round tins, pink or white powder and that was it. Hot chocolate came in a tin too. Hot chocolate, drinking chocolate. Blimey, I had more tins to play with than toys, come to think of it, tins, both round and rectangular, were my toys. Aerials then became far more sophisticated, becoming indoor equipment as opposed to outdoors and my job was to stand in the corner of the room when my Dad ordered me to and wobble the thing around so The Lone Ranger and Tonto weren't blurred.

Saturday morning picture shows
How we whistled when the film broke down
Frozen jubblies, flying saucers, liquorice wood
Lead soldiers in a box for half a crown
Having friends to tea but never in the week
Trying to ask a girl out and forgetting how to speak
Roy of The Rovers in his red and yellow shirt
Building roads for Dinky toys in the garden dirt

I remember bags of coloured rubber bands
Streets that never had those yellow lines
Snake-belts mine was red and blue
Shops with metal Ovaltiney signs
Fags behind bike sheds when my brother was a Ted
Transistor radio we smuggled into bed
Cold winter mornings when school milk froze
Third pint bottles I still remember those

Blaney Crescent was such a great place to live, a friendly community in the old East End tradition whereby people left their front-doors unlocked and were subsequently burgled with great regularity. Some of my neighbours were so poor that burglars sometimes put jewellery in jewellery boxes.

It consisted of a collection of brand-new council flats, literally in the shape of a crescent, obviously, with a green in the middle where we played football, cricket and run-outs, morning, noon and night. It was our very own Wembley Stadium, Lords Cricket Ground or White City Athletic Stadium. The narrow road around the green was exactly the same shape as a running track. I have a photo of me sitting on the green during a street party to celebrate The Queen's Coronation in 1953 and do you know what? I haven't changed a bit. I still vaguely remember that day, we were all presented with a small tin of custard cream biscuits and a little toy stagecoach.

In 2019 I took my youngest daughter, Rosie, back to see the place where I grew up for the first time. The green had sadly gone, the cup-finals replaced by a massive spread of concrete that is now a carpark. When we moved there, only four cars were owned by the many families in the flats. Mr Duly, Frank but I always had to call him Mr Duly, had a blue and white Hillman Minx KHV 543, don't ask, I've no idea. Mr Pearce had an Austin Ten, HTW 466, still no idea why I remember these things, the size of a tank and Mr Clatworthy had an MG sports car. An MG sports car no less, he must have been a bank robber. He also wore leather driving gloves and a bri-nylon polo-neck jumper, well above his station. To this day I have no idea what he was doing living in Blaney Crescent alongside the rest of us.

It made me gulp as I looked around at the changes with Rosie. Blaney Crescent had so many amazing stories to tell, stories that would forever remain a secret hidden away and forgotten in most cases. The big wooden gates were there, where girls would tuck their dresses in their knickers and play handstands and boys would clatter footballs against them until neighbours got the hump.

I used to clean the brass
Now it's old faded
As faded as the dreams that seem a million miles away
Kiss chase I played here
Getting caught on purpose
Hopscotch when the girls would tuck their dresses up their drawers

The Duly family lived upstairs to us, at 43, and the daughter, Margaret, and me, once hatched a cunning plan that eventually back-fired and got us into seriously hot water.

We built a wooden pram thing, pulled by string, we called them jiggers in the East End, and we raided allotments on the Barking by-pass when it was dark. The following day we would knock on doors flogging sticks of rhubarb and potatoes around the crescent. It went well until we tried selling our bounty to someone, Mr Snow to be precise, whose allotment had been raided the previous day and that was the end of that. The real bummer was Phillip and Keith Snow were mates and Gillian Snow went to school with my sister, so it was all rather embarrassing. I made a few pounds, of money not potatoes, but the business went bust after our capture. Mr Snow threatened to take the pair of us to East Ham Police Station but Mrs Snow talked him out of it. My Mum went mental, unlike my Dad who was far too busy fixing a neighbour's car to be bothered with my criminal activities. I think Mum told him and I think he shook his head in mild dismay, I'm not too sure. Maybe he was proud of me, maybe it was what East End kids did, I have no idea.

Those allotments are now buried underneath the M25 motorway and I wouldn't be surprised if, one day, sticks of rhubarb start sprouting from the hard shoulder or potatoes raise their heads in the fast lane. If Margaret and I hadn't been caught the motorway would be a far safer place today, let me tell you, and there I rest my case. Don't blame me if you swerve off the road and write your car off one day after meeting a stick of rhubarb head-on, Margaret and I did our best to keep you safe.

I think something that hurt me more during my visit recently was not the demise of the allotments but the sacred memorial by the public telephone box, commemorating the bravery of Captain Blaney, a bomb disposal officer in The Second World War. It had gone too, dismantled in a far safer way than he dismantled objects during the war. Us kids respected that memorial, our parents made us, never to be used as a goal or a climbing frame, yet it seemed the years had diminished the soldier's bravery because it had disappeared along with our stadium where we re-enacted so many cup finals and test matches. It's sad how time moves on and leaves the past ever further behind.

We should give further mention to Captain Blaney as his name has cropped up so many times. Captain Michael Flood Blaney, of The Royal Engineers, was born in our area and he was killed at the tender age of 30 trying to defuse a bomb down the road. He was well worthy of a monument and we respected it.

Time moves on, it doesn't wait for no man
Time moves on it never turns the other way
Time moves on, we can't turn back the hours
Maybe I was wrong, I think it turned today

It amazed me how small everything seemed to be so many years later. The wall I climbed with remarkable bravery and without a Sherpa was only half a dozen bricks high and the slalom course I skated down each winter, from our flat's entrance hall down to the kerb was just three paving slabs in length and yet I still fell over every time I imagined I was in Switzerland making my way down the steepest slope in Europe. The flats on three different levels seemed smaller too, as though they'd diminished over the years like old people seem to do.

As I began my early years there were no clues as to how much music would play such a major part in my life. I lived for football, I played football, watched football and read football magazines when I could lay my hands on second-hand copies of Charles Buchan's Football Monthly. I don't have much interest these days in the huge corporate business it became but I loved it when it was a sport, goalposts for jumpers and all that stuff. I played every single day of my school holidays, plus weekends when I'd done my part of the household chores. Every birthday someone bought me a new red Frido ball. A brand-new ball was always used for a cup-final. Every single day I was the goalkeeper, striker and commentator all rolled into one. When I played on my own the goal was a washing pole in the backyard but a goal only counted if you hit the pole without the ball touching the ground. They were the rules, approved no doubt by the FA. When the summer came along the same washing-pole became my stumps where I bowled at an Australian team in the hope I would win back The Ashes, rubbing a tennis ball on my groin to make it shine, just like the grown-ups did. Why on earth did I think I could shine a furry tennis ball?

Cricket was nothing more than a sunny interlude from football. They say you need to be a nutcase to be a goalkeeper and so it may come as no surprise to you that I played in goal. I did indeed, but for another reason other than being a nutter, I didn't have any football boots so I couldn't play in the outfield. Thinking back, I never seemed to have the right stuff for anything. Goalkeepers at the time wore green or yellow roll-neck jumpers but not yours truly. Mine was a beige crew-neck jumper that belonged to my older brother until it shrunk in Mum's wash tub and my gloves were a pair of yellow stringy things my sister wore out at the riding stables.

It was even worse when I played cricket. As a wicketkeeper I wore a pair of my Uncle Dick's motorcycle gauntlets. Blimey, I sound like some sad refugee dressed in hand me downs, but it didn't seem like that at all. It was all rather inventive. At least I was unique and it may have been the start of cricketers these days wearing motorcycle crash-helmets. Hey, maybe I started something. Maybe we'll see the return of motorbikes and sidecars.

Anyway, it was sport and more sport that consumed my early years and certainly not music. I swam a width and won a ribbon in The Olympic Games, ran the last leg of the men's relay without other runners to help me so I also ran the other three legs, but most of all I was an international footballer of high regard. I played for England with great pride and scored over a thousand goals in over two thousand appearances for my country.

Rosie got it, every single bit of it as we stood in Blaney Crescent. There wasn't much to see to be honest, just a collection of council flats, but she loved my mental guided tour back to the days where I grew up and went to school long before her arrival.

I'm just eleven but I aint stupid
My feet are firm on the ground
I was born on the wrong side of London
To see the sun shining down
But at least I have my dreams
And some people don't know what that means
So don't pity my bashed about shoes
I can be anyone that I choose

I started school in 1955 when I began my education at Vicarage Lane Primary School. It was a mixed school, those in trouble with the police and those who'd kept their noses clean.

I still recall every teacher and every shop I passed along Vicarage Lane on my way to school each morning, none of which are there anymore.

On that trip with Rosie I drove down Vicarage Lane itself and it was unrecognisable. Most shops had been converted to dwellings and gone were all the retailers, banished to my memory bank forever.

The oil shop that stank of paraffin, I even had to explain to Rosie what paraffin was and how it warmed our flat on cold, winter days and nights. Then there was the junk shop and Turners the newsagents for whom I did a paper-round until I realised a bundle of Exchange and Marts on a rainy evening were far too heavy for me. Bill the barber was a huge man and the only man outside of France to wear a beret. Wilson the butcher, the wool shop, Victoria Laundry and oh so many more. Collets sweet shop had to be my favourite stop-off as they sold bubble-gum with football cards to collect. I swapped Brian Clough six times because I had no idea who he was. I met him once and he didn't know who I was either. He was the only card in the set who played for Middlesbrough, which probably explained why I'd never heard of him. It must have been quite something to be featured on a cigarette card, especially in the days when most footballers smoked and thus collected the very same card themselves.

Guided tour done, I smiled to myself as I turned right into Gooseley Lane as Rosie and I headed for home. Gooseley Park had memories a-plenty with its five football pitches, a cricket pitch in the summer, tennis courts, even a bowls green behind evergreens where only half dead people were allowed to wander and arch their weary backs as some kind of sporting event. Then there was the playground area that housed a slide, a see-saw, jungle Jim for climbing and a roundabout on a concrete base, an accident waiting to happen and an accident that often did.

I once played football there with Bobby Moore and his mate, played cricket, kissed my first girl, also called Rosie funnily enough, by the tennis courts, and rode my bike through the park until the parkie blew his whistle and I had to get off. That parkie was a stickler for rules and regulations, shutting the place every night at 7pm. Luckily there were a couple of bent railings we could climb through when he'd gone home. I checked them out and they weren't there anymore. I mean to say, surely there are far more important things to do than straighten bent railings? What about world famine and that nasty Russian bloke?

I turned the car left at Charlemont Road, passing my piano lessons and then left again at the High Street. Up to Botha Road where Mum was born, passing Robertsons fishing tackle shop where I used to buy my maggots and then on to the rhubarb-free M25 as I headed for the sanctuary of my home in Wiltshire.

In that East End maze I realised Gooseley Park must have been a hell of a sanctuary with its green grass and flower beds, even if I did take it all for granted when I was a kid. It was also the home ground for my school football team that played in the sacred claret and blue.

I played football for Vicarage and a couple of times for East Ham Schools, once actually, where I played alongside Roger Cross, a Shaftesbury School inside forward who had a kick like a mule. He played for West Ham and Fulham before becoming a scout for The Hammers and then Southend United. We actually met up forty years later when he came to my gig at The Barn in Essex and, strangely, I recognised him straight away as he stood at the bar. We chatted for ages and kept in touch, we still exchange Christmas cards.

The regular East Ham goalkeeper played for Monega School and I wouldn't say for one minute he was better than me because I don't think he was, but he had a yellow roll-neck jumper so he looked more suitable in the team photograph, thus becoming first-choice. He had blonde, curly hair too so I always questioned his sexuality during the days when I didn't know any better.

An old school photograph
A black and whit school photograph
An old school photograph
Full of way back whens
Young kids starting out
Not knowing what the world's about
An old school photograph
Of old school friends

Obviously, my days at Vicarage are patchy but I did fall in love for the first time with Christine Lawrence, a sports day sensation who had her own white running spikes no less, and enjoyed many other firsts too, though sadly not in exams. For example, my first ever coach trip. Ah yes, my first ever coach trip, such excitement.

My class teacher was Mr Stitson, Mr Percy Stitson, a fine man who lived in Kent. It's hard to believe he cycled from Belvedere to the Woolwich Ferry, crossed the mighty River Thames and then cycled to the East End, every single morning. He looked after us reprobates then took the same route home every night. At weekends, on his days off, he ran our school football team. Anyway, Mr Stitson's local school in Kent, Bedonwell by name, wanted to play Vicarage in a friendly match and so it was that we boarded a coach, a bloody big coach, crossed the mighty, swirling river, and played so far from home. Honestly, it was just like being in Europe, confirmed by the fact that people in Kent had slightly different accents to me. Most of the game I stood between the posts feeling quite homesick. Sitting on that coach was something else, something magical, a bunch of excited kids who had never sat on a coach before or rarely travelled so far from home, and yet the excitement wasn't to last through my years because I hate sitting on buses so much I haven't done such a thing for nearly half a century.

That coach trip was a first. As for others, I had my first puff of a cigarette on my way home from St Mary's Church choir practice with my brother and my first ride in a car, an Austin Ten, happened when I was six, although I hasten to add I wasn't driving. At that time my grandfather died peacefully, unlike the passengers in his car who were screaming their heads off, just a joke, granddad was killed in the war on board HMS Ajax, which he wasn't driving either.

My first true death experience was my mate Kevin Sullivan's Mum, Daisy I think her name was. I'd never seen a funeral before and all the net curtains in the crescent parted as the big black car made its way from Blaney Crescent to Manor Park Crematorium, five miles away. Kevin had a guitar, a proper guitar, but I never realised its importance, or rather how important such an instrument would be later in my own life. He couldn't play it but he was a brilliant hard-tackling footballer so it didn't really matter. Ah, Kevin and his brothers Patsy and Danny Sullivan, I wonder where his family turned up in the East End from. I doubt very much if it was Scotland or the mountainous regions of North Wales.

John Lacey formed a skiffle group called The Happy Outlaws. His stepdad had made a tea-chest bass kind of thing, Kevin played the only guitar any of us had and Keith Williams played washboard. Me? I borrowed one of Kevin's brother's guitar. It was a cream plastic thing that didn't really make much of a sound. Our world tour took us to our classroom and then the classroom next door. We were wrecked after such extensive travelling. I hasten to add and hereby give credit to John, the whole thing being his idea. I simply made up the numbers. We split up after a week due to musical indifferences but not before Mr Stitson put us in the school Christmas play where we had to mime Michael Holliday's The Stairway of Love. We smashed it, well we would have done if his record-player had worked. Someone nicked the needle which confirms what I rough school Vicarage was.

As I sit here now, an old man with a few strands of stubborn hair on my head and grey stubble, it's hard to imagine the boy I have described in this opening introduction, a boy who dived between goalposts, saving penalties, wearing a pair of sandals and long white socks that belonged to his sister. Yes, it feels weird alright, but I'm so enjoying re-living the early days of a life well lived. I'm actually enjoying writing this more than I enjoyed the trip there in later years with Rosie. Don't get me wrong, it was great to show her my humble beginnings, of course it was, but how the place had deteriorated really got me. We were quite a proud gathering of families and I didn't sense that atmosphere on my return visit, it was a bland council housing estate and the magic had gone.

The sandals in particular make me smile, brown things with little holes cut out the top which were supposed to resemble flowers. On rainy days I waddled around between the goalposts like a duck trying to escape from quicksand. When I kicked the ball and caught it on the buckle of the sandal it really hurt, but I never screamed and rolled around on the ground like they do today. Mind you, I wasn't earning half a million quid a week either. Have you realised yet that the more a footballer who has tripped over an ant writhes in pain on the ground, the longer he appears on television showing off his boot sponsorship? It's the only time the cameras do close-ups of feet, just a thought but I bet you it's a consideration.

Round about this time in my schooldays those brown leather football boots were replaced by 'continentals,' black boots with white stripes down the sides that didn't protect the ankles but apparently made you run faster. I never knew in those days that professional footballers would one day wear pink, slip-on boots, have hairbands, bobs and ponytails. If my Dad had seen that one coming he would have made me play rugby or got that weird, confused lot to play netball.

The continentals were a blessing because my brother's friend, Martin Beak, who lived across the way in Folkestone Road, had a pair bought for him for his birthday and so I was given his old brown boots that I folded over so they looked like ankle-high continentals too. They resembled miner's boots with those rock-hard toe caps. Ants didn't stand a chance I'm afraid and even hippos would have been at risk had they frequented our playing field.

From the age of five to eleven I played every game for Vicarage, never missing one through injury or other stupid distractions like girls and cigarettes. All eleven of us played together for those six years and not one of us pulled out for any reason. Injuries didn't really happen back in the 1950s and footballers certainly didn't wear ear-rings for goodness sake. Nobody ever got booked or sent off, we just loved playing football. We never asked for ridiculous wage increases or demanded a transfer, we just played football until a red plastic ball burst and then we waited for another birthday to come around so we could begin playing again. A burst ball was our close season.

None of us appeared on Question of Sport or on adverts for smelly cosmetics, we just played football until it got dark, went home for our tea and went to bed. Floodlights had just about been invented but not at Blaney Crescent sadly. I remember once we asked Mr Duly if he'd turn on the headlights of his Hillman Minx so we could finish a very important game, but he refused, the miserable bastard.

Bedtime meant a cup of cocoa with horrible skin on the top and a couple of rich-tea biscuits, a hot-water bottle in the winter and a chance to cuddle the cats, Monty and Sooty, that had also wandered in for the night like me. They both slept on my bed, Sooty at my feet and Monty on my pillow, a strange threes-up if ever there was one.

This will mean absolutely nothing to you, so please forgive my utter indulgence as I put myself to the test and see how many team-mates I recall. In goal, yours truly, full backs were the aforementioned Kevin Sullivan who lost his Mum and slightly overweight Geoff Bright who didn't have a Dad so lived with his Mum and sister Carole in The Hameway. Geoff was the only team member who wore glasses, National Health glasses at that. He had a huge pink plaster on the left lens and so he played as a right sided midfielder, he had to or he would never have seen the ball.

Ah yes, National Health glasses, an essential almost compulsory piece of bodily equipment. Brown ones if you were a boy and pink ones if you were a girl, oh and white ones if you were The Milky Bar Kid. Nearly all of us wore them and it was indeed, as was the case with Geoff, a fashion for your mum to cover one lens with that pink plaster. Our eyes were both the same so it was nothing more than a pathetic protest to achieve some kind of sympathy. Additionally, they kept buzzing bees away and thus stopped them flying behind your glasses and stinging your eye. That was the national costume of the day. National Health glasses, a duffle coat, idiot mittens and black plimsols, never white. England may not have its own national costume now, unlike Scotland, Ireland and Wales, but back then we all looked more or less the same as we toddled off to school.

Centre-half was towering George Hilsdon, our captain, whose granddad played for Chelsea and had his wrought iron sculpture on a weathervane on the roof at Stamford Bridge once upon a time. George was considered special because his dad was a film extra and was often seen walking behind big stars or in a pub setting standing at the bar. In war films he was one of the soldiers who never spoke. Wow, such a famous dad and granddad, it was almost worth getting George's autograph. Then there was Kevin Bearman, a rarity in that he was an intellect, top of the class, who played football too and Happy Outlaw Keith Williams, a hard-nut fellow resident of Blaney Crescent whose brother Colin was a tough piece of work and troublemaker too who went on to become a prison warder on The Isle of Wight. Colin Williams was the only hard-nut I knew who also wore the dreaded National Health glasses but that didn't stop him beating kids up with gay abandon for no real reason. Tony Catchpole, Norman Armour, also both of Blaney Crescent and my best mate John Lacey, from adjoining Folkestone Road, played up front, and that's about it.

John's stepdad took me fishing for the first time at Walton on Thames and I caught a gudgeon with my home-made rod, a rod made from an old army tank aerial. It was very heavy and floppy, the aerial that is and not the gudgeon. I just made myself laugh when I realised that my first radio announcer when I joined the BBC was a certain Tim Gudgeon and I can't help wondering if they were related. I doubt it because there was no physical resemblance whatsoever apart from possibly bulbous eyes.

Whenever John and his stepdad, Les, went fishing they took me with them in a big white Ford Zephyr 4 and it was to become my great hobby through my life and still is to this day. Sitting in the car was special because we never had one. My Dad never took me, he just assumed fish came in batter, wrapped in an old Daily Mirror with a picture of Bobby Charlton on its arse where the print had seeped off. Anyway, that was our school football team, I'm a few short but not a bad exercise. Oh, I've just remembered our right-winger John King who lived in Brighton Road and had a back garden. To ease your thorough boredom, which I understand perfectly, I now apologise for such dreadful self-indulgence and move on to a far more interesting subject matter. I so wanted to find out team photograph but it never reached old age. I wonder if those boys suffered a similar plight.

I'm just eleven but I ain't stupid
My feet are firm on the ground
I was born on the wrong side of London
To see the sun shining down
So don't pity my bashed about shoes
I can be anyone that I choose

I'm just eleven but I'm not stupid
For an hour every night after school
And an hour before assembly
This back-yard is my Wembley
I've sure hit some goals against this wall
I'm an international
A back street international

Yes, I could be anyone I chose. I dribbled like Stanley Matthews on more than one occasion but more often than not I was a West Ham player, usually Vic Keeble who they signed from Newcastle United. I was the greatest goalscorer in the history of the game, the fiercest header of the ball, but I was a goalkeeper when the real games for my school came along.

If we spat on the pitch we would be punished with a back-hander, imagine that today, and if we feigned injury we were told to get up and grow up, all so unlike those footballers of today that I just mentioned who roll around in their own spit, and demand a week's wages that my Dad never earnt in his entire life.

And this is where this old man ponders and gets things into perspective.

My Dad's wages as an ambulance driver, believe it or not, when I was born would have been ten shillings a week in old money, or 50p, yes 50p for a week's work. The average house-price was £1,700, so well out of reach of the working class families like mine, and the average weekly grocery shop was less than a modern pound which is why both parents had to go out to work. How could life have changed so much in one man's lifetime? I have no idea, but that was the world I knew as a youngster living in the East End of London. It just goes to prove how many years I've been alive.

Mum and Dad never bought a home of their own and checking out such facts it is fairly obvious why. Two hardworking people who never stood a chance of getting on the property ladder, confined to council flats for their entire lives. When I started doing well on television I insisted they had a lovely house of their own but their inverted snobbery, a common East End thing, wouldn't allow them to accept my offer, my Dad reminding me that if they wanted a place of their own then they would have got it for themselves. 'Son, this is where I was born and raised and if it was good enough for my parents then it's good enough for me.' They both died whilst living in a tower block, Austin Court, Forest Gate.

I don't remember nasty gangs with guns, jellied eels, boiled beef and carrots and sing songs around the piano. No, we didn't do or see any of that kind of stuff and neither did any of my mates as far as I recall. None of us went to school singing The Lambeth Walk or dance down the street like Dick Van Dyke. I woke up, went to school, played football and helped Mum with the shopping and the household chores, oh and sometimes I was the class milk monitor. That was about it, boring as you read it now but complete happiness at the time. To close this opening burst of nostalgia, please allow me to tell you all about my shopping job because, as I think back, it's as unreal to imagine today as Dad's wages. I'm going back over 65 years now, before anyone had even a black and white television.

Uncle Dick and Auntie Winnie, who were not real aunts or uncles but Winnie was my Mum's friend as they worked together at Marks & Spencer so we had to pretend they were related, that was the way it was back then, stupid but at least I got an extra Christmas present, owned a butcher's shop and once a month I would be sent to the shop to pick up some meat that Uncle Dick kindly donated to us. I obviously wasn't too aware at such a tender age, but Mum and Dad were having a tough time financially and he helped us out with his generosity.

Now then, believe this if you will, to visit the shop I had to catch a bus and then a train, at the age of just five or six years old, because the shop was situated right outside Leytonstone tube station, a fair way from Blaney Crescent, let's say a million miles. This little bundle of tender years walked, on his own, to the bus-stop at The White Horse terminus, three-quarters of a mile away. From there I caught a 101 bus to

Wanstead, where I boarded a London underground train to Leytonstone. On the way home I lugged a hefty carrier bag of beef, ox-tongue, liver, mince and sausages, vegetarians hadn't been invented at that time, but never chicken. Now also bear in mind we didn't have freezers in those days either, just a Hotpoint fridge not much bigger than a box of cornflakes, so we ate like kings every one week in four.

All this was done on a Saturday morning, early enough to get back and play football for the school. Just imagine sending a five-year-old on such a journey, before it got light, in today's scary world. It just wouldn't happen would it? If it did you wouldn't ever see them again for sure. The bus-fare was a penny-halfpenny and the train fare was threepence. There and back, therefore, cost 9 old pence, let's say 5p with some change in today's dosh. My god, as I write this I can't help wondering why I never slept with Queen Victoria, surely I would have remembered.

I lived at 39 Blaney Crescent through my primary schooldays and, having failed my 11-plus as predicted, through my secondary modern schooldays too. My secondary school, Thomas Lethaby, was a slightly longer walk in the mornings and to be honest it doesn't rate as the happiest or most exciting time of my youth. I hated the school, never did my homework, was dropped from the football team, a ridiculous decision as I was one of the best goalkeepers in the whole wide world once I had boots, and when it came to GCEs time I flopped once again, gaining just four passes in English, thanks to Mr Jones, Art, thanks to Mr Rush, History, thanks to Mr Hurst and Technical Drawing, thanks to Mr Wernham, although I did get my National Cycling Proficiency Certificate and triangular badge though so not all was lost, even though I didn't actually have a bike. I know that doesn't sound too bad but I sat eleven exams so it represented quite a dismal failure rate that included maths, the important one. Something in my life just wasn't adding up so no wonder I failed maths.

Only one day really stands out whilst at Thomas Lethaby, the 28th October, 1962. That evening the school had a cricket match and one of the boys had gone home feeling ill and so I was chosen, or bludgeoned to be more accurate, to take his place in the cricket team at the last minute. I was a brilliant cricketer who should have played for England at the age of eight, but I never got in the school side so I wasn't that bothered about playing. I had decided to wait my chance and make my debut at Lords against Australia where my 200 runs would be more appreciated. Anyway, back in the real world, the problem was that I had no white sporty stuff with me and so I had to run home and run back again as fast as I could after school. Just before I left for home, horrible Mr King, who ran the cricket team with as much rage as he showed during PE lessons, asked me to listen to the radio at home and find out what had happened regarding the Cuban blockade, the Bay of Pigs, which I duly obliged to do.

To explain, we were on the brink of World War Three that very day because Russian ships were carrying missiles to be stationed in Cuba, in firing range of America. Kennedy and Khrushchev were daring each other to take one step too far and if that happened the dreaded nuclear button would have been pressed. The USA created a floating blockade of warships to stop the Russian ships offloading their missiles that would be in close proximity of the east coast. President Kennedy was having none of it and the world was on the brink, oh and I had to find my cricket stuff in the dirty washing basket, which didn't help matters. The Russian ships turned back, Kennedy won the day, and I was delighted to tell Mr King and my mates at school the good news. Peacetime would stay a while longer, so long in fact that The Third World War was brought on by a nasty virus army a short time ago.

Khrushchev was as frightening as the new bloke Putin but definitely not as macho. He didn't ride a horse with no shirt on or wear combats, he just looked like someone's grumpy, stumpy uncle. Kennedy looked like a film star and a far more believable human-being than Donald Trump, hardly surprising. Politicians were different then. Each nation trusted their leader and never for one minute did they take backhanders or kill those who opposed them. None of us liked Khrushchev particularly but he never sent his mates over to poison our doorknobs or work out the height of Thomas Lethaby School's clocktower. Question to Mr Putin, should he ever find this book in a Moscow bargain bin, what the hell was that all about?

Bear in mind, World Wars were a fairly regular occurrence and it wouldn't have surprised me or anyone else if it was all about to start again. Anyway, no war and no white cricket trousers, such a strange day was 28th October, 1962.

I faced up to the bowler with more bravery than the Russian fleet that evening and I say that with the greatest of pride. I never backed out and I reckon I survived three or four deliveries before I was clean bowled, causing me to retreat back to the pavilion like those cheeky Russians from Salisbury Station, but at least I gave it a go. No, I never backed down, I just lost the war, but hey, someone has to.

The following year President Kennedy was assassinated in Dallas and all of us of a certain age, oldies, can remember exactly what we doing when we heard the dreadful news, I most certainly do. It was a Friday night and I was working as a shelf-stacker at Browns Stores in High Street South, East Ham. As the news came out over the radio I was stacking blocks of Anchor butter on the shelves.

I was 14 years old and didn't really know what an assassination was. Kennedy's was the first unforgettable occurrence of that ilk and then more followed through the years, but just a never to be forgotten few that held firm in our grey matter.

When John Lennon was shot on 8th December 1980 by Mark Chapman, a so-called devoted fan which I find rather odd, I was editing my folk programme on Capital Radio and the whole building shuddered and went into shocked silence whilst the station began playing endless Beatles records in tribute. John Lennon was a massive inspiration to me as a street-cred songwriter. I found McCartney's songs almost too melodic, strange as that sounds, maybe even a little insipid at times, but Lennon had the hard-hitting lyrics and the more earthy melodies in my opinion. I related to him and what he was trying to say through his songs. Oh yes, I would dearly loved to have met the great man. He got in trouble at times, serious trouble it would seem, but haven't we all? It made him a more vulnerable human in my eyes. He stood up against authority and I liked that. Off the wall? There's nothing wrong with being off the wall unless you're Humpty Dumpty.

You may say I'm a dreamer

but dreams sometimes come true.
You may say I'm a dreamer
as I imagine sitting next to you.
Staring through those glasses
straight into my eyes.
Dare I strum along with you?
Dare I harmonise?
Miracles have worked through time
Like water turning into wine
To meet the man himself is mine
Yes you may say I'm a dreamer.

You may say I'm a dreamer.
Your words I choose to borrow.
You may say I'm a dreamer.
Yesterday maybe tomorrow.
You may say I'm a dreamer
but dreams sometimes come true.
You may say I'm a dreamer
as I imagine sitting next to you.
Staring through those glasses
straight into my eyes.
Dare I strum along with you?
Dare I harmonise?
Miracles have worked through time
Like water turning into wine
To meet the man himself is mine
Yes you may say I'm a dreamer.

You may say I'm a dreamer.

Your words I choose to borrow.
You may say I'm a dreamer.
Yesterday maybe tomorrow.

You may say I'm a dreamer,
But so often you are here.
For three, maybe four of five minutes
I hear you singing in my ear.
You left me but you never did
He never silenced you
that's why I wrote this song
as a gift from me to you
You may say I'm a dreamer.
Your words I choose to borrow.
You may say I'm a dreamer.
Yesterday maybe tomorrow.

When Princess Diana died on 31st August 1997 I had just returned from playing a concert at Oxford Apollo. On the day of her funeral 6th September 1997, I was up in Benbecula, at the northern tip of Great Britain, doing a show to British troops stationed at one of our early-warning outposts. I happened to be trout fishing in a nearby lake that morning when the three-minute silence occurred and so myself and a British soldier stood in a tiny rowing boat, there was only the two of us, as it rocked around in the strong, northern, biting wind. The upright soldier stood to attention and saluted and I bowed my head. It was a mark of respect that had to be done by both of us.

I met Princess Diana, not once but twice. First at Capital Radio when she came in the edit studio whilst I was editing my folk programme. She was well interested and watched me piece a song together with an introduction. I was instructed to wear headphones and look busy if she entered the edit studio, which I did. As I turned around I could see her talking to me, even though I couldn't hear a thing. I apologised and she giggled and she started again, asking me what I was doing. She was soon ushered along to meet the top-knobs of the radio station but she smiled nicely as she left and wished me good luck.

The second occasion was at Buckingham Palace, after a Princes Trust Concert at The London Palladium where I supported Sir Elton John who, by the way, told me he used to listen to the folk programme on Capital. Can you believe that? Princess Di asked how my editing was going, she actually remembered me and I just couldn't believe it. She was so beautiful in real life, stunningly so, and loved her music, especially Dire Straits and Duran Duran. I read recently of the set-up she encountered through that devious BBC reporter and I hate the way she was manipulated. I know from experience how nasty the media can be when you become a target. Once those claws are in they won't let go.

It's so amazing how those three people were so revered that their tragic ends stay with us forever. I often wonder if Lee Harvey Oswald knew where he was when Kennedy was shot. Oh well, it's just another conspiracy story now, a bit like the Titanic not actually sinking or Americans not walking on The Moon. There's a Diana conspiracy too which I choose to ignore for obvious reasons, the main reason being that it's so totally ridiculous.

The day I left secondary school, July 14th 1965, I knew I'd made a dreadful mistake by not bothering to study. We all burnt our books as we walked through the school gates in Langdon Crescent, bit of an East End thing I think, and as the bonfire raged it suddenly hit me that I was out in the big, bad world feeling naked and unprepared for adulthood. That evening I sat down with my Mum and admitted I'd blown my chances of being successful through my lack of attention to lessons. She quite rightly said it was my own fault and that I needed to give myself a wake-up call. I agreed, things had to change.

To that end, change they did, I enrolled for evening classes at East Ham College and worked at Safeway, again as a shelf-stacker, a magnetic occupation it would seem, to pay for my courses in English Literature and Modern British History. Let me tell you, you concentrate when you're stacking supermarket shelves to pay for your lessons. I knuckled down and gained two 'A' levels and thus gained my route to college. Oh yes, things definitely were about to change as books replaced comics.

Through my early years I dreamt of becoming a professional footballer, even having trials with Leyton Orient. The offer of a trial seemed out of this world and my heart filled with ambition and desire when I made my way to their Brisbane Road ground. Talk about a comedown and a reality check. There must have been a couple of hundred kids all running around like headless chickens. I accidentally kicked a goalpost and broke my big toe, a tragic end to a worthless football trial. So glad I never signed up with Leyton Orient though, a job slightly above having a paper-round.

All set for college, I was playing guitar by this time, never thinking for one moment it would eventually be my career, but this football crazy kid was on the brink of becoming a guitar-playing student so I was about to enter a completely different world enriched by Donovan, Bob Dylan, Leonard Cohen and anyone else who wore denim from head to toe.

Dear Mum had taken out a thing called a Provident Cheque to help me buy the guitar, one a tad beyond a nylon-strung unsuitable beginner's guitar, on the weekly as it was known. And so it was that we made our way to J60 Music Shop in High Street North, Manor Park. I bought an Eko Jumbo guitar for £28 with repayments of £2 per week. The man behind the counter who served me was a certain Steve Marriott who founded The Small Faces and went on to join Humble Pie with Peter Frampton. Steve, who lived in nearby Strone Road, died in a fire-blaze in 1991 and he always remained a great influence to me as both shop assistant and leader of The Small Faces, my youth club band. Sadly, I would never meet him again when Mum and I walked from his shop with my new acoustic guitar.

I know I promised I wouldn't name-drop too much but I think a Steve Marriott mention is valid under the circumstances. It's worth a boast when your youth club band featured Steve Marriott, Ronnie Lane and Kenny Jones who went on to replace Keith Moon as drummer with The Who. They rehearsed at The Ruskin Arms, just down the road, and so I used to hear them free of charge at regular intervals. Then they were actually on television singing their first hit record Watcha Gonna Do About It. I felt so proud in an odd kind of way, people I had met, sort of met, were on the telly. They made such a nice change to black and white Coronation Street.

It may seem strange to you but I've never owned that many guitars. I'm not a guitar enthusiast, I'm a guitar player and there's a difference. In my fifty years on the road I've only used five. My sacred Eko my Mum sorted for me, a Levin Goliath, an Epiphone Texan which someone stole from me and the one I still use to this day, my Martin D28 which is worth a small fortune because of its unusual colour. The fifth involved the occasional appearance of my Gibson 12-string that I lent to my agent at the time, Bob Voice, never to be seen again. That's agents for you. He should have at least given me twenty per cent of it back. No, I've never collected guitars like some do, to me they are work-tools. I look after them for obvious reasons, but I've never fallen madly in love with a guitar like I did with my very first instrument for fear of it being broken or stolen. I've kept a kind of distance just in case. Strange but true until lockdown when I realised my trusty Martin had been locked down too in its case for months and needed some TLC. Let's amend my statement right now, yes I do love my Martin guitar and I missed him so much for a year and a half and I have a funny feeling my guitar missed me just as much.

Where did you go? I missed your tender hand
Where did you go? I didn't understand
I looked all around but I couldn't see your face
I lay here wondering why you never took me out the case
I used to play the notes while you sang the song
All the times we spent together suddenly had gone
I wish I knew what happened to you
I want to know where did you go?

Where did you go? I've fallen out of tune
Where did you go? I hope you come back soon
The way you tuned me up the way you polished me
The way I helped you sing in a complimentary key
Everything went silent not a sound was heard
Not a single note was played not a single word
I wish I knew my strings do too
I want to know where did you go?

Most professional musicians cannot afford such a luxury as a collection of nice guitars. It's usually the semi-pros with steady jobs that have bedrooms or attics that look like guitar shops.

With my new qualifications the time had come to say goodbye to the East End for a while as I headed off to college in Glasgow and then on to Strathclyde. In fact, I left and returned to Blaney Crescent many times as things often didn't go quite to plan, as you shall hear, so this was my first of many such moves from home, temporary moves from home. Honestly, I was in and out of Blaney Crescent more times that my left leg in the Hokey Cokey.

My move to Scotland would play a major part of my future life as I gained a huge interest in folk music at that time, particularly English traditional music. So, it was not just goodbye to London, but also goodbye to The Beatles, The Rolling Stones, The Small Faces and The Kinks, plus my associated friends who were into that kind of music along with the button-down collared, Ben Sherman shirts and Chelsea boots, as I discovered the sounds of Bob Dylan and Phil Ochs amongst others and the different clothes they wore. I lost touch with just about all my mod chums when I disappeared up north, all of them actually, and so it seemed as though I was starting my life all over again in a different direction.

My ears had suddenly opened to lyrics of social comment and meaningful subject matter, way beyond the usual love songs of the bands I had previously followed. I was reading far more into a contemporary song than just a catchy melody. My life suddenly became exciting in a musical way this waster had never expected. For no real reason I had become a hippie, grown my hair long and fully embraced the flower-power movement of the 60s. People were singing of love and peace and walking around in sandals and kaftans. Most of us seemed to look like Sergeant Pepper, whoever he was. Any girl who didn't have flowing, shoulder-length hair wasn't really playing the game, so at least we all know where we stood. I sang We Shall Overcome not having a clue what it was about and the guy who sang Three Wheels On My Wagon as a member of The New Christie Minstrels, Barry McGuire, was suddenly singing about The Eve of Destruction.

Glasgow wasn't really the best place to walk around with shoulder-length hair and flowery shirts back in the day but that's exactly what I was about to do and, against the odds, I survived. Hey, I was a rough and tumble East End boy after all. I suppose I looked a bit weird, a bit like Leo Sayer on stilts.

I continued to play football though as many of my fellow students played for Clydebank as part-timers, but I wasn't struck on the aggressive side of Scottish football, mind you, having long hair and turning up in a flowery shirt didn't help matters. I was even kicked and knocked around in the warm-up by my own team-mates who all had short back and sides. They were even reluctant to allow me in the dressing room and shower with them, certain I was going through some sort of a sex-change. Glasgow hadn't moved with the times as quickly as San Francisco or London, they were still up there smoking ordinary cigarettes. Fine ones to talk mind, blokes strolling around in tartan skirts with a dead badger on the front.

Scotland, despite it all, would become a major turning point in my life for sure. I would be alone, for the very first time in my life, fending for myself and discovering more obscure music in the process. I was suddenly listening to blues music, the very music that had inspired The Rolling Stones through their love of Muddy Waters and Howlin' Wolf. It was strange that hippies like me, who were supposed to be having a great time of things, were all belting out twelve-bar blues epics, songs of gloom, doom and despondency composed by the savaged black musicians of the delta regions, with great regularity.

I'll tell you much more about Scotland shortly but, for the moment, we must say goodbye to Blaney for the first time in this story as I head for the frozen north.

The tiny council flat in Blaney Crescent had so many stories to reveal and yet it seemed so insignificant all those years later during my re-visit with Rosie. I obviously have no idea who lives there now but I can't believe they are having as fun a time as I experienced during those first few years of my life. Rosie loved seeing where I started out and I relished the return visit too, even though it hurt inside. It was as though I'd gone to say a last goodbye, paying a final tribute to the place where my life well lived began. I could probably name all the families that lived in the crescent and it's so weird to think that all the parents would have now passed away as would so many of my mates who joined me for games of football and cricket on the green.

I came to say a last goodbye
It's breaking my heart but I don't know why
It was only a pile of bricks and a creaking door
Progress leaves another empty space
Where we sang songs around the fireplace
Three-part harmonies but not pleasant on the ear

Yes, it was only bricks and mortar
Some windows let in water
But we all go a little downhill as time goes by
It was only bricks and mortar
The roof let in water
But I still had to come to say a last goodbye

I still remember the old back yard
Flyweight fighters with our kneecaps scarred
Never thinking all those years ago I'd be on the radio

Chapter 2 - Hello Scotland

The Glasgow experience was astonishing in so many different ways. I was desperately homesick before I even reached Scotland but there was no going back. Thank god for that. Had I done so I would never have made music my life because I wouldn't have known how to begin. For this wet behind the ears teenager a new life was about to start in a way I would never have thought possible and it was about to all happen such a long, long way from home. Mum and Dad didn't have a phone and so I sent them a card to let them know I'd arrived safely, and then we lost touch for months because I ran out of stamps.

I didn't know much about Glasgow other than the fact it had a reputation as being a bit of a rough house in those days. That didn't bother me in the slightest, the East End where I was raised had a similar reputation so it didn't faze me.

Why did I choose Glasgow? I was just short of the right qualifications to go to college elsewhere and Glasgow accepted me. Had there been an option to college anywhere else in the country, anywhere in the whole wide world, I would have taken it to be perfectly honest, but I had no choice. I knew a little bit about the place but not much. They had lots of football teams and a river industry like we used to have at The Royal Albert Docks as I was growing up. To me, it just seemed more of the same so I packed a bag, slung my guitar on my back and headed north. It was no big deal really as I had very few friends to say goodbye to due to my musical swerve and I promised to write regularly to Mum and Dad, something, as I just said, I never got around to doing. It wasn't laziness or anything like that, or lack of stamps as I suggested, I just knew Mum would burst into tears and Dad wouldn't have bothered to read it, so I didn't really see the point. Besides, I only wrote thank-you letters after Christmas, the other eleven months of the year my pen remained redundant. Come to think of it Mum and Dad never wrote to me either.

Being short of cash I hitch-hiked up to Scotland with my rucksack and guitar. There was no M6 motorway in those days, I don't think there were any motorways at all then, and so I hitched up the east side of England and spent my first night having left home under the stars in the ruins of Scarborough Castle with a girl called Linda who I had met on the beach, before heading further north towards the distant country that would be my final destination.

Regarding motorways, the first I remember encountering was the M4, that long vein of roadworks that stretch from London to West Wales. When I first used it, it only went west as far as Heathrow Airport and then it stopped and returned to A4 status. Anyway, back to Scotland.

I'd taken on a sandwich course at college, employed by engineering company Babcock & Wilcox, and I rented a flat, 98 Minard Road in the Glasgow area of Shawlands. I lived opposite Crossmyloof Ice Rink. An Ice Rink? I didn't even know what an ice-rink was. I knew it would be cold up in Scotland, but an ice-rink? An indoor ballroom you skated on? What the hell was that all about? I was young and didn't even realise the country had mountains with snow on the top let alone massive buildings full of ice. My new friends watched ice-hockey games, a sport which allows all concerned to beat the shit out of each other. Back in the day that was how Russia and America sorted out their differences.

It took two and a half days to get there from London but, due to fun I had in the castle with Linda, so it turned out to be quite convenient and, in the end, a bit of a result that I couldn't afford the train-fare.

My first-storey flat was adjacent to a railway bridge, under which sped the Glasgow to London express train. Each time that train rattled my window-frames I felt a pang of jealousy towards the passengers who were heading towards my Mum and Dad. I wanted to be on that train so many times but I refused to be beaten by homesickness. I'd already messed up my life once by not bothering to work hard at school and it wasn't going to happen again, or so I thought. Unfortunately, that's exactly what did happen again as I messed up a second time. Bloody music, that's what did it. If music had never been invented I would have become an engineer with a decent pension that would have come in handy during the last year or so of interminable lockdown. I wasn't expecting to starve so late in life.

Speaking of starvation, being the first time I'd lived away from home I soon discovered how hard it was to pay the bills or buy food, even with a job, and so I began to lose interest in all things that took a little effort like studying. I took on an evening job to enhance my lowly apprentice income, at The Argus, I think it was called, tying bundles of newspapers together with pink string so they could be thrown out of the backs of delivery vans as they slowed down at various newsagents. The job cut my hands to ribbons and it affected my guitar playing, which wasn't great in the first place, so my flatmates considered the weary job a blessing.

Just imagine what was going through my head at the time, a young football-mad kid who genuinely thought I would one day play for West Ham, being hacked down on Scottish football pitches by opposition and team-mates alike, tying up papers with string nearly 400 miles from home, papers whose back-pages seemed to be obsessed with Rangers and Celtic and none of the other lesser clubs that were at the bottom of Dad's football coupon.

The only time I went out after dark was my weekly visit to The Glasgow Folk Centre in Montrose Street, run by a scary-looking Scot by the name of Drew Moyes. I seem to recall that many of the singers looked like that menacing man on the front of a packet of porridge, he who wore a kilt and tossed a caber. Most Scottish folksingers had beards and a majority of those beards were ginger. This is where things begin to make sense, I hope. This is where my initial dabbling with singing in front of an audience began.

If you get up and sing a song in a folk club you get in free of charge and so, not having any money, I got up and sang, simple as that really and thus my career in folk music began. The first song I ever sang was The Jolly Waggoners, an English traditional folk song from an album by The Watersons. Needless to say, I died on my arse as it went down like a cup of cold sick, but I was unknowingly on my way to a new kind of life.

I still remember walking into that club for the first time. Hamish Imlach was the main act and second on the bill was a certain John Martyn, a brilliant songwriter and guitar player and a close friend of Hamish. I sat on my own, not knowing a soul, until I plucked up the courage to tell him, John Martyn, how much I'd enjoyed his set. He joined me at my small, lonely table that sported a flickering candle and we became friends in a matter of minutes. I invited him back to Minard Road even though I didn't have any food or drink to offer him. Skint times. I never ever had any food and drink in the flat at any time now I think about it. John scrounged some crisps from the bar as part of his support act fee and so we dined like lords after all and we played guitars through the night, him brilliantly and me very badly. He'd just written a beautiful song called Fairy-tale Lullaby and we sang it over and over again.

If you want to ride a rainbow come with me
and I will take you to the magic dancing sea
And if you want your friends to come
then bring them all along

I'm sure he accepted how crap I was because he had a warm bed for the night and in return I received free guitar lessons from a musical genius, even though my fingers stank of cheese and onion. I reckon I learnt five years of guitar playing in just one year.

We began following The Incredible String Band, a duo comprising of Robin Williamson and Mike Heron. We both fell in love with their music and we went to see them whenever we could. They began as a trio with third member Clive Palmer but he soon left. I still recommend their album The Hangman's Beautiful Daughter to anyone who doesn't know their music, because it's the album that made me think out of the box with regards creativity.

John was reasonably well-known so he always managed to get us into places free of charge. I couldn't afford to buy many albums so I memorised the String Band's words while John, as brilliant as ever, played the guitar parts. That was my move across from the traditional folk music to the more contemporary style of the String Band. In those days it was as black and white as that, you were either traditional or contemporary folksingers and no half measures. There weren't any folk comedians at that time either, no folk bands apart from the odd duo, even my college folk club resident Billy Connolly was going down the serious route by teaming up with Gerry Rafferty, he who wrote Baker Street, in a duo called The Humblebums.

It was later, a few years later, when he pioneered the folk comedian movement, followed by the likes of Max Boyce, Fred Wedlock and Mike Harding. Billy was a great inspiration to me although I've only met him once in my life, at the Dunoon Folk Festival in Scotland. The inspiration rose from the fact that blokes used to buy him pints and girls used to chat him up when he came off stage and that was good enough for me, I wanted to be Billy Connolly, or certainly as popular as Billy Connolly, perhaps my luck would change on the social front in Glasgow too. Knowing my luck at the time blokes would have chatted me up and girls would have bought me pints of beer.

John Martyn went on to great things, becoming a huge-selling songwriter with even Eric Clapton singing his song May You Never. He worked with David Gilmour of Pink Floyd and Phil Collins of Genesis at the time, so he was a highly respected musician, unlike me. I'd learnt so much from him as I progressed with my guitar playing and I remember well the sad day when he told me he had signed a record deal with Island Records and was heading for London. 98, Minard Road would never quite be the same again and I so wanted to return to London with him. It was my first step to realising who and what I wanted to be. Glasgow had made my mouth water and I had a feeling there was more out there for me to taste. I knew John would benefit from living in London and, to be honest, I was as jealous as hell. My jigsaw of life still had a couple of corners missing.

He taught me how to tune my guitar in various ways the same as he did, his song Fairy-tale Lullaby being a classic example with its E bass string dropped down to D, and I smile as the young folk musicians today think it's cool and innovative to put their guitars into all sorts of weird and wonderful tunings such as DADGAD. We did it half a Century ago, yes, it's cool but hardly innovative. John Martyn did it all, years before they were born. Respect where it's due all you young guitarists.

In one instance he took a traditional song, Spencer The Rover, and with a different modal guitar tuning he put a new slant on a song that had been popularised on the folk scene by Shirley Collins and her sister Dolly and sung by most traditional singers of the time, yet John's version seemed as contemporary and ground-breaking as the songs he wrote himself at the time. To hear a lilting old English ballad sung, accompanied by a guitar stuffed with various effects including his early Watkins echo-chamber dabbles as we used to call it, was completely revolutionary. I would go so far as to say that one song was his constant connection with the folk scene as he moved away with his more avant-garde style of singing and playing along with Pentangle's Danny Thompson and his wife Beverley. There weren't many other guitar players experimenting in such a way with our beautiful, virginal traditional music. I don't know when Spencer The Rover was first collected by our nation's song collectors who travelled the lanes and byways of Britain, recording the songs sung by our farmers and country dwellers, but I do shudder to think what they would have made of experiencing John Martyn singing Spencer The Rover.

These words were composed by Spencer The Rover
who travelled Great Britain and most parts of Wales
He had been so reduced which caused great confusion
and that was the reason he went on the road

Such were the traditional lyrics of that song, not very John Martyn-like and yet he made that song his own for a while. It suited the unique guitar tuning he was dabbling with at the time. Because he was experimenting with echo, that Watkins CopyCat, reverb in today's jargon, he needed new guitar chords that didn't collide into each other and contort, causing a nasty musical crash.

On stage I never use different tunings because I'm too busy telling stories but in my studio at home I experiment as much as anyone else. DADGAD is the most used tuning these days, first deployed by Nic Jones I think. Nic ran The Three Cups folk club in Chelmsford and we all dreaded playing there because he was better than all of us. Nic was seriously injured when his car collided with a lorry on his way home from a gig and he was a huge loss to the growing folk scene.

My Eko jumbo guitar was as influenced by John Martyn as much as myself. It all began after we'd seen The Incredible String Band in Stirling. John noticed that Mike Heron had quite literally shaved the front of his guitar down to bare wood and John decided to do the same. Drastic stuff. It seemed to work though, his guitar sounded amazing and much louder without the plastic coating. Needless to say, I followed suit with the help of paint stripper from a hardware store on my first guitar, followed by frantic French polishing. It worked and it became a talking point later when I returned to London and a friend painted a scene from Middle Earth on the top corner of the guitar's body. Oh yes, we were all into Lord of the Rings and my guitar proved I'd followed the travels of Bilbo Baggins and Gandalf.

I made probably the greatest decision of my life by giving up life in Glasgow, dropping out of college, and following John Martyn back to London. I was penniless and couldn't afford the train fare home so I just shut the door at 98, Minard Road, leaving everything behind except my cherished guitar, and hitch-hiked my way back to Mum and Dad in East Ham. It took me nearly three days to get home as my first kind traveller was heading a few hundred miles out of my way. It didn't matter where I was going, so long as I was heading home. I spent the first night sleeping beneath the stars back in Scarborough Castle, in the hope Linda would still be hanging around, and spent the next morning busking on the beach next to some useless engraver who ruined people's identity bracelets, a huge fashion of that time. I made a few pounds, bought fish and chips for him and myself and then continued on my way home with a full stomach, a rare biological fact.

Comment [THG]:

The second night I slept by the River Cam in Cambridge, waking up every ten minutes because I was petrified by the scuffling of water rats. I tried my hand at busking for a second night and I made absolutely nothing, but hey, Cambridge had its fair share of great musicians, but it was a nice place to starve. I loved sleeping beneath the stars, something I would never have risked in The East End of London for obvious reasons. At least I could boast I went to Cambridge, even if it was for just the one night.

I was taking far more interest in history and folk music than engineering, plus I had suffered more and more huge bouts of homesickness, a horrible sensation of hopelessness if you've experienced it yourself, and so my return to the warmer climes of the south would be most welcome when I finally got there. I enjoyed the Modern British History tutorials though and became obsessed with those who created and expanded the Industrial Revolution, all of which contributed to my growing interest in folk music. Through the years I have made a special point of visiting the former homes of our pioneers such as Brunel, Abraham Darby, Samuel Crompton, just to soak up the ambient feeling of those clever inventors and developers. To stand where they stood is always something special to me and a strange hobby I fully accept.

In 2019, just before lockdown, I was allowed to examine letters at The Wiltshire Museum in Chippenham that were written to Florence Nightingale by Isambard Kingdom Brunel. They were original letters and so I touched his very writing. It made me tingle and I can't tell you how many people I bored down the pub with that one. None of them needed sleeping tablets that night. They all seemed far more interested in

EastEnders or Coronation Street, two soaps I still know very little about I have to confess. Brunel for heaven's sake, I more or less touched his hand. Sod Eastenders and Coronation Street, the tips of my fingers were touching history.

I don't think I've ever watched an episode of Coronation Street all the way through, although I recall Elsie Tanner and Len Fairclough, but I do remember The Daily Telegraph mentioning it a few years ago when they were giving an award for the best cryptic crossword clue of the year. The clue was 'a bar of soap' and the solution was six letters and six letters, rovers return. Very clever.

I stuck with living in Scotland for fourteen months in all before I chucked it all in and decided to return to London. I still remember the 'Welcome to England' sign by the side of the road because it brought a tear to my eye. I was ever nearer to home, via Scarborough and Cambridge, as I stuck out my thumb on the side of the road for the last part of my journey. People used to stop in those days, unlike nowadays.

Mobile phones hadn't been invented and so Mum and Dad had no prior warning of my return. Taking three days to hitch-hike back to Blaney Crescent I looked like some manky stray cat at the doorstep when Mum opened the door. I felt like one too if I'm honest. She opened the door and just sighed as if she knew I would return. Her first words to me confirmed she wasn't in the least bit surprised I'd come home.

'Cup of tea?'

I had grown my hair and wore a bright green Sergeant Pepper style mandarin jacket as I took my Mum and Dad by surprise. Mum hugged me for ages and didn't seem too bothered I'd slung everything in to become a professional folksinger and that I looked a right tit in the bargain. She made me a cup of tea and a huge fry-up as I told her how my life had changed so much over the past months. Mum understood I needed to follow my dreams. Considering my Mum finally went to art school when she was 63 years old I would imagine she would have so loved to have followed her dream sooner too.

My brother had moved to Wickham Road, Lewisham in South London where he was at Goldsmiths Art College and my sister, Jill, had become a nurse at Whipps Cross Hospital in Leytonstone, living-in, so, luckily, there was room for me and my guitar back in the tiny council flat. I remember my Mum telling me I slept for two days like some hedgehog awakening from its winter slumber. I wouldn't be surprised if I bathed for two days too when I woke up, I don't really remember but it would have been a damn good idea bearing in mind the tatty journey home.

There was a slight problem however. Dad told me I couldn't stay unless I cut my hair and got a job. Mum told him to get lost and hugged me again like a bear. Dad relented but mildly disowned me, thinking the neighbours would be embarrassed once again, in his words, dancing down the road like some ballet dancer. I'm not surprised those words came from someone who said The Beatles couldn't possibly sing properly with their ridiculous haircuts. It got worse when he saw those filthy Rolling Stones. He fought in the war for them?? Good old Dad, but he knew how to drive a lorry and change an engine on a Cortina. I had a horrible feeling I would be catching mice over the allotments and climbing in through the fanlight window again as he locked the doors again, but I stood firm and my hair remained long.

Thanks to John Martyn's lessons I wasn't too bad on the guitar at this point, not too great yet not too bad, and I'd been to a few folk clubs to gain some experience of what it was all about. Watching The Incredible String band helped me too, they had charisma, a word I wouldn't have ever heard at that stage of my life. John had bedded down in Lower Richmond Road, the other side of London, so we lost touch for a while as I couldn't afford the train fare to visit. The next time I saw him was at a coffee house called La Bourge, excuse the guessed spelling, adjacent to Richmond Bridge. He strolled in bare-footed, wearing a sky-blue silk kaftan, holding a huge Indian sitar of all things, something that may not have gone down too well in Glasgow back in the day. He couldn't play it but it looked impressive, like a wooden ET dummy with its thin body and bulbous head. It made him the centre of attention and I just tagged on, not looking quite so impressive. The place had a cute courtyard at the front where hippies sat and talked for hours in the open air for the price of a cup of coffee. I loved the place.

John's first album 'London Conversation' made the album charts and his next, 'The Tumbler,' was even bigger, so soon he was playing The Royal Festival Hall and headlining all the major theatres and university gigs around the country. We were at different levels, very different levels, but we kept in touch. He moved to Willoughby Road in Hampstead and I went there a few times as he put me through my guitar paces once again.

Another thing I remember about John at that time was that he'd developed a cockney accent. Although he was born in New Malden the year before me, 1948, as Iain McGeachy, he'd spent a lot of time up in Scotland and had a gentle, lilting voice, thus his vocal style, so it was odd he suddenly rattled out words as if he had been cast in Only Fools And Horses and swore like a trooper. A London Conversation indeed.

In 2016, at the Cromer Folk Festival, I sat drinking with Blair Dunlop, one of today's great musicians, after our gig and he was mesmerised by my time with the legend that became John Martyn and my occasional meet-ups with Nick Drake, someone I met with John half a dozen times or so and yet I never heard him speak a single word. He sat quietly and nodded a lot as though he was considering every sentence spoken in the room. Nothing changes no matter the differences in age, we all start somehow, idolising our contemporaries, and I remain proud to have known the great man.

John sadly died in Ireland in 2009 after years of ill-health. We drifted apart when I started singing funny songs. It wasn't his thing at all and he just didn't get it. It was cheap in his eyes and I didn't see him for many years but nonetheless we discovered The Incredible String Band together, a major influence on both of us as we built our very different careers. Thanks for the memories John, even though you despised what I did in later years. It was odd to me that he took such a stance of dislike towards me, particularly on a personal level, when he loved telling the funny stories himself in between songs but hey-ho, such was his choice. One thing for sure, you never argued with John Martyn. I shall always remember the nights in Minard Road when we shared packets of crisps and cheap bottles of wine that should have been sprinkled on chips.

Despite what you may think to the contrary I loved Scotland. The people were a really friendly bunch and I made many new friends during my short stay at college. Only one threatening looking native in a kilt and ginger beard came at me the whole time I was in Glasgow, but to be honest I didn't find her that attractive so I side-stepped out of the way and she crashed into a wall and burst her bagpipes. Just had to get a Scottish gag in somewhere and that was it. I've never been one to dismiss a cheap laugh.

Sadly, I knew I'd lose contact with all of them eventually, never to meet again, and that's exactly how it has turned out. Glasgow and London are 370 miles apart and with no transport, mobile phone or address book it more or less had to be that way. It may have been different if I hadn't failed my first-year exams due to musical distractions. A degree? No, sadly not. There was more chance of a rocking horse winning The Grand National. I may have stayed if I'd achieved a higher Workshop Technology grade, but I didn't. Thank goodness my daughters did better than me.

My trusty guitar was still by my side, stripped and French polished but intact, and it had become ever more important, a true friend and well worth the two quid a week repayments that my Mum made to pay off the Provident loan.

Not dissimilar to Blaney Crescent with Rosie I returned to Minard Road just a few years ago whilst doing a gig in Glasgow. My dear friend Jack Westwood took me there and I sat in his car and stared for ages at another part of my life that used to be. There was no ice-rink, that had obviously melted away and the whole area looked so different, apart from the window I stared out of at 98, Minard Road. It was the pending return to Blaney Crescent in my head all over again.

Strangely, as previously briefly mentioned I only ever met Billy Connolly the once, at Dunoon. Strange because we followed the same path of folk entertainment and we were both signed to the same record label, Transatlantic, but our paths were never to cross again. I have no idea why, it just never happened. He was a massive influence just the same and I would have loved to have had the chance to thank him for being such an inspiration to me.

Back from Scotland, my parents knew I'd blown it again. I knew it too. I'd given everything up to return home. With no future and no job I began working in a shoe-shop, True Form, in East Ham High Street. With my earnings I took driving lessons and much against the usual outcomes for me I passed first time, so no more hitch-hiking for me. All I needed was a car. Only skint people hitch-hike and I sold shoes. I no longer needed to mix with such reprobates. Oxford Brogues and tartan carpet slippers paid a much higher commission than any other shoes in the shop and so I sold them as if they were going out of fashion, a strange statement as they hadn't been in fashion in the first place. If I'd had my way everyone in East Ham would have been wearing Oxford brogues and tartan carpet slippers and I would have been driving around in a Bentley.

I still remember the name of the shop manager, Charles Sodeau, a really lovely, understanding man, who wasn't too struck that my entire wardrobe was denim. Instead of having a go at me he took me to a clothing shop a few doors down by the name of Brent & Collins and bought me a pair of sensible black trousers and a belt which were left on a hanger in the shop so I wouldn't forget to wear them. Thank you, Mr Sodeau.

I never appreciated his kindness until just now, nearly sixty years too late.

So, I was home from Scotland and settling into life back at good old Blaney Crescent, but, through no fault of mine or my parents, it wouldn't be that way for too long. I felt restless. I was used to playing strange music and sitting up all night, something my Dad wouldn't encourage as Bob Dylan was American and he didn't like Americans, which was something to do with the war I think, like most things he disliked.

Not all was lost though because East Ham had a folk club and I was meeting new people who also had long hair like me. I didn't feel as much of an outcast as I first thought but Dad just didn't understand any of it. He told me that if he wanted a kid with long hair, he would have had another daughter. We didn't talk for weeks but that was no big deal as words failed us both.

Mum was so happy to have me back home and that was all that mattered, but Dad kind of demanded I only went out at night so the neighbours wouldn't be scared by his son on the brink of a sex-change. I remember when I got home from Scotland he was working underneath a neighbour's car and his first words were to ask me to hold a spanner while he adjusted the clutch. Oh, to be back in the world I thought I had left behind. I didn't know how long I would be back with Mum and Dad for, but the time had come to get a proper full-time job beyond the shoe shop and save some money as opposed to selling shoes a couple of days a week.

I started paying rent when I got a job at Chappell's Music in New Bond Street, Posh London. It had little to do with my interest in music, purely coincidental, it was just a job advertised in the paper. I became a print-order clerk, making sure they never ran out of sheet music or songbooks. Mr Len Bishop was my boss, my very strict boss with a PA called Barbara Hayes who was even stricter, and he caught me doodling on a scrap of paper one day when I should have been working. Instead of a bollocking he got me designing front pages for the sheet music. I loved the freedom and I remember my first two designs were for Neal Reid's Mother of Mine and Rod Stewart's Maggie May. The year was 1971, the days of flower-power and the 'do as you please' attitude of a newly liberated world were fading fast from view and it was time to look towards growing up a bit. Well, it seemed like a good idea at the time but thank god it didn't work out that way.

If I'm honest I could have made a career in music publishing, but I wanted to be the songwriter and not the printer, thank you very much. Despite how it sounds it wasn't a particularly interesting job. I think the highlight was meeting Johnny Marks who wrote Rudolph The Red Nosed Reindeer, he just wandered in one day whilst in London on a visit from America, while Mr Bishop was at lunch, and I made him a cup of tea. Just listen to this conversation.

'I'm afraid Mr Bishop isn't here at the moment, would you like a cup of tea?'

'That would be most welcome, thank you. So what do you do at Chappell's?'

'I make sure we never run out of sheet music.'

'Ah that's good, that means you must print some of my songs.'

'Quite possibly, would I know any of your songs by name?'

'Yeah, probably. Have you heard of Rudolph The Red Nosed Reindeer and Rocking Around The Christmas Tree?'

My bottom lip hit the carpet as I handed this musical legend his tea. I'd only made Johnny Marks a cup of tea. He wished me well and went on his sight-seeing way. You should have seen Mr Bishop's face when I told him he'd missed Johnny Marks while he was at his lengthy lunch break. He went absolutely mental, even running out into the street to see if he was still around. The very thought of him running up and down Regent Street shouting Johnny's name makes me really laugh, going up to people and asking them if they had seen an American tourist. Eight million people in London and he raced around looking for a man with a straw hat and multi-coloured umbrella. What made matters worse was that he blamed me when he couldn't find him, as if it was my fault. His rage turned him as red as Rudolph's nose.

Time for me to move on yet again though. I wasn't keen on the daily commuting by tube from one side of London to the other, especially as I sat up so late most nights playing my guitar. Many's the time I woke up on a tube-train to discover my head resting gently on another passenger's shoulder. I often wonder if I snored back then like I do now.

Ordering sheet-music print wasn't really for me but when I handed my notice in I was surprisingly offered a far more interesting job as a sheet music cover designer. I genuinely didn't realise Mr Bishop thought that much of me. It was very flattering and any sane person would have jumped at the opportunity and the pay-rise, but I had un-started business in the music business as a performer as opposed to the other kind of artist and nothing was more attractive than the distant dream of being a professional musician. I'd bought a stereo record player and my collection of blues albums had grown, well I say that, I only had half a dozen but that was a huge rise from the zero number I had before.

Rudolph the Red Nosed Reindeer
He went down in history
As for the man who wrote it
I once made him a cup of tea

Chapter 3 - East Ham Folk Club

East Ham folk club ran every Friday night at The Central Pub in Barking Road, next door to a block of flats made famous by The Kray Twins when they found Mad Axeman Mitchell hiding there. It was to be where I would really learn my trade, music I mean and not gangland crime. It was run by Dave Van Doorn and his brother-in-law I think, Ken Brown. It was an amazing oasis for us folkies, even though it was in a typical, working class, East End pub which has since been demolished.

There was some man on the piano downstairs who sang ballads with no teeth, a female singer called Vi who sang with a roll-up in her mouth and the whole place stank of stale beer and rotten carpets, but once I climbed the stairs to the upstairs function room it was pure heaven. In that drab room I saw all the musicians who inspired me and with whom I became good friends as time passed.

I rarely sang there as they had so many fantastic resident singers. I remember each and every one of them. There was Martin and Bone, Martin Scragg and his student mate, a duo from Devon who were studying in London, an unaccompanied trio called Home Brew, a pair of female vocalists Jennifer Beeching and Christina Williamson, The Farrows and a superb guitar player, Roger Moss. Dave and Ken knew I was totally broke and so they always let me in for nothing, even if I wasn't singing, for which I remain eternally grateful. In return, I sold raffle tickets for them and put the chairs away at the end of the night before walking back home to Blaney Crescent. I certainly began to feel part of the folk scene at last. I muscled in to all the conversations as I swept up the fag-ash, empty glasses and failed raffle tickets before I went home.

My biggest inspiration at that time was Ralph McTell, famous for writing Streets of London, but who wrote so many other brilliant songs too. He became a big friend through the years but at that time I just watched his fingers and listened to his words. His guitar style, unlike John Martyn's, was heavily influenced by the American ragtime style of blues legends Blind Blake, Willie McTell, where I assume Ralph adopted his stage name although I've never asked, and The Reverend Gary Davis. As Ralph learned from them, I in turn learned from Ralph, just by sitting at the front and watching every move of his hands. He was generous with his help.

One of my prized possessions at home is a leather-bound book of Ralph's lyrics which he gave me at The Cropredy Festival in 2015. It's signed and says 'To a dear friend, with so many memories.' I couldn't have summed it up better myself. Without any doubt I owe my ragtime guitar style to Ralph, a musical genius just like John Martyn. When I did a 'Desert Island Discs' programme I named his Factory Girl as one of my favourite songs and a truly modern-day folk song if ever there was one. My Mum was a factory girl in the Romford Road, maybe that's why I loved the song so much.

The old London term for a factory cleaner was a washerwoman and that's what mum was. She used to scrub the floors and clear up the mess left by thousands of jelly-babies that had just started out in life. The natural assumption of a washerwoman is an old dear at a sink scrubbing the old man's collars along with pants and pillowcases, but no, it was someone who scrubbed floors. That's what mum did until she went to art school at the age of 63 and realised her dream.

She's just a washerwoman with teardrops in her eyes
Wondering as she scrubs the factory floor
She thinks of all the faces and the places she has seen
And other things she'll never see no more

She was born into the backstreets in 1919
Was began when she was 21
So she never saw the flicker of a silent movie screen
But often heard the cracking of a gun

Given the chance again oh how she's dance again
Oh how she'd take to the floor
But no knight in shining armour will take her by the hand
Like they did in the days before the war

Many well-known performers climbed up those stairs at The Central pub to perform at my local folk club, including many who developed a wider appeal such as Paul Simon, Peter Sarstedt, Sandy Denny and Barbara Dickson, but there were others who were a great inspiration to me, particularly with their guitar playing. John Renbourn of Pentangle was one of my favourites. He smoked twenty Gold Leaf cigarettes during the course of his gig and he played guitar like a demon. Again, I watched his fingers and learnt so much. I don't wish to sound arrogant but many young musicians have told me how I inspired them to play the guitar through YouTube and other means but I can assure you, flattering as that is of course, I have my own influences without whom I would never have made music my career, Ralph McTell, John Martyn, John Renbourn and Roger Moss, not so well known on the folk scene as the others, but who I should really tell you about shortly. Oh, and I think I should throw in Bert Jansch for good measure. I met up with Bert many times at The Half Moon in Putney and we got on really well even though we were opposite sides of the performance and musical spectrum. Unlike John Martyn he liked my stuff and we laughed often.

Ralph will tell you that Roger Moss was one of the very best guitarists around and I agree. Roger lived in Redbridge, near Ilford in Essex, worked at Ilford Films, and could have been a huge musical star but his strict parents, in my opinion, held him back. Hang on, not in my opinion actually, they really did hold him back. He certainly wasn't a rebel with a cause at all costs like I was. We formed a duo for a very short while called New Mythology and Roger taught me so many guitar licks in the short time we were together. What went wrong? Neither of us had cars and we lived a fair distance apart so we were restricted on where and when we could play. I suppose this was the real beginning of my fifty and more years on the road even though it began via various Eastern National bus routes and not a trendy transit van.

We took up a Sunday residency at The Starting Gate folk club in Wood Green where I so wanted to hang out after gigs but we had to get back home on the last bus as usual. Roger was never allowed to stay out all night so it was always out of the question. New Mythology lasted just a few months but it was invaluable, working alongside a brilliant guitar player like Roger. Don't have a clue what happened to him. He would certainly have moved on to great things if his Mum and Dad had taken the shackles off him. Parents eh? Who'd have 'em? Well, I suppose it's better than being an orphan. New Mythology, ha what a crass name. That Mr Tolkien had a lot to answer for. Back in the day musicians argued for hours over what to call themselves when they teamed up. Agreement would often take days. It probably wasn't that difficult for Chas and Dave, they obviously couldn't be bothered with all the arguments, a sensible decision.

I suppose our one real claim to fame was that we supported T Rex at Rush Green College near Dagenham or, more accurately I should say that T Rex supported us. Marc Bolan asked us if he could go on first or he'd miss the last tube home, which we agreed to, so theoretically I suppose, going on first, Marc Bolan was my first ever support act. Imagine that? Every time I watch the Billy Elliott movie, particularly when they dance to I Love To Boogie, I recall that night and smile. It really is a funny old world. Bloody hell, I spoke to Marc Bolan. I liked him too, a nice gentle soul. I hope you're enjoying all this name-dropping stuff. Marc was a devout folkie for a while, his surname being the first and last letters of Bob Dylan. He was a good-looking guy, destined to be a pin-up, unlike myself, and so I wasn't surprised in the slightest when he entered the world of glam rock. Actually, I have a funny feeling he may well have created glam rock in this country. It definitely wasn't me or Les Dawson.

After New Mythology split I began to hang out at the all-nighter folk joint Les Cousins, a cellar music club situated below a Greek restaurant at 49 Greek Street, in the heart of London's Soho, where all the big names from here and America played. Roger definitely wasn't allowed to participate in such debauchery of an all-nighter and that was another ingredient that forced my return to solo work. I started going there on Wednesday nights too, a weekly jaunt run by guitarist Gordon Giltrap.

I never got to actually play on the big weekend nights but Wednesdays was easier to get on. Wednesdays became a ritual, a tube to Tottenham Court Road, buy the Melody Maker, look through the windows of the guitar shops in Denmark Street and then a gentle saunter to Greek Street. I used to get so nervous as Gordon was a wonderful player and I was still verging on the fairly average. Contradiction again, I seem to be putting myself down again. I wasn't useless, I just wasn't that enjoyable to listen to, a bit like a modern jazz concert, I knew all the notes but didn't necessarily get them in the right order as Eric Morecambe once told Andre Previn. Giltrap was different class.

Les Cousins was the only place of its kind then and there's been no other place like it since in this country although there are such through the night venues in America and Holland funnily enough. It ran from 8.00pm to 11 and then opened again from around midnight to 4.00am when people went to sleep where they sat as there weren't any tube trains running that time of the morning. The most regular compere was Al Stewart of The Year of The Cat fame.

Al was playing a residency down the road at Bunjies in Little Titchfield Street and he then turned his allegiance to Andy who ran Les Cousins, a smart move as it became the in-place to hang out. There were two main acts on every Friday and Saturday as opposed to the usual one. In one single night you could sit in that dingy, small cellar that stank of kebabs and watch young singer/songwriters like Steve Adams. Steve Adams? You've never heard of him? I think you have if I told you he changed his name to Cat Stevens before changing it yet again in later life in support of his religion. Donovan played there a few times too, I once saw him there with Sandy Denny.

Closing this chapter of my musical career, hanging around in sleazy clubs in Soho, and serious name-dropping, I remember Sandy Denny coming back to Mum and Dad's to stay the night after appearing at East Ham folk club as, unlike Marc Bolan, she'd missed the last tube back to the other side of London and had nowhere to go. I was her last chance saloon because everyone else had gone home as I swept the floor and put the last of the chairs away. I obliged, we walked back to Blaney Crescent and she slept on the couch with our cat Monty. I couldn't do the chivalrous thing and offer her my bed as I shared a room with my brother. The next morning my Mum made her a bacon sandwich before she headed off west.

I seem to remember she was a nurse at Brompton Hospital in West London and her boyfriend was an American folksinger called Jackson C Frank. She was still semi-professional at the time but we all knew she was destined for big things. She was about to take the folk scene by storm like no other performer has ever done since or ever will again.

Sandy more or less created the entire electric folk movement on her own. It just wouldn't exist today were it not for her. She joined Fairport Convention and turned them from a band doing American covers to the inspirational folk band they became, indeed the most inspirational folk band in the world. I often wonder what would have happened if my dear old Mum hadn't made her that sandwich and she'd died of starvation many years before she sadly did. But for my Mum's bacon sandwich there would have been no electric folk scene that exploded in the late 1960s after Mum had turned off the frying pan. There would possibly have been no Fairport, no Steeleye Span or other such famous bands. Sandy went on to form Fotheringay with her new Australian husband Trevor Lucas and my Mum went on to cooking ham, egg and chips, so both benefitted from the short meeting at Blaney Crescent and went on to far greater things.

A few other singers stayed with Mum and Dad too. There was Shelagh McDonald, a Scottish singer who was doing really well until she simply disappeared off the scene without trace. She'd made a beautiful album in 1970 with such musicians as Richard Thompson and Danny Thompson and then she was gone a year later. Some journalist from The Scottish Daily Mail found her in 2005, thirty years later, and she had been living in a tent after a particularly bad LSD trip.

Dave Cartwright, a singer/songwriter who was a great friend of Clifford T Ward, one of the few folkies to ever have a number one hit record with Gaye, stayed with us too on quite a few occasions. He lived in The Midlands, in Kidderminster, and stayed when he had gigs in London. Dave was a very polite man, so polite that even my Dad liked him. We were both signed to Transatlantic Records and we became good friends.

We lost Sandy Denny many years ago now, a tragic loss to our folk scene. She died in 1978, falling down a flight of stairs, I lost my Mum seven years later. My Dad didn't like Sandy because she swore a lot and was a bad influence but I adored her. Oh yes, and all female singers sounded the same to him. He would have been shot down in flames if Toyah Willcox and Gracie Fields had formed a duo. There was something radical about Sandy Denny that I envied. She said the kind of things to my Dad I would never have said myself, yet she sang like an angelic cherub. Such beautiful songs like Solo and Old-Fashioned Waltz. I'd seen her sing first with Alex Campbell at The Central and then The Strawbs but it was when she joined Fairport that we all realised something magical was happening with songs like The Banks Of The Nile and Matty Groves. Fairport Convention were nothing more than a covers band singing songs by American songwriters but with Sandy and Richard Thompson in their ranks, things would change in a short time. She later went on to sing with Led Zeppelin too. I say here and now she was the best female singer I have ever heard in my 50 years of performing. Simon Cowell would have hated her, that's how bloody good she was. All that creative energy from a solitary bacon sandwich. I think this is the point where we all raise a glass to my mum.

To digress for a moment and speaking of rubbish talent shows I got slagged off on New Faces once and I wasn't even on the bloody show. How unfortunate was that? There was some guy from Doncaster, Steve Womack, singing a funny song and one of the panellists, Nina Myscough, again excuse the spelling if wrong but who cares in this particular instance, told him he sounded like Richard Digance and that one Richard Digance was enough thank you very much. Bit harsh. Someone once asked me what I would do if I ever met her and my reply was I'd get her pregnant and if it was a boy I'd call it Richard. Another Richard Digance. Another journalist once called Ken Dodd the greatest dinosaur of comedy next to Richard Digance. Even harsher I would suggest. I would have got him pregnant too if he hadn't been a bloke.

It goes with the territory to be slagged-off once you are on television, maybe that's why I struggled so much in that industry. Sometimes it hurt. It's a British disease that doesn't happen anywhere else. Stand-up comedians of that time had been toughened up by playing the working-men's clubs around the country. They took all the insults and barracking, giving back as much as they got. I'd never played such a club in my life and so found it harder to take all the slagging-off on the chin. But it's something you have to get used to.

Britain loves to slag-off people as they get older, be they singers, movie stars, comedians, sports personalities. Once you reach a certain age in this country you have to work very hard to not become surplus to requirements. In America you are respected and revered, in other countries too, but not here in unforgiving Britain.

I remember American comedian George Burns, aged 99, being asked what he would do on his 100th birthday and he replied he would like to play The Royal Albert Hall if it was still standing. Fantastic reply. Mature performers are respected over there, not quite the case over here where we really do become surplus to requirements.

Even when I make my annual performance at The Cropredy Festival I get slagged-off mercilessly by some who think it's clever but actually it isn't. The clever thing is to get up in front of 23,000 people on the Cropredy stage and have them shouting for more. It's Fairport Convention's festival and they even slag off Fairport Convention at times. Weird people. The simple answer is not to go into the field during my set. There are loads of other festivals around The British Isles. It's a shame that a few music-lovers are filled with such hatred.

At 2016's festival I chose to dedicate a song to absent friends. After all, the folk scene has lost so many in recent times. I chose to re-write one of my older songs Goodbye My Friend and it worked well I reckon. I know you shouldn't read your own reviews unless you want to slip into a bout of deep depression but it got hammered. In my eyes it was a respectful thing I chose to do and I stand by me decision. I know only too well you must take the criticisms and I've been around long enough to take my fair share of them, but sometimes it confuses me. As I say, the song was for those no longer with us so, good or bad, it deserves a little respect.

Goodbye my friend goodbye
I must turn as you take to the sky
I know you have to go
The cold winds came to tell you so
It seems so hard to me
To accept what has to be
I know the time has come
For you to follow the sun
So take your place in the sky

Goodbye my friend goodbye

When I got on television I still held the folk clubs in high regard. We toured for a while in a small 15-seater coach and I always bored my team rigid by making the driver stop whenever we passed a pub where I once sang. I sat and stared for a minute or so, taking in the memories, and then we drove on. They all respected my gesture and went along with it. They all knew had I not played those rooms at the back of pubs they wouldn't have been on my tour coach, and these were acts who'd never set foot in a folk club in their lives.

The 15-seater, supplied by Wakes Coaches of Wincanton along with driver Steve Scarsbrook, made a nice change for me from driving everywhere on my own as I had up to that point. It had tables and we played cards and Trivial Pursuit as we rattled around the country in comfort and splendour. We stayed in hotels too, pure luxury. British tours were organised by the promoter and the tour manager took care of logistics, an important part of any major tour but someone I don't have to use these days. I've had a few tour managers in my time but certainly not as many as most. Sadly, I can't remember all of their names but most went their ways when they demanded more money or were offered a better tour. They've never been known for being the most loyal species within the music industry. My first and last, without doubt the most loyal, were Dave Bubb and Matt Hampton.

Dave was around in the 70s with me and he was ok. He sang in a Kent duo with Damien Aked when he wasn't working for me and, although we got on well, he had this dreadful habit after every gig of telling me where I went wrong and what songs he would have sung if he was me. He even started writing songs for me to perform, which I didn't use as I wrote my own, so needless to say, it didn't last.

Matt Hampton was the best tour manager by a mile. He's still a close friend to this day and he helps me with all things technical. Matt was a quick learner and I was pleased to have offered him the work until he found his feet as a TV and film cameraman. He became a huge success in that field but we still meet up on Saturday mornings every month or so for a breakfast and a natter at my house. I knew I was holding Matt back from a more lucrative and secure career but we had some great times together travelling the world, from The Caribbean to The Arctic Circle.

Unfortunately, most of my touring during my fifty years on the road was during the Autumn or Winter months. There was the odd summer season to negotiate but summertime has never been a good time to tour, what with public distractions such as holidays, kids off school, barbecues in the garden, people saving up to go away. We toured mainly in the colder months, and still do. It isn't always great and sometimes needs drastic measures to keep going.

I remember one time, during my heady television days, we were in the tour coach driving through the Essex town of Great Dunmow towards a gig at The Mercury Theatre in Colchester. It was a wet Tuesday. We were freezing cold and it must have been close to Christmas because we were all wearing Father Christmas hats to cheer ourselves up and keep warm. We'd been on tour a while and we were all in need of a rest to ease the depression caused from cold condensation dripping down the inside of the coach windows. Things were damp and miserable. We were all sneezing and sniffing as we sat at a set of red traffic lights in the High Street and as we did so I glanced across and saw a travel agents on the other side of the road. It looked most inviting I have to say. I told Steve to park the bus up on the kerb and in I went. The conversation went something like as follows;

'Can I help you, sir?'

'Yes,' I replied. 'Where's the warmest place in the world right now?'

'I beg your pardon?' she replied.

'Where's the warmest place in the world right now? I repeated.

'Probably The Gambia.'

'Right, in which case I want a holiday for eight, a week in The Gambia, please.'

She stared at me for a while and I stared back. She seemed a little on the shock side.

'Aren't you Richard Digance off the telly?'

'Yes.'

'So, is this a wind-up is it?'

'No.'

'So, when is this for, this trip to The Gambia for eight?'

'This Sunday please,' I replied.

She stared at me once more before getting to work tapping away on her computer.

That really happened. That weekend I was to take my team to The Gambia including tour manager, merchandise seller Rachel Ivey, support act, driver and tour photographer Keith Curtis. I climbed back into the bus, clutching brochures and posh envelopes, soaking wet from the pouring rain and told them what I'd just done in the travel agents. They didn't believe me at first but within a few days we were swimming with turtles and barracuda fishing in the beautiful blue waters, things that aren't that easy to do in the outskirts of Colchester. One of my moments of sheer madness I must admit but we all had a bloody good time, re-charging our batteries for the final stage of the British Tour in yet more horrible, cold weather. Two of that tour team left the minute we finished that tour, suntans still intact, that's why I haven't listed their names. That wouldn't be very nice. Loyalty and gratitude aren't always seen in the same sentence and those two leavers also proved that loyalty and gratitude don't always exist amongst members of a tour team either. I've always been lucky with a great bunch of workmates through the years but there were the odd exceptions.

A tour bus and a friendly audience was a far cry from experiences on stage in my earlier days. Once I was shipped off, by an agent by the name of Ann Dex, to Sweden in 1974 and I took my fellow Plaistow chum, Doug Morter, with me. The venue was The White Corner in Gothenburg, an eating house and bar that had been granted a late licence if they booked English acts as it had been marketed as a good old English pub. It was coming up to Christmas so the country was plunged into darkness for most hours of the day, twenty-three to be precise. Depressing or what? We needed the money and it was five weeks abroad so it was really a no brainer but I don't think either of us had ever been so bored in our lives, nor have we been since.

The ferry trip from Felixstowe over there seemed an eternity, hardly surprising because it was a bloody eternity, and

I hated the place, full of pretend pissheads and noisy to boot. We had to play four 45-minute sets each night, yes four.

Nobody was ever there for the first set so every night the first three quarters of an hour consisted of just one song, The House of The Rising Sun. The deal Doug and I made with each other was that neither of us was allowed to sing any of the original words so we made the words up as we went along. There were verses about our schools, catching crucian carp and where we'd rather be and what we'd rather be doing. Nobody was in the room so it didn't matter what the words were, and when the room filled up very few of the punters understood English anyway so it didn't matter much then either.

Before the second set, during the break, we would eat, compliments of the restaurant. We had steak every single night for five weeks and I'm sure that prolonged my life. I'd never eaten steak before, nor salad. Mum never did salad because Dad would have complained it was cold and the food with which they fed rabbits. No, Dad would have none of that, he didn't fight in the way to be given a plateful of cold food. We tried different sauces on our steaks, sauces I'd never heard of let alone eaten before. We dined like lords, making the most of the offer as we prepared for the second music session.

Set two was Doug bashing out some blues in good fashion and long-drawn-out guitar solos that thankfully lasted an equal eternity to the ferry trip. His raunchy guitar style was more suitable than my delicate fingerpicking so most of the time I just left it up to him. I was, if you like, the rhythm guitarist and it was a tedious task playing the same three chords of a 12-bar blues for 45 minutes.

Set three we sang songs to the audience and set four we sang songs to a drunken audience who didn't know what day it was or the time, judging by the constant darkness. And we did that for five weeks! Strangely we built quite a following and after the first fortnight we were packing the place for the late-night sessions. All I remember about Sweden other than drunks, were the freezing cold weather and rump steaks the size of the late Ronnie Corbett. I never saw Gothenburg as it was pitch black most of the day and it forever snowed so we stayed in most of the day. I don't remember the countryside either.

Sweden was cold, we kind of expected that, but Doug was surprised when he washed his pants, his only pair of pants, on the first night, hung them on the windowsill of our flat above the gig, never thinking they would freeze and never thaw out the whole time we were there. You could have smashed plates with them and I think we did. All those beautiful Swedish women and we spent every day doing a jigsaw of mostly sky, until the final day when we kicked it around the room in total desperation as if we were members of The Who. Neither of us could wait to get home.

We were met at Felixstowe by Steve Kemp, Rick's brother, who broke the news to me in the car on the way home that while we were away he nicked my girlfriend at the time, Alison, who just happened to be sitting on the back seat when he told me. We all just shrugged our shoulders. Worse things had happened at sea, or across the sea to be more accurate.

I suppose the very worst time was one night, during set four, the drunks set, when some nutcase went up to Doug on the stage, knocking over a pa speaker, and asked him to sing I

Never Promised You a Rose Garden. Neither of us knew the Lynn Anderson song as indeed Doug told the drunk, an answer that led to the man putting a knife to Doug's neck. We both promptly sang I beg your pardon, I never promised you a rose garden, along with the moonshine, with additional made-up words we were able to do what with our set one rendition of The House of The Rising Sun. After the song the drunk burst into tears, hugging Doug whilst telling him it was the best version of the song he'd ever heard. Such a tosser. When you endure and survive five weeks of that pure hell together, then you are inseparable friends forever, as indeed we are.

The House of The Rising Song by The Animals was a massive hit record in the 60s. It was a very long song for a 45rpm single and for most of us it was the first real blues song we'd ever heard. I remember buying it, never thinking it would come to my aid in Sweden so many years later. Everyone of my age remembers that song, it being a common song to play for rookie guitar players. And of course, there are those for whom the songs means more or less nothing at all, depending on your age, as is the case with so many other things. The House of The Rising Sun was up there with all The Beatles classics, sung by Eric Burden who seemed to pull his throat to shreds as he bellowed out the song about a brothel in New Orleans. The Animals came from Newcastle but that didn't stop them having an affinity with such a grubby establishment. Most of us knew the words, I repeat, it all depended upon your age.

Depending on your age it's either ladies drawers of knickers
Depending on your age it's either marathon or snickers
Depending on your age it's either Beatles or Oasis

Depending on your age it's either holdalls or suitcases

Depending on your age it's either texts or conversation
Depending on your age it's hopscotch or Play Station
Depending on your age it's arthritis or its cramps
Depending on your age it's bonus points or Green Shield Stamps

Depending on your age it's either 8 tracks or CDs
Depending on your age it's either Brie or Dairyleas
Depending on your age it's Adele or Sandie Shaw
Depending on your age it's Daniel Craig or Roger Moore

Depending on your age it's Pink or Billy Fury
Depending on your age it's The Voice or Juke Box Jury
Depending on your age it's either Buzzcocks or The Goons
Depending on your age you play the keyboard or the spoons

Chapter Four - And So To Essex

West Ham's former football ground, Upton Park, wasn't actually in West Ham. In actual fact, it was a fair distance from West Ham, a bus journey at minimum. The actual postal address was East Ham but it was far more confusing than that. It stood where Green Street meets Barking Road, the main road into the city of London. Barking Road at this point isn't in Barking, but in East Ham and Green Street is in the area known as Forest Gate. Where they meet is The Boleyn pub, where Anne Boleyn apparently stayed. If you think that's complicated it gets more so because the real name of West Ham's ground was The Boleyn Ground and not Upton Park. At the start of the 20th Century, The Thames Ironworkers, as they were known then, moved there from The Memorial Ground, which wasn't in West Ham either or on the banks of The Thames, but in Plaistow where I was born.

So why is all that useless information important to my story? My parents three-bedroom council flat in Blaney Crescent was, according to the council, surplus to requirements as all three children, myself, my sister Jill and my brother Leonard, had all moved on and so they decided to move my parents on too, to Forest Gate, so a larger family with children could move into 39. And so it was goodbye to Blaney Crescent and the monumental, ornamental garden as they were moved to the seventh floor of Austin Court in Kings Road, not the famous Kings Road. The high-rise flats were about a hundred paces from Upton Park tube station and overlooked the south bank of the football ground. That was where Mum and Dad would spend the rest of their lives. I moved there too but it wouldn't be for long as I craved to be a musician on the road and find a new place to live away from my parents.

My first ever paid performance, crap as I was, my first outing as a professional musician to be more precise, was at The Bus Folk Club in Cooks Road, Stratford, in London's East End and not Shakespeare's gaff, not that far from where they built the Olympic Stadium or whatever they've decided to call it since West Ham United moved in. I was paid three pounds. Yes, a whole three pounds and there was no agent's fee, so it was all mine, every single penny. I can't remember if I blew it on champagne or a packet of fags. And it really was a bus, a grubby, smelly converted London Transport double-decker that had been painted sky blue before being dumped in a scrapyard to die. The seats had been taken out and the small audience, in number not size, sat on old blankets or moth-eaten cushions on the floor. The singer stood with their back to the driver's cab, if you can imagine that, and there was no pa system, of course there wasn't, it was tiny.

When the interval arrived we all went upstairs and supped oxtail soup and crap coffee served by a woman who looked like the late Queen Mother. I don't have a clue who she was or how she got there, she being much older than the rest of us, but she was always there just the same, dishing out the soup and coffee that resembled yacht varnish. It definitely wasn't The Queen Mother, she didn't come to the East End too often once The Blitz had ended. More to the point I think she preferred salmon fishing on the Tweed up in Scotland to boiling up soup for dodgy folksingers in Stratford by the banks of the River Lea. Think? I know.

I never dabbled with drugs, none of us did, they were for headaches or constipation. I indulged in that possibly royal oxtail soup though. I'm not sure they even sell it anymore. They probably do but I never buy any. I've just checked, yes, they do still make it but very few buy it. They don't make kidney soup any more though, hardly one of the biggest surprises you are going to discover in this book. Whoever had a spoonful of kidney soup? That must have tasted like a muddy puddle and if not it would have looked like it.

So just imagine such a scenario today, a filthy scrapyard with the gates wide open at night so a bunch of hippies could walk up to a double-decker bus, painted sky blue for some reason, sing some songs and walk back home. Let's just say the chances of such a thing happening would be slim.

My first ever paid appearance was important to me as I needed to impress a girl I really fancied called Barbara Thompson, not the famous jazz musician Barbara Thompson, but just Barbara Thompson. Ah yes, the gorgeous Barbara Thompson, as fit as a flea. She had long, brown hair, wore tight jeans and everyone in the bus fancied her rotten, but none more so than me. It mildly worked as I once walked her back to her home near Blackwell Tunnel, so I got further than anyone else at the bus. She never invited me in, in more ways than one. I'd been the star of the show for the first time in my life, she was bound to want to go out with the biggest singing sensation since Elvis Presley, or so I thought.

I got home at 2am and my Dad had bolted the door so I had to climb through the fanlight window like Sooty my cat did most nights, usually with a mouse from the allotments in his mouth. I never understood my Dad's decision because he too must have chased the opposite sex at some point or I wouldn't be here. I think my Dad's actions stemmed from the fact he didn't like folk music and didn't want his son to sing folk songs for a living. He would have preferred me to go out at night in search of those mice on the allotments and become a toolmaker, that's how much he hated folk music. Little did he know I didn't like eating mice. That old bus in Stratford shall remain forever close to my heart.

On a summertime day down Stratford way
We forgot all out troublesome strikes
Me and Gillian Johnson
Would go for a ride on our bikes
We only reached Bow cos we peddled really slow
But we sure had a whole lot of fun
That Stratford day seems so far away
But that's when your dad met your mum

A few years later, along came my trusty four-tyred friend after a visit to Dovercourt Showrooms, a Volkswagen dealer in Plaistow. I'd watched the film 'Alice's Restaurant' starring American folk-singer Arlo Guthrie, son of the legendary Woody Guthrie. He went everywhere in a VW Camper van, lived an amazingly liberated life, and that movie inspired me to do the same.

Moving on to 1969, now a long time ago and yet it's a year that goes down in history, because Neil Armstrong walked on The Moon, the first Concorde roared overhead, The Beatles played a gig on the roof of their new Apple offices in London, and, more importantly for me, the Woodstock Festival took place.

According to Joni Mitchell's song nearly half a million free-loving, brightly dressed, beautiful children of the 60s turned up at a dairy farm in Bethel, New York, on August 15th to enjoy a weekend of music and head-spinning substances. A ticket for a day cost 7 dollars, or 13 dollars for two days. Those who played there became music legends, every single one of them. From Jimi Hendrix, to Crosby Stills and Nash. Thirty-two acts in all, mostly performing in the pouring rain, the last performer being Hendrix himself at 8.30 on the Monday morning. I rate Hendrix highly but I'm not sure even I could have handled him that early in the day. I prefer Weetabix to heavy rock music when I rise.

More importantly, as far as I was concerned, folk-singer Arlo Guthrie sang at Woodstock, all on his own. Just him and his acoustic guitar. I had this stupid idea he drove there in his Volkswagen Camper van. Yeah, right, of course he did, but that was the reason I found myself at Dovercourt, I wanted to live the dream in a VW of my own.

There they were, lined up like soldiers on the forecourt, Volkswagen camper vans of various shapes and sizes. Some had split-windscreens and some had split tyres, it was the East End after all, whilst others had the spare-wheel bolted to the front. I reckon there must have been a selection of around a dozen or so, but my mind had already been made up quickly due to the size of my pocket. I could just about afford the cream one on the end, the sad one no-one else wanted because it didn't have a roof that raised for more headroom. It needed to be adopted rather than sold. I'd chosen the bedraggled, miserable-looking animal at the dog's home, for which I paid £799 and my dream became a reality. Don't get me wrong, £799 was a lot of money then and it was quite flash to be a folk singer with a VW camper van like Arlo.

It would become my Ritz on wheels, a constant place to get my head down as I travelled Britain in search of whatever it was I searched for and whatever the music industry had to offer me. With luck it would soon pay for itself as an alternative to other overnight accommodation. Oh yes, and it did 60 miles to the gallon, 20 miles to the gallon uphill and 60 miles to the gallon downhill. I sensed it had been a showroom fixture a while without attracting any buyers, causing the dealer to nudge the poor thing along the line until it finally found its rightful place on the end. Any further to the side and it would have been in the gents' toilets. I didn't care, I had a Volkswagen camper van and that's all I needed to kick-start my career as a solo musician. I couldn't wait to taste the open countryside and the miles of excitement it afforded me. In Arlo Guthrie's movie his VW acted as a magnet to attract beautiful women, I hoped my cream camper van would have the same affect after my lack of success previously mentioned, but I wasn't really holding my breath. Just as well. Magnets repel as much as they attract. It had been worth the wait and it was better than staying in people's spare rooms.

Hotels? Of course not! Hotels were for rich people who could afford to have a fortnight's holiday somewhere along Britain's coastline. These days hotels welcome travellers, wedding guests, corporate meeting attenders and dirty couples, rarely musicians, but back then they didn't really welcome anyone other than holidaymakers without noisy kids and If they weren't holidaymakers they were couples by the name of Smith. They were respectable places where they didn't encourage any form of how's your father, preferring to play host to the clean-living Smiths, Browns and Jones's. Musicians like myself weren't welcome, whatever our names were, which didn't matter in the slightest as we couldn't afford such a luxurious stop-over anyway. Please note Motorway Services owners, we didn't have to pay to park then. They were just glad of our custom, even if it was just stopping off for a cup of tea. We slept in car-parks free of charge then. We used to call them welcome breaks, not unwelcome breaks.

There was something romantic about sleeping in a lay-by too, even if you did wake up covered in condensation and a damp sleeping-bag. A shower? No such luxury. A change of underwear? Sometimes, even if it didn't need changing. The thought of it added fuel to my dream of the open road and the freedom I craved for. If Arlo could do it in Stockbridge then so could I.

My time in Glasgow, my starting out time in East Ham, it had all been worth it, but now the time had come to put on long trousers and prove to myself that my dream could come true. No-one around thought it would, particularly my Dad, but I didn't listen. They all had jobs and girlfriends whereas I had neither but a burning ambition down another road, a road I would travel with my new VW Camper Van. I still recall the excitement when I parked it outside Mum and Dad's for the first time. Dad wasn't sure about it because it was German and I don't need to tell you what my Dad thought of that place. Germany wasn't part of East Ham so it was a horrible place full of horrible people who were the reason he went off to fight in Africa while back home they bombed his local fish and chip shop. No, he didn't want a German tank outside the flat.

No budding musician or singer back then ever wrote a song believing it would be a massive hit and turn them immediately into millionaires, apart from me I suppose. Greed within music and the idea one can simply swan into the charts without learning the trade is a relatively new belief brought about through talent shows that are sometimes nothing more than karaoke. I hate X Factor as much as I hate the bloke who owns it and hogs it. He once said on that show that he hated people who sang funny songs. The feeling is mutual Simon old boy. The thought of a panel being more important than the performers I find totally horrifying. Back in the day all musicians had to complete a kind of apprenticeship if they wanted to make headway in the music business. Fame didn't come with a single appearance on television. Blimey, Dixon of Dock Green was on every single week and he never had a hit record.

Suddenly I was travelling further afield than East Ham Folk Club in my dream machine, not as far as Germany but further afield just the same. My friend Jazz Summers and I opened our own club at The Angel Pub in Ilford High Road and our claim to fame was refusing Mark Knopfler a floor spot because we didn't have time to put him on. I don't think it affected his career. He sang with his brother David at the time and then along came Dire Straits. We wouldn't have booked them either if they'd asked us because folk clubs didn't welcome electric guitars and drums in those days. Noisy buggers. We had Spencer Davis there though, remember Keep On Running?

In days long gone now, musicians, particularly vocalists, were mindful they needed to look after their well-being and, to that end, most smoked roll-ups as opposed to tailor-made cigarettes. These days they encourage the five a day plan for fitness and health, in those days they enjoyed twenty or thirty a day. Five of what and twenty or thirty of what isn't probably the same what, well it obviously isn't referring to the same thing but that further confirms the difference between then and now. Everyone smoked in those days, even trains and car radiators.

Ask anyone, like myself, who was around half a century ago what they reckon stands out as the biggest difference regarding life on the road then as opposed to now and most will give one of two responses. Roadworks, the dreaded disease that has struck Britain's roads today, or the demise of transport cafes, the luxurious pause of yesteryear, two subject-matters that sum it all up. Let's begin with the latter before we attack the former. There was a time when we all ate white bread and some of us are still here. Ah yes, good old transport cafes, free copies of Spotlight magazine and a smell of fried bread in the morning and stewed cabbage at lunchtime. Whilst some musicians were taking drugs I sucked Rennies. They were an institution, something that anyone under forty years of age have sadly missed out on, and I'm speaking of both transport cafes and Rennies. People didn't eat bananas and yoghurt in those days, they scoffed chip sandwiches smothered in brown sauce and sucked Rennies. Winston Churchill won the war by sucking Rennies. Bananas were for the middle-class types who didn't like apples when they first appeared in Britain in the 1950s and yoghurt tasted like milk that had been left on the doorstep for too long on a summer's day. Salad? I don't think so. Rabbits ate salads, not starving musicians. Spaghetti? He could have been an Italian World Cup player, playing in defence alongside Lasagne for all I knew back then when your stomach knew exactly what headed its way.

The only time things changed and shocked the system was on a Sunday when a transport café cooked roast beef and Yorkshire puddings. It was always beef and never chicken, and it came with a beige-coloured gravy that you couldn't find, or want to find, anywhere else. It had the consistency of paint and really should have been much darker like gravy at home, but it never was.

They didn't serve vegetarian food. I'm not sure there were that many vegetarians around in those early days as we were forced by our parents to eat what they placed in front of us. There wasn't any choice. We ate it or went without. I don't think I met a vegetarian until I was in my 30s. Her name was Sue Holland and although being a vegetarian she looked perfectly normal to me, two arms, two legs and everything in the right place. Yes, I weighed her up alongside my other pals that ate sausage sandwiches smothered in brown sauce and she didn't look any different. I have to admit she looked a darn sight better than most of my spotty pals who didn't eat properly or regularly. I don't know when the first vegetarian smuggled itself into Britain but it must have been around about that time. Maybe Sue Holland was the first ever to reach our shores from another planet. Sue played classical guitar and she taught me the piece of Johann Sebastian Bach that I still play on stage to this day. Anyway, regardless of that she didn't eat meat. I loved Sue but she wasn't keen on coming to Mum and

Dad's because the cuisine centred around Dad's burnt sausages. He fought in the war against vegetarians to save the burnt sausage from extinction.

These days, transport cafes are as rare as rocking-horse droppings but they used to be an essential stop on any long journey. It wasn't uncommon for us to park up overnight in their carparks, so we were ready and waiting once the café opened at 7am. The lure was that good wholesome grub and a chance to meet up with other lonely souls in white vests that housed large bellies. It would be fair to say if it weren't for transport cafes the whole Country would have been over-run by now with sausages like Dad's by the million and baked beans by the trillion. Brown bread? What the hell was that?

Tea came in mugs the size of a toilet bowl, unlike the silly cups and saucers handed out in a guesthouse. Slices of bread were huge, they were known as doorsteps, sometimes needing a Sherpa to reach the top of the sheer crust and steep glacier of butter. As I said, we're still here, albeit with reduced arteries yet we're a darn sight healthier than the roads we travel on. Most of them are terminal.

Lorry drivers we shared the road with scanned the back pages of The Daily Mirror to read about the previous night's football before thumbing to page three to eye the finest pair since England's 1966 World Cup heroes Geoff Hurst and Martin Peters. There was no big deal about sexism, political correctness or equal rights when I started out on the road. Hey, it was the swinging 60s, a time of free love or a tenner in the back streets of Portsmouth. Swinging means something else these days, something I can't indulge in being a single man. Let's tell it how it is, some women were more than happy to show off their milk-churns in tabloid newspapers as a step towards a lucrative modelling career, showing their bumpy chests to a few million of the working-classes ensured fame and fortune for many, or certainly fortune as they knew it then. Just one appearance guaranteed a massive hundred pounds for a modelling assignment. If they didn't like it, they could have easily covered themselves up and become secretaries like so many other less brazen types had chosen to do. I myself never chose to be a topless model so I feel qualified to comment. Come to think of it, I think I auditioned once but never got the job. No, I didn't.

There were saucy calendars too that boasted two naked bumps for each month of the year, produced by a tyre company, though I never understood the connection other than having to tread carefully when you met such a woman. In this modern world of equality all such pictures are a thing of the past with the more discerning lorry-driver engrossed in crosswords while they wait for their food. I remember back in 1971 having a thing about February. She was a corker. I call her a corker because she would definitely have floated in the sea. Of course, we all welcome the equality in society but young ladies seeking modelling assignment didn't do their sex any favours.

In all honesty I never bothered with such attractions. The big deal for me was getting a Melody Maker music paper on a Wednesday night and scouring the back-page ads in the remote hope somebody wanted a ropey guitar player to join their folk band. I rarely saw such an ad, if at all, but it kept my hopes up at a time when it would have been easier to give up. Then I would turn to the folk page. Ah, sheer bliss. It was called

Folk Forum and it listed all the folk clubs and who was appearing. With that page I would plan my week depending on how much petrol I had. I would visit some of the clubs and hope they would let me get up and play, even maybe book me for a future date if luck was on my side, which it rarely was as unknowns never really stood much of a chance.

I remember when I appeared in Folk Forum for the first time. It was so exciting and it made all the hard work well worth it. There it was; The Ram Folk Club, Wandsworth, South London, Richard Digance supported by Jon Wyse. I cut it out and showed my Mum. I'd made it. I was mentioned in the same paper as Bob Dylan. I remember that gig too. It wasn't exactly bursting at the seams but it went ok and someone, John Townsend actually, came along and booked me for The Nags Head in Clapham. It was time to buy a diary!

The New Musical Express, a rival music paper, had a folk page too but it was no great shakes and so did another music paper, Sounds, but I could only afford one paper a week so I stayed loyal to Melody Maker, the one that gave me my first mention, thus telling the world of my arrival on the scene.

Ok, let's talk about the smallest gigs I've done. I know the smallest for sure. The Hole In The Wall folk club in Chichester, Sussex. I have a thing about Chichester because it's where the Digances landed from France in the 18th Century. It seemed Chichester didn't have a thing about me though. There wasn't anyone there when the club started at 8.00pm. Just the organiser and me watching. He did half an hour of chorus songs so I had to join in. Then it was my turn and he returned the favour. When we reached the interval he climbed on the stage, apologised for the small crowd and proceeded to cancel the raffle. The rotten bastard, I would have won. I was paid £5 and he promised to book me back, which he never did. The rotten bastard again.

Guitar sound was and still is important, particularly in the early days when clubs didn't have pa systems and buying new guitar strings was a luxury I just couldn't afford. For those of you who have a guitar at home you probably never have to change the strings. They're on there and that's that. These days I put fresh strings on every two gigs. It wasn't financially possible then but I was taught a trick by the late John Renbourn of Pentangle. It's a tip I'm delighted to pass on to you. Impurities dull strings and that kind of thing comes from sweaty fingers, dust or dirty digits. John told me how strings could be brightened up by taking them off, boiling them in a saucepan and then putting them back on. It gets rid of all the impurities and they sound as good as new for no extra cost. It doesn't stay that way for long however and the strings are slightly weakened by being taken off the guitar, so be warned, but it really works and you can thank John Renbourn for that one. Try it if you have a neglected guitar at home. Anyway, I digressed once again so back to the transport café.

The transport café represented a haven for all and sundry, as welcome as a lighthouse in a storm. The good old tranny knew no class difference, thus allowing the truckers to mix with the hairy musicians without raised eyebrows or comment. We all lived in perfect harmony on the road, both knowing the other had to eat so they all considered each other as equal knights of the road. Bands travelled in Ford Transit vans in the main whilst solo singers travelled in bashed-about cars, often with broken windscreen-wipers. It didn't really matter so long as they made it to their next gig, that's when the egos were raised. Folksingers and flash cars didn't seem to gel somehow. I wouldn't have swapped my camper van for the world, certainly not for a Ford Transit that stank of an oil refinery by day and cheap perfume by night, if you see what I mean. I say that, but that's exactly what happened as you shall hear.

Transport cafes exhausted, we now turn our attentions to roadworks. They're more of a threat to musicians these days than sexually transmitted diseases were way back in the day. Diseases go away but it would seem roadworks are here to plague us forever. They make us scratch our heads, unlike other experiences on the road that made us scratch other areas in days gone by. I knew people who were more populated down there than Southend beach with the tide out. Some were itching for a partner, others were just itching having chosen the wrong partner. You weren't a professional musician until you'd had a course of penicillin. Rock bans had groupies but solo folksingers had those who felt sorry for you because they thought you were lonely. It was all about pubic health as opposed to public health.

Ah yes, bloody roadworks. Those dreadful things that spread quicker than scurvy on an old British man-of-war galleon, a finer analogy than Southend beach it has to be said. Motorists hate them and it would seem those who instigate them, in turn, hate motorists. Mile after mile after mile after bloody mile of traffic cones with installed 50mph speed limits to protect the handful of conscientious workers, sitting in vans talking to their mates on their mobiles, in their luminous yellow jackets and hard-hats worn in case something drops from the sky. What's it all about? I don't ever recall my camper van having its way blocked by a road-closure. It's a relatively new pain in the backside. Arlo Guthrie didn't have to keep stopping at temporary traffic lights as he travelled America.

I heard from a very reliable source that red and white traffic cones cost 90p each to manufacture and the labour costs in picking them up when their work is done is so prohibitive it makes more financial sense to just leave them where they are for as long as possible. It makes sense to me. I often wonder if there are more traffic cones living in the country than humans. Just imagine if they rebelled against us. We wouldn't stand a chance. So, what's the population of traffic-cones on this island of ours? Who makes the damn things? Where the hell do they hide them all before letting them loose on the unsuspecting motorist? Do I hate the red and white beasties so much because I don't support Arsenal? Why is there the occasional blue one and what's so special about it? Answer any one of those questions if you can, though you probably can't. They seem to multiply by the year, like rabbits in an asparagus patch. Ah blue ones warn of electric cables overhead apparently. Excuse my ignorance. Public health and safety in my day was a bottle of TCP and a decent eyesight. Cars didn't have seatbelts and beer glasses were washed with a grubby dishcloth that had seen better and cleaner days.

When I began my career most of the venues I played consisted of small rooms in the backs of pubs or upstairs where they held wedding receptions or fishing-club meetings. Most looked rather dingy, in need of attention, like some singers, and some still stank of stale wedding-cake, but that didn't matter as a collection of musical outcasts in duffle coats and jeans who'd said goodbye to pop-music in the charts gathered to sing songs of our past or the worries of the future. Anyone could get up and sing at such gatherings as I told you I had done many times myself, supporting a paid guest, myself or someone like me in later years, who'd travelled from afar to entertain them. Yes, I happened to be one such wandering minstrel. It was all so enjoyable and easy then, because every pub had a nice big carpark and if they didn't you could park right outside in the high street.

The venues were easy to find as there weren't any one-way systems designed by pissed architects who doodled with their pencils before going home early on a Friday afternoon. Sometimes a kind landlord, aware of your pending arrival, placed a couple of beer-crates in the road with a plank across to make sure you had somewhere to leave the car as you entered into the world of folk music. Beer crates were the earliest form of traffic cones and for those of us who dared to nick them they also made fine coffee tables and stools in flats where furniture was as scarce as rent money. You couldn't beat a piece of natural wood, far better than plastic, even if they did have the name of the brewery painted on the side. Having said that, my first coffee table boasted Fyffes Bananas on one side.

I remember when crisps appeared in pubs for the first time. It was so exciting, a cardboard box full of wondrous bags of sliced potatoes, made by Smiths, with a little blue bag of salt thrown in for good measure. There were no flavour options, just potato. They were a welcome alternative to pickled eggs and gherkins. Ah yes, we undid the bag and then untwisted the little bag of salt, shook the whole thing as if it had been a naughty boy and then scoffed the ingredients. There was something quite grown-up about it, almost like preparing a meal of your own instead of enduring Mum and Dad's cooking.

The Romans invented many wonderful things but they didn't bother with irritating traffic cones, or crisps for that matter, they didn't use plastic moulds, they hand-crafted everything. They built things perfectly well and did us proud for hundreds, if not thousands, of years. Suddenly their efforts have been diagnosed as crap and that's cruel. Yes, they too wore silly helmets with red plumes, metallic as opposed to yellow plastic, along with steel skirts, but they knew how to build a road or a viaduct better than anyone. Now it appears everything has gone wrong.

Hang on, most roadworks are on motorways and the Romans didn't build motorways so we cannot blame them for that. They didn't build service stations either because they knew they wouldn't get away with charging a week's wages for a sandwich of limp lettuce and a £100 fine if you stopped for a two-hour snooze instead of causing a road accident. Welcome break on offer? More like an unwelcome break I say for the second time because it annoys me so much. The Romans were mightier and more upstanding than that. I'm certain they would have invented the fair-trading corner shops if they hadn't built their roads so long and straight. I do presume, however, they gave us Italian restaurants bearing in mind where they came from. Oh yes, I have a great respect for The Romans, apart from candles because I've been a great fan of fireworks, such a waste of money. I don't rate their numerals either, surely it would have been much easier if they had used proper numbers like the rest of us.

It's a shame they're not around anymore to sort out the dismal, never-ending attempts at road maintenance that goes on today. After all, they did create those superb washrooms in Bath, so they would come with an amazing track record. Strange thing about The Romans is they built the longest garden wall from Carlisle across to Newcastle, along with endless straight roads like The Fosse Way and then they buggered off, not even bothering to plant any daffodils. All that work for no apparent reason seems strange to someone like myself who never excelled in vintage history at school, although I don't suppose it's any different to us building sandcastles on the beach as kids and leaving them there when we went home.

Yes, the Romans left us with many fine things that we still appreciate to this day, but they didn't invent the 'roadworks' sign and they didn't build too many of the roads under repair today while they were here. It seems the dodgy ones that are falling apart were built much later. Three cheers for The Romans, the roads they built are still in fine nick and the long wall keeps Scottish sheep out of England one assumes. Road works is a red vision, which also happens to be an anagram of diversion for those who have never seen me on Countdown.

As the European framework ebbs and flows with the Brexit vote and the political world changes at alarming speed I can't help wondering if Hadrian's Wall will have a new lease of life before too long, a new sense of purpose as certain Scottish political party leaders crave for independence. Yes, I know it's fifteen miles south of Scotland, but it would certainly save on building materials. Perhaps Hadrian, all those years ago, had some kind of inkling as to what would happen in later years, long after he'd gone. It's just that he got his bearings a bit wrong. Maybe it was snowing in Scotland so he edged south a few miles. I've no idea, I'm only guessing. Back to the music I think.

The amazing thing, the thing all musicians and other entertainers are proud of, is the fact that a gig never starts late despite the constant attempts by road construction companies and speed cameras in pointless locations to scupper the performances of anyone who has to travel more than ten and a half miles to the next venue. Against all the odds we are always there, side of stage, waiting in the wings to take to the stage dead on time. It's an incredible achievement on our part, even if I do say so myself. If only the audience knew what the performers go through to give them their evening's entertainment. On second thoughts it's probably best they don't know.

There's so much more to a working day in my industry than falling out of a plush hotel bed at midday for a late champagne breakfast, getting rid of the groupies, and arriving at the next venue by helicopter. That's a style of life for the very few who enjoy a hit record or two and ram their success down people's throats, the very people who bought their songs and put them where they are. If only it were like that in the real world but it isn't.

The life of a musician is a tough battle, both geographically and financially and yet very few fall totally by the wayside, starving but never dying. Against all the odds they win the day and then the day after that. They are a hardy bunch and yet there's more than a hunch that they are now an endangered species as roads become ever harder to negotiate. Getting to a town is one thing, finding the venue is another thing altogether. Getting home, in my case, can be even worse an experience. The show is the easy part. All very well but 2020 saw the end of live shows as we all knew them. Pubs and theatres closed and performers were told to find jobs elsewhere, a difficult task for a guitar-player in his 70s. Some believe it's only a matter of time before the travelling musician disappears with the dodo and the giant panda and it's fair to say their lives on the road as we have known it will be a thing of the past. Bills had to be paid in 2020 and 2021 and so many professional musicians slung in the towel and found different ways of earning a living, mostly driving jobs. Live music would return but performed mostly by those who had day jobs and sang in the evenings for pleasure in the pubs and other venues that managed to survive. As the months passed by in 2021, I wondered if any music venues would ever return to life. There were more false starts than an under-fives school egg and spoon race.

Some of our great musical icons have moved on to pastures new in recent times, too many of them. Fair enough, the Dodo did reappear a few years ago and bashed out a few songs, or was that Dido? Giant pandas? Their disappearance is their own fault, they won't shag each other, so it's hard to feel sorry for them, difficult to like them when they don't even like each other. Apparently, a panda warns another panda to keep their distance or they'll be given a black eye. Hang on, I must have made that one up.

It was all so different once upon a time, a romantic, free-wheeling job to quote the words of Bob Dylan, the

American music legend, disliked by my Dad, who also claimed the times they are a-changing. It is equally fair to say the times have now changed, proving the icon of American folk-music to be right. My god, let's hope that not everything Dylan, Nostradamus with a mouth-organ, wrote about becomes a truth, heaven forbid we have to listen to some odd-ball singing a song accompanying himself on a tambourine like some Salvation Army lassie. Staying on that subject, American songwriters have the ability, well maybe not the ability but certainly the luxury, to romanticise and PR the towns they travel to on their way to or from work. Galveston, Tulsa, New Orleans, Phoenix, Nashville and so on. The aforementioned Arlo Guthrie sang a song about a train called The City of New Orleans, nice song written by an old friend of mine, Steve Goodman. Imagine us Brits writing songs about trains. The only stroke of luck on our side would be the fact stations rhymes with cancellations. That said, I am surprised there hasn't been songs about The Flying Scotsman or The Mallard in our more traditional folk clubs. The American writers had it easy, they still do. Their British counterparts do not share the same luxury and the reason may well be the fact that the Brits can't wait to get to where they're heading through the tangled mess on the side of the road so they ignore the towns on either side while they try to work out where to go.

There are very few pleasant views along the way to inspire lyrics these days, our eyes fully consumed with bone idle cement mixers, speed cameras, diversions, road closures and platitudes of signs that we are supposed to read with one eye whilst keeping the other eye on the road. It is all an impossibility, except for the never to be beaten musician who needs to always be on time, even if their eyes are popping out like organ stops. Well let's be honest if he was out of time he wouldn't be a very good musician. No, they do not have the time or inclination to see the passing towns and write lovingly about them while they crawl along like snails through an average speed limit zone that's been there for the best part of six months. I am dubious to write a song about an English city because Roger Whitaker wrote a song about leaving Durham Town. He left and we never saw him again.

The Scottish brothers in arms, The Proclaimers, decided to walk 500 miles, an alternative to getting tangled up in road-works for a few hours. It is a great song, my only doubt being that if I walked 500 miles to a special woman would I bother to take my brother with me? I somehow doubt it. At least they wrote to each other when one of them went to America.

The late David Bowie, himself a folkie who ran a folk club at The Three Tuns in Beckenham, did once sing about the Norfolk Broads in Life On Mars, but it hardly counts when it is an area where most people travel by boat at an average speed of 4mph. So it's The Highways Authorities, or whatever such folk call themselves as I'm sure I've got the title wrong, who must take the blame for the serious lack of British names in songs. '24 Hours From Milton Keynes' doesn't really cut the bacon, neither does 'get your kicks along the M6.' It's no good writing songs in Britain about the time and length of any journey because it all depends whether or not they've decided to shut down a road without warning. That is the reason most British song-writers pen songs relating to the safer subjects of love and rejection. It did not used to be like that. Songs were happier. Songwriters were happier. The country was happier.

None of us could have ever have envisaged what happened in 2020 and 2021.

My first song, and I use the term loosely, I wrote in the back of my Volkswagen Camper Van. Actually, quite a few first things were done in the back of my Volkswagen Camper Van but that's of no consequence right now. I called it 'Song of a Childhood Dream' this masterpiece scribbled with a BIC biro whilst parked up in a lay-by somewhere in Devon. It was crap, most of my songs were, but I was in heaven that day as I qualified as a full-on, full-time professional, British songwriter on the road. I wouldn't call it a risk as I had little else in the pipeline as my schooldays only gave me the qualifications to become a milk-monitor, or a calcium anthropologist as they prefer to call themselves. Oh my god, Song of a Childhood Dream. Crap of the highest order, but hey, it was my very first song of my own.

I know when I'm falling
you can pick me up and place me on the shelf.
Then I know you never loved me
From the start I only loved myself

Dreadful words, even for a first attempt. All these years on I have not written a single verse sitting in sprawling, crawling traffic on a motorway. I've sworn and cursed a few times but never put such naughty words to music. But neither have I delivered a single bottle of milk. There was nothing more enjoyable in my first few years on the road than parking the camper in a country lane, opening the sliding door, sitting there having a bash at a new song and swatting flies at the same time. I always arrived at a venue by late afternoon to give me time to relax and enjoy the solitude. Audiences were small and I do not mean in physique. I remember that trip to Devon in my new, second-hand, VW bus, HTW 177H. Today a journey from London to Devon would take about four hours were it not for the aforementioned obstructions. Back then I set off at 8am, even earlier if hangovers allowed, and journeyed through the day in sheer bliss, even though I had nine or ten hours ahead of me behind the wheel. It is odd that I still prefer that ten hours of yesteryear more than the flexible four hours I need to negotiate today. Surely it should be around the other way? Yes, but it isn't. I hate motorways, I hate service stations, I hate roadworks, I hate idiotic drivers, and I hate satnavs who don't always knows where they're going and yet argue the toss with you. I loved to start my day scanning the pages of my road atlas, plotting a new route if there was a page missing. In fact, I hate the whole day that I take on these days to go on stage and perform my show to an audience who have travelled a few miles at the least. It all changes when I get out on that stage, it is then that nothing matters in the slightest. All a bit one-sided. Yes, it would be fair to admit I hate many things, but I truly loved my camper van and I think my camper van truly loved me as it idled around the country once I'd rescued it from the end of the line at the Plaistow showrooms. It had a distinctive smell too. All VW Campers had a distinctive smell. I have a feeling I had a distinctive smell too after a few nights kipping in lay-bys but it was all part of my first few years of many on the road.

I still remember that Volkswagen well, some fifty years or more on. It was nothing like a present-day vehicle. It chugged along at a sensible, placid speed and yet few overtook me. We, the nation, all chugged along at a sensible, placid speed so we rarely overtook each other. There were no boy-racers with their baseball caps round the wrong way or posh speed kings in BMWs.

What did my Dad think of my VW camper? What do you think? I'll give you a clue, it was built in Germany. Enough said.

It had a bed in the back with various drawers and cupboards that I filled with stuff until I got sick to death of the sound of items of cutlery unable to control themselves when I went around a bend. If only I had tied them together with a rubber band, that would have worked, although it would have offended my sister who bought me a white plastic cutlery tray as a going-away present. Ah yes, that was part of the distinctive smell, Tupperware mugs, dishes and boxes. Tupperware parties of yesteryear were like Ann Summers parties of today. You bought stuff but you didn't often use it.

A sink by the sliding side-door allowed a modicum of hygiene when you woke up in the morning. Its size allowed a brisk brush of the teeth and a gargle before the tank beneath it needed emptying. It had a swan-neck tap too although it looked more like a starving duck. I never used it because the hand-pump sprained my wrist and the water tank was no bigger than a shoebox. To assist with the hygiene my dear old Mum bought me an enormous plastic water carrier from the camping shop. It worked a treat until one night, after successfully luring a young lady into my swish mobile abode, she stuck a stiletto heel through it whilst attempting a position I had never seen before, one that I thought at the time was verging on the impossible, which turned out to be right. The resulting tsunami I swept from the floor with a brush and dustpan next morning, another gift from my caring Mum. It was like shovelling smoke up a hill but I got there in the end. I never saw that aquatic girl again but for a while I was the only VW camper owner with a waterbed. I don't even remember her name or what she looked like, but she left her toothbrush behind so she definitely had teeth. I have to say that was a bit of a result.

I was never done for speeding in those days, I couldn't have sped if I'd wanted to in that camper van. Unlike many struggling musicians I also had a tax disc proudly displayed on my windscreen and insurance, third party fire and theft, so proud was I to have my own transport, something that took the pressure off having to board cancelled trains. How odd, third party fire and theft. I feel the description needs analysis. Firstly, of course it's third party, no-one would steal their own car and set fire to it. Secondly, fire and theft? I never got that part back then either. Why on earth would you steal a car that's on fire. It was an era when nasty little Herberts wouldn't steal a car for a joy-ride before torching it for a laugh. It just didn't happen. That trend of yobbos being total shits would surface thirty years later. Sometimes they climbed up a tree and stole an apple or chalked some comment on a toilet wall, but that was about it. Back then young kids were scared of portly policemen on bicycles. The cops didn't need pepper sprays and Taser guns shoving a few volts up the arses of the guilty. It's so different now, a young hooligan today gets a lawyer before they get pubic hair.

It angers me so much that I get fined £300 and penalised three points for driving at 58mph in a 50mph average speed zone at 1.28am in the morning, as I did in Yeovil a couple of years ago, wrong I admit, when there was nothing else on the road, and yet an under-aged rogue the same week stole a car, drove it into a shop wall and set fire to it before running away. He was caught on CCTV and they gave him a £30 fine and told him he was a very naughty boy. They couldn't put any points on his licence because he didn't have one. £30? I would have transported the little shit to Australia in a rowing boat. I bet he wouldn't have set fire to that, or hopefully he would. The Ashes spring to mind for some strange reason.

Third party, fire and theft, was a common grade of car insurance back in the days of my camper van, now it would be an insurance scam, a great way of getting rich without bothering to get a job, so sadly, third party, fire and theft, had to go and go it did along with handy tins of lighter fuel. Now there's just plain car insurance that never goes down if you drive well, like it used to once upon a time, but gets more expensive each year despite your driving skills. I used to be quite proud of my no-claims bonus, I considered it an achievement in a life that, back then, hadn't achieved much else. Considering my decision to go on the road it felt like some sort of university degree, a recognition that I'd chosen the right occupation and knew what I was doing, despite my Dad's objections. I hasten to add that I didn't have the foggiest idea what I was doing but at least I was in the world of music, where I wanted to be.

I remember all the items in my glove compartment as though I opened it yesterday; a road atlas, a Green Shield Stamps book, a spare fanbelt, a couple of free wine glasses that came with the purchase of petrol, an Esso keyring too tasteless to put to good use, a penknife stroke bottle-opener, a first-aid kit I never once opened and a car manual. There were no airbags, no windscreen washer fluid or silly, smelly pine trees hanging from my rear-view mirror. I should also add there were no face-masks ready for action. There were no bottles of mineral water either, I was driving to a gig, not crossing the Sahara Desert. I didn't need water, I'm not a bloody elephant or hippo for god's sake. I was on the road and that was all that mattered.

I had blue and white gingham curtains in the back that absorbed condensation while I slept in the lay-by. I learnt how to check my oil with a dipstick, to look at my spark plugs and brush off the black stuff so the van started easier. I even discovered the engine was at the back and not the front. Sometimes I checked the tyres and then kicked them in the belief that would give me some idea if the tyre pressures were correct. People still kick tyres when they're buying a second-hand car, which is totally pointless, like kicking the arse of a cow before you drink a pint of milk. Due to the strange position of the engine the spare wheel fitted on the front, beneath the window, like a squashed nose. I remember, when I got the van home, my Dad thought it looked like Sid James, the star of the Carry On films. I wasn't Isambard Kingdom Brunel but I had some idea of the workings of my trusty new travelling companion.

Today I don't have the foggiest idea what's going on beneath the bonnet. Sometimes it makes a funny noise, so do I occasionally when I take to the stage. Back then I lifted the bonnet, not a hood as we're supposed to call them today, but a good old bonnet. In my earlier life hoods were people who caused trouble by threatening and hustling for protection money. They certainly didn't sit on top of car engines. I used to take out the sparkplugs and blow on them if the van coughed and spluttered. If it squeaked I knew it had to be the water-pump or a slipping fan-belt. Yeah, there wasn't much I didn't know about cars and how they worked. No, there wasn't much I didn't know about car maintenance and as a back-up I joined the AA for £12. I upped the subscription to £25 when they introduced AA Relay, a service that guaranteed the good people in yellow would get you home if all else failed. I had a plan that seemed a good one at the time whereby I didn't have a car at all but instead would just use the Relay service to get home after a gig, a stupid idea that I didn't even try to put into practice.

Blimey, I'm so old that I remember when AA patrolmen drove motorbikes with sidecars and they saluted you if they saw your AA badge on the front grill. Imagine that today.

That girl's discarded toothbrush came in handy for cleaning sparkplugs by the way.

Sometimes that skill of mechanics enabled me to fill my car battery with distilled water. Distilled water? What the hell is or was distilled water I hear people say. Distilled water was a bottle of water that had been boiled, not unlike boiled water I assume. You were only allowed to top-up a car battery with distilled water or else the car exploded and all the tyres deflated, dark clouds filled the sky and birds flew south. So what exactly was it? Sadly, I have no idea. All I remember was buying it at a garage at a time when garages didn't sell bottled water to drink. There was indeed a time when garages only sold things for cars. Mangos and beach-balls came much later, as did bonfire kindling, luminous yellow waistcoats, pot plants and hidden cabinets where they hid cigarettes from people who wanted to buy cigarettes like a health-conscious hide and seek.

My cream VW with no elevating roof, but with a thoroughly scrubbed floor, became a sincere friend for a couple of years. Its actual description was a Danbury Conversion which means it came over from Germany as a shell, a bit like a doodlebug, and was kitted out in Danbury, a place near Chelmsford. That was where they fitted the sink I didn't use because the water tank was too small and the table that rocked around on a single leg like Long John Silver. Despite all that I loved my VW. Sometimes I spoke to it as I travelled along with a smile on my face, it was cheaper than buying cassettes. I stroked it with great fondness, I could park it right outside venues without fear of being clamped. Clamps? They were things that kept your mouth open when they took out a wisdom tooth as opposed to an occupation invented for retired army blokes and out of date police officers. I can't help thinking there must be other occupations for that lot other than wheel-clampers and football referees.

Multi-storey carparks? What the hell were multi-storey carparks? Parking directly outside the venue allowed me to make a cup of tea after a sound-check if I'd saved enough water. Yes and it had a little cooker should you want to prepare a Sunday roast or fry a sausage. No wonder Jamie Oliver still owns a VW van, he may well have discovered the art of cooking by staying out all night in a VW Camper like I used to. You seldom see him burn a sausage so he must have learnt his skills somewhere. The VW style of food preparation certainly gave a different meaning to a slow cooker. Arrive at venue, park up, cup of tea, a stretch out on the bed and then the gig.

Nothing in that vehicle was particularly convenient in truth. The bed took ages to make up and then collapsed at the slightest opportunity. Fuses blew with more regularity than a rubbish Premier League referee I just mentioned, of which there are many, the cupboards were about as useful as a British Rail timetable or a chocolate poker. Despite all that the camper van represented total freedom, just like it had for Arlo Guthrie. Nowadays I chug along at a slightly faster speed, whenever possible, in a sheepish manner though, full knowing I have nine points on my driving licence and thus on the brink of not driving anywhere for six months if I'm caught by yet another officious copper with a speed gun. Of course they have nothing better to do or they wouldn't do us, so there's no point at all in asking them. There's no crime on our streets, no terrorists threatening our little country, they have every right to stand in the pissing rain holding their cameras, pretending they're on holiday. They moan about too much paperwork in the modern police office. Simple answer, pretend to run out of paper and buy a mood-music CD of whale noises or some Thai bloke bashing something out on the panpipes. I'm sure they'd sleep better at nights if they calmed down a bit.

Coincidentally, my highest snooker break is also nine points, red, black and then another red, so not only am I a crap snooker player but I'm apparently a crap driver too. Yes, just three points from an enforced rest. Three points from my next tour being cancelled unless I go on one of those 'awareness courses' where they sit you down with a cup of tea and a digestive biscuit and you're told what a bloody awful driver you are by some know-all sitting behind a school desk with some walkie-talkie phone strapped to the side of his armpit. No thanks. I'm completely aware of my driving skills and I'm equally aware that after sitting in drab roadworks for what seems half a century, I have to walk on stage on time or get home before lunchtime TV shows begin. Those awareness chaps should themselves be made aware of why we sometimes have to put our toe down, they should get in the real world and sit in roadworks for hours instead of being holier than thou. I've often said that all speed limits should cease an hour after midnight so sensible drivers could reach their destinations quicker. I often have such strange ideas, for example, professional footballers should all be over 70, giving them time to learn how not to spit on grass they're about to roll around on. My god, this world would be a far better place if I became Prime Minister. It's strange it's regarded as maybe the most important job in the country and yet you don't need any form of qualification other than a wealthy education.

So, my camper van took me around when I undertook my first ever tour as a professional singer. Again it was odd because it was a tour along the valleys of South Wales. The first gig was a lunchtime event at the Hoover factory in Merthyr Tydfil, a promising gig with people sucking up to you. Someone had the bright idea of putting folk shows on in the canteen while weary factory workers were eating their lunch. Can you imagine the chaos and the din? There was the crashing of trays, the rattling of knives and forks, the constant gabbling of workers around tables and the crashing of crockery as the canteen workers cleared and cleaned the empty plates. Not a particularly conducive atmosphere for singing nice little songs on an acoustic guitar but it paid £15 and that was quite a bit of money back then, certainly worth dying on your arse for.

I got out as quickly as I could and made my way down to Aberdare where I was performing the next night in The Railway Hotel. And so the tour down the mining areas continued. Mountain Ash, Ebbw Vale, Newport and the golden nugget gig at Llandaff College, Cardiff. I came home with money in my pocket for the very first time, a nice change and I felt I'd finally become a fully qualified professional folksinger. I was able to help Mum and Dad with the rent, a rare occurrence.

That week, making my way south through the valleys from Ebbw Vale truly my first legitimate tour, a string of gigs slung together, I began to feel special, finally doing what I really wanted to do. The Hoover factory gig apparently went down so well they said they would have me back. I'm still waiting but it was flattering nonetheless. Wales was the first place that took a gamble on me and I returned home full of it. I was only a bloody touring artist no less. Not only that but I returned to Cardiff just a few weeks later with a gig at The Locomotive in Frederick Street followed by the next night in Bridgend. I was taking Wales by storm, so much so I even thought about moving there, a good idea apart from two points, I didn't know anyone and secondly it was a long way from home. Oh yes and another thing, it was a time when Welsh people set fire to English people's homes if they dared to move there, and I didn't fancy taking the risk as it took me back to the third party fire and theft conundrum. One more tour and they will have me at their rugby stadium singing their national anthem instead of Katherine Jenkins. Wales loved Max Boyce when most of us non-rugger types weren't sure what he was all about, jumping on stage with a giant spring onion and a coat he borrowed from

Father Christmas, no-one quite git it this side of the Severn Bridge.

Seeing as we're talking about days gone by on the road I think you may find this interesting. Let's go back even further when there weren't any cars in Britain at all. Touring and doing gigs in those days must have been so difficult, shoving your pa system on the back of a horse and cart, I don't know how they managed to do it. Lighting crews with bundles of candles, yet another fire risk to throw into the melting pot of confusion.

Entertainment is a fantasy land that doesn't have room for moaning and groaning from those up on stage, as it's an industry that takes people away from their troubles for a few hours as the wicked world passes by, outside the theatre, without notice. What do they say? The show must go one. Yeah, but to paraphrase that boast remember the only people that can stop the show going on are the audience when they boo you off. That's a sobering thought. The last thing a paying audience want to hear about is the grief of actually being an entertainer, the most rewarding job in the world. They don't care about broken-down cars and road diversions. Heaven forbid we tell others of our misfortunes when the lights go down and the curtains open. Heaven forbid even more that someone should write a bloody book about it.

I used to cleverly carry a set of spanners around with me in the camper van days but I can't think why. Of course I mean in my vehicle and not in my hand as I walked down the high street threatening old age pensioners. I carried a set of sockets too, even more bizarre. I did have to change a wheel once on the side of a busy road, but I didn't need my shiny blue toolbox to come to my rescue. Oh no. The spare wheel on my

Volkswagen camper van was at the front and the relevant tool that undid the wheel-bolts had been very kindly donated to my glove-compartment by the manufacturer. By the way, why is it still called a glove compartment when nobody has put gloves in them for half a Century? Since I started out on the road in fact. I've never worn leather driving gloves so therefore I've never carried leather driving gloves in my exclusive leather driving glove compartment. You do see the odd chap wearing them whilst driving a vintage car to a rally with the roof down but they aren't really for modern day use are they? I do wonder if they should change the name from glove compartment. I still reckon it's amazing how that description has stayed the test of time. A young teenager buying their first car will be told of the manual in the glove compartment. You tell me the last time you saw a young teenager bombing past you wearing leather driving gloves. If manufacturers have managed to keep that part of a car intact through the years then why isn't there still some chap walking in front of the car waving a red flag, warning people on the cobbled-streets about a speedy hazard coming their way? Oh well, that's my pointless rant over. I just don't go with the term glove compartment.

Now I'm old and reminiscing
There's my old van that I missing
My friend who made journey's end of time
As I think back on the winning
The losing and the singing
I think of my VW with this rhyme

I may be a writer and a singer of the songs
But I'd a friend few people knowed

Many men have written songs
For friends before but this belongs
To you my friend upon the road

It wasn't long after that period that I became a member of a folk trio, Pisces, along with John O'Connor and Tim Greenwood. The time had come to leave Blaney Crescent for a second time. The flat in Glasgow had given me a taste for independence and I wanted more, especially as I'd developed a keen interest in the opposite sex. I seemed to wallow in being skint and my Leytonstone experience at 87 Fairlop Road would be no different. Before Tim joined as a bass player John and I survived in various dubious ways which are best left unsaid. Let's just say that we developed a habit of forgetting to pay for our shopping. John worked in the post and packaging room at Transatlantic Records and so we also seemed to have a few albums to sell. How ironic that I ended up on Transatlantic four years later.

We had a brilliant creative time in Fairlop Road, learning to write songs and play instruments and forgetting to go to sleep on numerous occasions. We were so serious about becoming a successful group that we even bought a Ford Transit van, a blue one that had been an insurance write-off. It enabled us to stop at The Watford Gap services on the M1 and park alongside all the other transits owned by bands who were stopping off for a very early breakfast or late midnight snack, whichever way you look at it. We had arrived and at long last I had become a professional musician way beyond the description of a solo folksinger.

We stayed together for just over a year before, like all groups, we had more disagreements than rehearsals and split up. It was a shame as we had all become good work colleagues, but all living under the same roof had become way too strenuous.

To be honest, our odd games of football were the few times we socialised. They were both in serious relationships and I wasn't. When we spilt up I never heard from Tim Greenwood ever again and John O'Connor went off to live in America, becoming very wealthy indeed after writing Star Trekkin' in his tiny eight-track home studio in Ritchings Avenue, Walthamstow. It was a massive hit worldwide, a follow-up to his previous hit Arthur Daley He's Alright which reached number four in the UK charts, a song he originally wrote for Chas and Dave but they turned it down. We haven't kept in touch, a shame I suppose, but these things happen in all walks of life when work colleagues disappear without trace when you change jobs.

Thinking back, no we weren't great friends or anything like that, apart from those football sessions, simply musical business associates. Once John's girlfriend Carol had moved into the Fairlop Road flat they kept themselves to themselves, sometimes I didn't see them for days on end when they chose to just stay in their room. Tim and his girlfriend Fiona were very much the same. For me Pisces was a stepping stone, although I didn't think of it as that at the time, learning how to work in a recording studio and how to stand my ground and write the material I believed in. That belief caused the splitting up of the trio, but we'd done well and we'd all become names on the folk scene, which was all I wanted.

Sadly, we were about to record our second album on Bill Leader's Trailer label, when we went our separate ways but it didn't matter to me as I had a funny feeling none of my songs would feature on any new album so I hadn't lost much. Richard Digance, John O'Connor and Tim Greenwood were passing ships, nice enough guys but still passing ships. I warned lovely Bill Leader we were splitting as I didn't want him to spend time and money on a second album that wouldn't sell. Maybe the other two weren't impressed? I've no idea.

As a trio we had elevated ourselves to a headline name on the British folk scene, something I hadn't managed to do on my own, far from it. We played at folk festivals and our album was in record shops. Richard Digance, John O'Connor and Tim Greenwood had arrived, three failed solo acts who had finally got up there with the big boys. It was a proud time. Sadly, I haven't thought much about the three of us over the years, if at all, until I began this book.

I remember that we didn't eat very often, which probably didn't help our mood swings, and many's the time we'd gone to Mum and Dad's for a full English breakfast. Mum knew it was a different scenario though when I knocked on the door with my case of clothes and my guitar, just as I had when I returned from Scotland, but this time from Leytonstone, not such a long journey. Her response was exactly the same as then.

'Cup of tea?'

So, no sooner had I settled into a hippie life in Fairlop Road, Leytonstone that I was back home to Mum and Dad. Well, we had a nice view across London towards the Thames but it wasn't the place for a musician to live. The walls were paper-thin and everyone on either side, plus those above and below, seemed to spend their days arguing. I didn't fancy living there for too long but, sadly, Mum and Dad had no choice.

Who do they think they are?
Do they think we have no pride?
It's not that they've forgotten us
They've joined the other side
Up on the seventh floor
Lonely shadows on the skyline
Up on the seventh floor
Like wayward mountaineers.

So Pisces had gone, John O'Connor and Tim Greenwood had disappeared into thin air, I had my dreams and I was well and truly on the road. During the year of being in Pisces there was a rival London band called Hunter Muskett. On a social level I was friendlier with that band than I was with the members of Pisces. Terry Hiscock was their main songwriter, a superb wordsmith and a really nice guy, Rog Trevitt played bass, and sometimes went to watch West Ham with me on Saturday afternoons, while Chris George and Doug Morter played additional guitars. Doug and I, as you have heard, became big pals, even brothers I would be tempted to say. We were raised in the same streets.

After Pisces and before the Transatlantic record deal I was broke again and so it was the inevitable return to Mum and Dad's place. Doug lived just down the road. Although he was married and had a child, Alice, he still lived with his parents in Prince Regent Lane, Plaistow.

Hunter Muskett were a great folk band but finances eventually forced them off the road, a great shame and a great loss. They re-formed in 2014, good news for all. I didn't actually go to school with Doug but we went to rival schools. Doug went to Avery Hill College in South London when I went to Glasgow and that's where he met up with the other members of Hunter Muskett.

Between splitting up and re-forming that band, a good forty years' gap, Doug did many things. He played guitar with Home Service on, I think, Lark Rise To Candleford, he played in The Maddy Prior Band, a splinter group of Steeleye Span and, coincidentally he played with John Martyn. Oh yes, he also played in Acoustic Gathering with Ray Jackson of Lindisfarne and Fairport's Jerry Donahue, Magna Carta and various other mixes.

Doug is a master guitar player and he was way back then too. He's a well-respected name on the folk scene and the first guy on the club scene who played an electric guitar to my knowledge. Some of the bigger bands had electric players like Richard Thompson but they didn't really play the clubs. He used to bend notes and everything. I didn't have to ever do that because I got the right note in the first place so I didn't have to bend anything. Those electric guitar players should practice more, that's what I say. I once wrote to Eric Clapton and told him that but he never replied. I didn't mind as I knew he was probably too busy.

Yes, it's fair to say Hunter Muskett were my mates and members of Pisces were my workmates. Terry came to my house this year with his wife Dee to work on a documentary in my studio, and Doug stayed last year and drank a full bottle of whiskey before stumbling into the spare room. As for Tim and John of Pisces, I'm not even sure I'd recognise them if I passed them in the street. It's just like any other workplace, you don't need to get on well with your colleagues and my industry is no different, fact confirmed by the number of bands that split up before they see out more years together.

Doug spent more time at Mum and Dad's than he did at his own parent's place. We played snooker, darts, Subbuteo, went to West Ham together along with Roger as I mentioned and enjoyed endless night-fishing sessions at The South Essex Carp Fisheries at South Ockendon, when everyone else thought he was off playing a gig. He had a blue mini with a white roof in which he somehow squeezed a guitar, amplifier, fishing tackle and spare un-ironed shirts. We both loved our fishing sessions, driving off late evening to Ockers as we called it, our secret code word for a getaway. Back home the next morning Mum would cook us both a fry-up before Doug returned home after a quick scrub-up to wash off the evidence of groundbait aroma. We were two naughty little boys together, sponsored by my Mum's cooking.

I remember we were travelling to Ockers one night in Doug's clapped-out Mini and we were stopped by the police. Doug had no insurance, no MOT and tyres as bald as I am today. Things didn't look too promising until the copper notice our fishing tackle in the back. As luck would have it we got talking about the best ways of catching crucian carp. Doug owned up to the boy in blue that he was driving illegally but he let him off with more advice about how to attract the beautiful fish using sweetcorn. Doug got away with murder that night, as he often did, he being such a likeable person.

Doug and I started doing gigs together after my first album. He was alongside me when I supported Jethro Tull, Richard Thompson, Elkie Brooks, and additional dates with Steeleye. Doug had moved to a flat in Aldersbrook Road, Wanstead for a while, a flat I took over when he bought his first house in West Street, Hertford. We never made any money and so Doug had to spread his wings to pay for his first ever mortgage and support his family. He played on my second album and numerous gigs, once on my TV show, but we went our separate ways for financial reasons, yet remaining the very best of friends still to this day.

Being broke can cement great friendships and myself and Doug Morter are classic examples. Because we had no money, nothing new there, my social life was zero except for visits to the home of fellow folk-singer Michael Moore in Barwick Ford, not far from Doug's new house in Hertfordshire. We listened to music and played darts all night, the three of us inventing our own darts game which we called Micky Marathon, a game that always lasted about ten hours. We listened to Kate and Anna McGarrigle albums all night and drank far too much. Some darts didn't even travel in the right direction.

My greatest memory of Doug though was when he got married, he bought a green, velvet suit and the cheque bounced, so after the wedding he took the suit back. We are still big friends to this day, he sometimes pops over to my house if he has a spare few moments, when he's working in England, bearing in mind he moved to Denmark. It's a forever friendship as it is with the other members of Hunter Muskett, especially Terry Hiscock. As for the members of Pisces, as I said earlier I sadly have to pass on that one. The only connection I have with them these days is that album that's just been re-released in Japan. The experiences we shared together was worth more than that, in my opinion, but we drifted apart when they went off my funny songs, just like John Martyn had earlier. It's odd how audiences love the fun stuff but some fellow songwriters look at such songs with utter disdain. I accepted long ago I would never be totally accepted with such fun material, particularly on the serious side of the folk scene but it has never bothered me. The strange irony is that others get up and sing my songs in folk clubs far more than I do myself.

I still think of Doug and myself as two East End boys who made it out of East London, both born in Plaistow, both finding the folk scene at an early age. Both failed students, both Hammers fans and both having endless stories that are best left un-said. Doug continued to make his way with Steeleye's Rick Kemp while I set about strolling on stage alone yet again, both of them becoming members of The Maddy Prior Band. This time I had the confidence to do it and I would remain solo to this day. It was my fourth and final attempt. All the guys I've mentioned were very important to me, they helped to build my name and I appreciate them all, I just don't see any of them apart from Douglas William Morter, carp-fisherman extraordinaire.

We weren't the only Plaistow kids that made music our lives. There was Joe Brown, one of the nicest guys I've ever met, David Essex and Linda Lewis that I know of, though probably a few more. No, not Chas and Dave, they were from North London. That's like calling a Canadian an American. Billy

Bragg came along later, so East Enders didn't contribute that much to the folk scene apart from Billy, Doug and myself.

Doug and I mastered the art of changing drivers in the camper van without stopping. I would simply get on a straight road, move out the driving seat and Doug would slide in without any reduction of speed. Can you imagine doing that today? There's a lot of things Doug and I did that I couldn't imagine doing today.

I look back and it seems strange that I didn't quite have the confidence to go it alone back then. Having Doug by my side was important and had he not been around as I tried to build my name at that particular time I would never have built the career I did. For that reason I give full credit to Doug Morter, but more importantly we caught some nice fish and mastered the art of slinging darts all night without stopping. Doug cried as much as I did when my dear Mum passed away, he being her adopted son, and that, as far as I am concerned, is true friendship.

When the darkest clouds are rolling in
And you're at your lowest ever
Look all around they'll be thin on the ground
But friends they are forever

My former neighbour in Blaney Crescent, Richard Cole, lived in a house with various others in North London and it was one of those shared-house jobs where you put money in the meter to get hot water. Anyway, Richard had put his money in the slot and a naughty man by the name of Jazz Summers jumped in the bath and thus stole his hot water. That was how

Richard and Jazz met, in rage, and the latter played drums in a pub-band in Palmers Green, North London, and so I was invited by Richard to go and watch them one night. I got on well with the fellow musician and when he bought a house in Romford he invited me to have a bedroom. The problem was I had no money to contribute financially and so I became a house worker as a means of paying my way, cleaning, cooking meals and making copious amounts of tea. I was off again.

Before we go any further, and to digress slightly, when I made it to the giddy world of television I tried to move Mum and Dad into a nice place in the country but they were having none of it. There's an inverted snobbery with Eastenders, particularly so with their generation, a kind of I was born here and the only way I'll leave is in a box kind of attitude. Anyway, back to the plot.

Jazz worked at Oldchurch Hospital in Romford and got me a job there as an x-ray assistant. He became my first full-time manager until he went on to manage Wham, George Michael, The Scissors Sisters, Snow Patrol, The Verve, Nigel Kennedy and Boy George. We moved from Pettits Lane to Upper Brentwood Road in Gidea Park. On Sunday nights we would go to our local pub, The Squirrels, and talk about our future plans, neither of us really thinking we had much of a future anyway. I spent really fun times at 456 Upper Brentwood Road but it didn't seem right when Jazz and I parted company and he moved on to things far greater than I. And so it was back to Mum and Dad's for the third time and final time. My pride never really enjoyed me being back there for the first time and the second time I found far harder. Mum was having a tough time of it too if I'm honest. The only real saving grace was that Mum had enrolled for art lessons and was making a fine job of her flower paintings and landscapes. As she didn't drive, I loved lugging her artworks around to the different exhibitions. On one occasion, in Bishops Stortford, she exhibited four paintings and sold the lot. I had never seen her so happy and proud. My Mum began her art lessons at 63 and she died at the age of 68 so I always say she had five great years doing exactly what she wanted to do and five years had to be better than none at all.

Given the chance again
Oh how she'd dance again
Oh how she'd take to the floor
But no knight in shining armour
Will take her by the hand
Like they did in the days before the war

I don't believe she enjoyed living in Forest Gate either and her art was a distraction from the new abode she never really wanted. I only returned for a summer and then, at last, good fortune came my way and a music publishing advance represented the deposit of the very first home of my own. For a reason that still seems a little strange I bought my first house in Whitley Wood Lane, Reading. Why Reading? A damn good question with a damn good answer. There were two reasons, the first being that it was central to the motorways that were springing up everywhere, an important factor as I gained more and more work as a support act to the big names in the music business, and secondly, I would be close to the band members of Jethro Tull, whom I became good friends with what with being their support act on two British tours, Songs From The Wood and Heavy Horses.

Drummer Barrie Barlow lived near Henley on Thames and the river flowed past the bottom of his garden. Being a keen angler I loved the honour of being allowed to fish from his old boathouse. I fished there with Deep Purple's drummer Ian Paice and he caught a dozen pike in less than an hour. I preferred the tranquillity and less barbaric pastime of fishing in the lily pads for roach and the occasional bream, nice interruptions to my beer drinking by the river's edge. I used to sit and look at all the unworthy peasants on the other bank, crowded into each other, and I often heard them saying is was alright for some as Barrie's wife brought me a bacon sandwich for my lunch. It was great to pretend, albeit for a couple of hours that I was a decadent man of great wealth, a rock star. I must admit I enjoyed being a downright snob, I loved pretending I lived in such a splendid house on the banks of The Thames. When the unworthy peasants had packed up and gone home I loaded up my knackered Fiat and I drove home to Reading too, back to where my finances allowed.

I visited Mum and Dad whenever I could in the tower-block in Forest Gate and often stayed over if I was working in London. They loved me staying because they had a spare room and nobody ever stayed there except me. It was also handy for popping across to the football without parking issues. Every year I bought my Dad a season ticket for West Ham United and it was great to meet up with my cousin John, my mate John Cooper who worked for Arista Records, sometimes Roger Trevitt, have a cup of tea at Austin Court with my folks and then mooch across to the ground ten minutes before kick-off. A great way to spend a Saturday afternoon.

After Dad died I never went to Upton Park again, the moment had ended and I didn't want to sit beside the empty seat. We didn't speak too often, he still never quite grasped the fact I'd become a long-haired musician, not any son of his, but we always went to the football together, the four of us, a Dad, son, cousin and mate, all with claret and blue scarves around our necks like Alf Garnett. Great memories. By the way, did you know that Warren Mitchell, the actor who played Alf Garnett, was a staunch Spurs fan? For that 90 minutes there were no barriers as we called the referee all sorts of names and every single player from every single visiting team was a right dirty bastard. Mum always had tea and cakes ready after the game as we waited for the crowds to disperse. It all went when Dad died and of course Upton Park was about to die too, to be reincarnated as a housing estate.

It's all about the money
So sang Jessie J
But you cannot take 100 years and throw it all away
As though it didn't happen
As though it wasn't there
And make a famous football team
Go and play elsewhere
Goodbye Upton Park
Thanks for all the fun
I'm really going to miss you
And I'm not the only one

So let me tell you more about this sharp left turn in my life that sent me to a place in Berkshire I didn't know at all. There's not much more to add than what I've already written but it was a part of my life as I went through numerous transitions. Hello Reading.

Chapter Five - Reading And Back To Essex

Still to this day I find it strange that I bought a house, my very first house, in Reading, despite the two reasons I mentioned. I had no real affiliation for the place and it's easy for me to forget I actually lived there at all to be honest. Having said that, it was a time of achievement as I secured my first mortgage after paying the deposit with my Transatlantic Records publishing and record advance. The advance was £400 recording advance and £400 publishing advance and the house cost £14,500. I couldn't really afford it but it was time to find a way forward in a life that had experienced more false starts than my second-hand Fiat that I was driving after the death of the camper van. I had two bedrooms and a garden, along with a very proud Mum and Dad too.

At the bottom of the road they opened the first ever Little Chef, a small, square, red building. It's all changed now as they rebuilt the tiny roundabout just off the M4 to accommodate the Majeski Stadium and all that went with it but it was quite a cute area back in the day with a church next to the Little Chef and a row of friendly shops.

I enjoyed going to the local folk club every Thursday at The Red Lion and spent lots of time further down the river pretending I was wealthy enough to live in Henley like my rock pals.

I had a Belgian girlfriend at the time, Nadine, who lived in Brussels, and she was all set to move to England before changing her mind. It was a shame because I adored Nadine, a clever, stunningly beautiful lady who recommended so many amazing books for me to read, particularly Salinger's Catcher In The Rye. Like an idiot, I never realised she had a boyfriend in Belgium too. It was the first time my heart was truly broken.

If you break my heart
Please don't throw away the pieces
For I will mend it some day
When my new love increases
Not needle and thread
But happiness and smiles instead

I saved up and decided to have new windows fitted by a company called Tudor Glass. The man who came to do the deal, Ray Whiteman, sang in a folk group, The Romany, at Windsor and Eton folk club, a club I'd played a few times, so you can imagine my surprise when he turned up with his wife Debbie. To cut a long story short I ended up marrying Debbie, yes a very long story with a sad ending, and for the first time in my life I was feeling settled. Debbie sang in The Romany too and it became a very musical house. We were together nineteen years and that's the only mention I make of our relationship, one that came to a particularly nasty end. Nobody's fault particularly, but it came to a very nasty end just the same as yet another solicitor bought another flash car. It was an event that drew me and my two daughters, Polly and Rosie, ever closer as we negotiated a particularly difficult time as a formidable trio. Enough said.

More and more dates came in and my new manager after Jazz's departure, Jo Lustig, signed me up to Chrysalis

Records. It was a time of advancement in so many different ways. I was in a stable with Ralph McTell and Richard Thompson, plus Irish band The Chieftains, excellent company, and my name grew bigger on the folk scene. Yes, all was going well but I yearned to be back where I kind of belonged and so, with better earnings, we moved to Essex, the dreamland of all Eastenders made good. Wherever you lived in Essex there was a fair chance your neighbour was a taxi-driver with his cab parked in the drive.

I didn't want to return to London, I'd spent enough years there thank you very much, and so I bought a house in the lovely village of Debden, near Saffron Walden. Fern Cottage was a thirty second walk from The Plough pub, run by a guitar nutcase landlord by the name of Brendan. Heaven. My eldest daughter, Polly, was born at The Rosie Maternity Hospital in Cambridge and with her arrival we soon needed another house with an extra bedroom. I didn't want to leave the area and so we bought Appletree Cottage in Cherry Green, just outside the beautiful town of Thaxted.

I made many excursions into London as I had my own show on BBC Radio 2 at the time. The journey wasn't much more than an hour, the M11 motorway being nothing like the clogged beast it is today.

So, let's forget my attempts at hospital radio for a moment, I joined the BBC in the early 1970s and appeared on numerous radio shows for seven years on BBC Radio 2, including various series of my own. It all began with Braden's World, a show featuring the satirist of the time Bernard Braden. The series didn't last long as Mr Braden's health deteriorated but the show was re-formatted and re-named

Stop The World, produced by Alan Nixon. It was presented by Francis Matthews and Sally Grace with me providing the music and silly rhymes along with certain strange one-liners I wrote for a certain Mr Fletcher. It became a very successful comedy radio show, broadcasting twice a week, on Thursdays and Saturdays, and it led me to various BBC Radio 2 shows of my own, Digance Does It Locally, Digance Does It Sportingly, The Richard Digance Show and The Animal Alphabet. They were recorded at The Paris Theatre in London's Lower Regent Street and I loved making them so much. Let me tell you all about The Paris Theatre sessions.

In those days you could park your car right outside the studio, imagine that in modern day Regent Street, and leave it there the whole day through rehearsal and broadcast. Ah, those were the days. No wheel-clamps, no nasty men with winches, trucks, or shaven heads, not even a yellow line. Retired soldiers and coppers got proper jobs after they'd completed their years of service. Traffic wardens were so new I had barely had the time to write a song about the coming of the black and yellow human wasps. The world really was a simpler place back then. Computers? I don't think so. Scripts were written long-hand or on a typewriter until basic word-processors arrived in the late 1970s. Tippex? Anyone remember Tippex? I remember the smell of the stuff as it was nearest I ever came to taking drugs. Words ending in the letter x seem to be reminders of my past; Tippex, Airfix, Ajax, Playtex living girdles, Asterix, all long before sex limped into my life.

The additional reason I loved working at The Paris was because I stood on stage where so many others had stood before me. Peter Sellers, Sir Harry Secombe, Michael Bentine,

Spike Milligan and of course Tony Hancock. Who wouldn't have wanted to have stood on that stage, that bastion of comedy? Oh yes, and my old mate, the late Roy Hudd, the master of British music hall, he recorded The News Huddlines there too, and now it was my turn. I'm sure you can imagine the excitement of following in all their footsteps and stepping out from those thick red velvet curtains that I still see as I write this.

After every recording we went to a pub round the corner between Regent Street and The Haymarket, The Captain's Cabin, which Spike Milligan lovingly referred to as The Captain, and we stayed until closing time every week, laughing and drinking. Strangely my car was still there when it was time to head on home. There was the very odd occasion when I'd had too much to drink and so I left the car in Regent Street overnight, went and stayed at the producer's, Alan Nixon's, house in Finsbury Park, North London and tubed it in the next morning with the car still sitting there, guitar in the boot, waiting for its irresponsible owner. It all sounds too ridiculous for words when compared to the modern world, but that's the way it was fifty years ago and the differences make me smile. Just imagine leaving your car in a street in the heart of London for twenty-four hours, guitar in the back, and you will realise how much the world has changed in my lifetime.

It was whilst living in Cherry Green I made a sweeping decision of leaving the BBC and joining the vibrant, new Capital Radio. I needed the change.

I was playing in a spaghetti house in Romford Road, Manor Park, a break from supporting other people. It seemed a huge mistake as I sat in the corner, strumming my guitar to hardly anyone. When I say hardly anyone I mean two people. It didn't really matter to me though as I was playing my guitar so I was happy. A solitary couple sat at a table as I sang my songs, tumbleweed roaring past me. They didn't seem to be taking much notice but when they stood to leave the male of the couple came across to me and asked me to call him the next morning. He gave me his business card and left. I forgot to call. Two weeks later he returned to the restaurant and asked me why I hadn't called. I remembered him but didn't really have a sensible answer so I just apologised and promised I would call him the next morning, which I did. When I got home I checked out his card and you could have knocked me down with a feather. The man in question was Aiden Day, the Programme Controller of Capital Radio, London's new commercial radio station, indeed the country's largest independent radio station serving over 8 million Londoners. He wanted a folk programme on the station and he'd chosen me to present it. Can you believe I didn't bother to call him first time around?

That's how I presented Britain's first ever commercial radio folk programme, Richard Digance and Friends. It's a warning to all performers that you must never ever throw a gig away because you never know who is in the audience, even if there happens to be just two of them. Every member of an audience is important, no matter how big or small, as I eventually found out.

I'd signed for an initial six weeks but ended up at Capital for over four years. That was how I ended up supporting The Beach Boys at Knebworth, and Dire Straits the following year, and how I interviewed two of my greatest influences, Joni Mitchell and Arlo Guthrie, he who inspired me to buy my VW camper van. It all came from playing in a spaghetti house to just two people. It goes to show you just never know.

Capital were behind the Knebworth Festival and me being a member of staff meant I was a part of it too. A fluke but much appreciated Capital Radio, accepted with thanks. Other presenters weren't folkie enough to interview Joni Mitchell or Arlo Guthrie, they weren't really that interested, so I was grateful for that too. In the canteen was a notice board on which were pinned upcoming interview opportunities if anybody wanted to do them. The offers for Joni and Arlo were blank so I put my name down and had them all to myself.

I interviewed Joni Mitchell at Capital Radio in 1981 and it was an honour, a sheer delight, and I mean for me and not her. She had released a new album and was doing the usual rounds of interviews that record companies demand. She looked tired but the first thing that struck me was how tiny she was. A huge name with a huge voice and yet she looked so diminutive. I was allowed thirty minutes by the record company representative as we sat down in a small studio the size of a bathroom. The first thing Joni did was light a cigarette, it was allowed in the work-place in those days. She chain-smoked all the way through the interview and yet it was one of the highlights of my musical life. There she sat, opposite me, the woman who gave us Big Yellow Taxi, Woodstock, Ladies of The Canyon and my favourite album Blue. And so the interview began with the usual plug of an album and what she was up to. Joni answered politely, the same as she had many times that day at other radio stations. She plugged her gig at The Royal Festival Hall, job done. It was a chore we all go through from time to time.

It was all going par for the course until I asked the lady how she created her own guitar style by tuning to the chord of G. I'd never known anyone else do it at that time and the sound was certainly distinctive. It was the album Clouds that alerted us all to a new kind of folk guitar playing. As I asked the question her eyes came alive, telling me no-one had ever asked her that before during a radio interview. I remember her saying I'd done my homework and I'd replied by telling her I didn't need homework because I knew her music inside out. She told me how she could find certain chords on the piano which she couldn't find on a standard-tuned guitar due to the fact her left hand had been affected by polio when she was a child and so she tuned to a chord thus allowing her to play the piano with her left hand and the guitar with her right while writing her songs. That way, she could find the piano notes on her guitar and the rest is history.

Late last night I heard a car door slam, and a big yellow taxi took away my old man.

She loved talking about her early stuff, giggling lots as she recalled the early days in between lighting cigarettes. I remember thinking she must have had some chimney in her lounge at home or she wouldn't have seen her TV.

The record company chappie kept tapping his watch, reminding Joni my time was up, but she was having none of it. We spoke for an hour and a half, a complete packet of cigarettes for Joni and when the job was done we had coffee in the café area, forcing the man to cancel the next interview. I adored Joni Mitchell, she was everything I wanted to be, a singer, songwriter, poet and painter. One of my favourite songs is Case of You from the Blue album, a song I sang with Marc

Cohn, he who had a massive hit with Walking in Memphis, when he came onto my TV show a few years later. During a coffee break at rehearsals at The London Studios I told Marc, a massive Joni fan himself, the story of how I had interviewed Joni just down the road and he was highly impressed.

'Richard, you met Joni Mitchell?'

'I certainly did.'

'I'm so envious of you, man.'

Hey, I'd just met Marc Cohn and that was quite something too.

During the afternoon rehearsal Marc was fiddling around on the grand piano as the crew were sorting their camera angles and I joined him on my acoustic guitar. We busked an impromptu version of Case of You, my favourite Joni Mitchell song of all time. We decided to do it during the evening recording and I loved every minute of it. Unfortunately, the editor sent it, unceremoniously, to the cutting-room floor and our efforts never saw the light of day. Oh well, Marc sang Walking in Memphis on my show and it reached the top twenty by the Monday morning, just two days later, such was the power of television when there were only four channels.

I've looked at clouds from both sides now.
It was such a celebration
You were such an inspiration
To spend some time with you
Even just an hour or two

Another very interesting fact that Joni told me during our interview was how difficult it was to perform in Canada, as musicians had to pay a 200-dollar union fee. Sometimes musician unions can take away work from those who are their struggling members, which is very strange. Her most popular song 'Both Sides Now' has been recorded by 1,200 different artists and yet she struggled to scrape the money together to get herself started in the music business due to the union demands. It's a strange world out there. Musicians of today trying to make headway in such a topsy-turvy world would never be in a position to raise such cash just to keep legal. I don't think they'd even bother. 2021 sees musicians in an equally dubious situation but for an entirely different reason.

As for my good mate Mike Smith who was sitting next to me when I noticed Joni's name on the noticeboard, he sadly died in 2014 at just 59 years of age during major heart surgery. It was so sad.

Smithy and I laughed so many times as we made our way through the years at Capital Radio and out the other side. He became a national figure on BBC Radio One and TV too, hosting the That's Entertainment TV series, I didn't make Radio One myself, I had no real desire to if I'm honest, but I interviewed Joni Mitchell and that's good enough for me.

I felt equally humbled, four weeks later, when I interviewed Arlo Guthrie, son of folk legend Woody Guthrie, in the same tiny studio. We shook hands and he warned me not to ask questions about his father, which I totally understood. I knew all about Woody anyway, I'd read Bound For Glory from cover to cover but I really wanted to get him onto the subject of Alice's Restaurant, the album and movie that convinced me I needed a VW camper van to be a true folkie. We got on well, so much so that when we met again at The Cambridge Folk

Festival he remembered the interview and we ended up doing a banjo/guitar duet in the club tent much to the shock and hopefully the enjoyment of the crowd.

The London folk show I presented didn't get the biggest ratings in the world to be honest but it was respected. It was all a bit odd because I was still signed to the enemy, the BBC. I'd started there with Bernard Braden and it was now twelve years on as I prepared for my fourth series on Radio 2. I had a new producer, Andy Aliffe, a complete nutcase with a wardrobe full of creative ideas. He opened my eyes to radio production. The last time I saw him, just a couple of years ago, he was doing Jack the Ripper tours for tourists around the East End.

Capital Radio was really, really exciting, something new, and I joined a stable of fantastic presenters such as Kenny Everett, Alan Freeman, my mate Mike Smith and Michael Aspel. Of those names I single out Kenny Everett for the moment and Smithy in a short while.

Kenny, a shy, introverted man, made most of his programmes from home and rarely came into the Capital studios, something I was to do myself as time passed, making my own shows, under my own steam, in my own recording studio. He was a great inspiration to me and he gave me a great tip when I became a disc-jockey, DJ to younger readers, as opposed to a presenter.

It was when I took over Midnight Special, speaking to London for four hours from midnight until Phil Allen or Phillip Schofield took over on The Early Show. Oh yes, I was hugely popular with insomniacs and burglars. Kenny told me to place a photograph of someone I knew on the control desk in front of me and talk to that person as opposed to the whole of London, which would have been quite daunting. It worked. It was all about impressing and so I put a photo of my football hero Bobby Moore on the control desk in the hope I would impress him as much as he had impressed me with his skills.

Not only did we have the big names of the folk scene but also those from other musical walks of life who fancied going acoustic and showing what they were made of. Examples? I recorded the only acoustic performance ever by rock icons Jethro Tull. Then there was country legend Carlene Carter, with her Johnny Cash connection, who performed with Dave Edmunds who'd had a massive hit with Sabre Dance on one side of her and Nick Lowe, who sang I Knew The Bride When She Used To Rock and Roll, on the other. As I said, there were no boundaries, just musicians showing what they were made of. An acoustic set by blues legend Rory Gallagher, Elkie Brooks on the piano singing blues standards, and folkies who had moved on to bigger things such as Gerry Rafferty and Dave Brock of Hawkwind. Of course there were the regular folk club performers too, but I just wanted to show you the diversity that I knew I would never discover at The BBC and why I moved on to pastures new. The John Peel inspiration was there for all to hear. He pioneered acoustic music long before anyone else did, highlighting the talents of Marc Bolan and Bridget St John to name just two. I loved and admired his diversity and I wanted to emulate him at Capital and I did my very best to do exactly that.

At the start of it all I only went into London from my home in Essex on that one recording day of the week, but that was to change as my extra broadcasting opportunities sprung up. I completed a radio production course with fellow presenter, Mike Smith, at Elstree School of Broadcasting and so then, being a qualified radio producer, I spent far more time at Capital's studios in Euston Road making other programmes. Once again, just like in Regent Street, I could park my car outside all day and not get a ticket. Try getting away with that one in Euston Road today, another Monopoly stop-off by the way.

I was presenting, as well as the folk programme, Midnight Special, R2D2, Monday Matters with Adrian Love and Sunday Funday and my career seemed to be moving away from performing in the folk clubs to being on the radio most days of the week. I made sure that wouldn't totally happen as music was firmly in my blood, so I built a recording studio at my home at Thaxted where, incidentally, Dick Turpin worked as a butcher, but not during the time I lived there before you ask. My friends, Rod and Marian Stokes, ran a folk club at their pub, The Bluebell, which was once the home of that famous highwayman and I actually slept in Dick Turpin's bedroom, but I digress.

My radio production course with Smithy had been beneficial way beyond my wildest dreams. If I'm perfectly honest Mike Smith and myself saw it as a bit of a jolly away from the constant studio work but we both got really into it. Mike, who qualified the same as me, went on to be a successful Radio One presenter and TV celebrity, a qualified pilot too, surviving a helicopter crash in 1988. Whatever we both went on to do we both had our production qualifications to fall back on if it all backfired and I have great memories of a really nice guy who, incidentally, was once Noel Edmunds's driver. They were both Romford, Essex boys and so I assume Smithy must have learnt so much from his boss as he drove backwards and forwards to the studio with Britain's most successful presenter of the time, someone we can all forgive for creating Mr Blobby. Can we? Can we really? I'll just go and make a cup of tea while we ponder that one!

There's no doubt my days at Elstree Radio School with Mike Smith were invaluable in learning my way around a studio. I've mentioned Smithy a couple of times in my story. His dream came true when he married the lovely Sarah Greene and he died far too young in 2014. He was my big ally at Capital at a time when I struggled to find my feet in commercial radio. Timing was of paramount importance with station idents and adverts flying in and out, left, right and centre. It was nothing like making programmes at the BBC as I had in the past, so it took me a while to get the hang of it. It was a brave new world for me and Smithy often used to come and sit alongside me, teaching me how to be a self-drive presenter. I liked him a lot. He had a great sense of humour and was a fantastic Breakfast Show presenter, such a friendly guy. At my age I've obviously lost a few pals along the way, but I can honestly say the passing of Smithy and my close friend, comedian Dave Lee, both made me burst into tears with deep regret.

My time as a radio presenter and producer at London's Capital Radio spanned from 1979 to 1983 and it was a highly enjoyable time of my life. And yet it was the epitome of loneliness at times, talking to a wall through the night. It's time to rectify that and have you sitting beside me once again, just like you did at The Troubadour. So many people through the years have asked me what it was like working as a radio presenter in London, so I'm about to do my best to describe in greater detail by trying to stir your imagination by taking you back there with me.

Having become a qualified radio producer at Elstree it enabled me to stretch my radio appearances way beyond the folk programme that I originally went to Capital Radio to present. You are about to sit beside me as I go on air, Midnight Special.

We are sat in Studio 4, a room the size of a kitchen in a one-bedroomed flat. In front of us is the desk that I 'drive' that's the term used, whilst I speak live on air to the people of London, Bobby Moore's picture in front of me. I can reach out and touch all four walls, it's that small.

I've pushed a chair up beside mine so you can be there. It's a bit of a squeeze but we manage it. There is now so little room I can barely move around to the turntable, the tape machine behind me from which I play various concert tracks, and the pile of cartridges, big cassettes if you like, by my right elbow that I need to load up every time there is a commercial break. The whole experience of Midnight Special is solitary confinement in the extreme. Four hours, from midnight, obviously, to 4am, just sitting in a tiny cupboard of a studio playing music to Londoners.

The only link to the outside world was a telephone that listeners could call if they wanted a dedication. During the day such callers would have heard a telephonist on the other end who would pass messages to the in-demand disc-jockey live on air, but this wasn't during the day. I had no such telephonist, no such luxury, and so I answered the phone myself, something you will be doing shortly on my behalf, trust me. The phone never rings, it only flashes up a light on the receiver, and, believe me, the light will never stop flashing for the whole 4 hours, so you're in for a busy old time.

I presume when anyone thinks of a major radio station such as Capital Radio they think of a busy hive of media industry. Well, yes it was during the day, but at night-time it was a different kettle of fish. Although situated in the giant Euston Tower, a real skyscraper of a building beside the Euston Underpass, it gave the wrong impression because it was only on one floor and the rest of the building was taken up with offices related to MI5. When I presented Midnight Special for those three years I was the only person in the building other than an overnight security guard who spent the whole time chatting to his girlfriend on the phone downstairs. As I've already said it was solitary in the extreme.

One night in 1981, out of complete boredom, I had a bit of a lightbulb moment and it was this very night I'm returning to now as I take you into the dimly-lit Studio 4. Please let me set it up. Sometimes it was difficult to even stay awake and on two occasions I didn't even manage that, but those nights are of no consequence to this book in general and this night in particular. I invented a London Grand Prix for bread delivery drivers, so many of whom were carting their vans around London delivering bread and cakes for the high street shops and supermarkets in the middle of the night, doing their best to stay awake at the wheel at such an unearthly hour. The rules were simple.

'Hey guys, I'm all on my own here, just like you are, so if you're listening to my show while you're driving round town drop by and leave me a nice cake at reception. Be the first winner of My London Bakery Grand Prix. I'm waiting. Call me when you've dropped one off and I'll give you a name check.'

So, we sit here waiting for the action to start and you see the light on the phone begin to flash like part of the Blackpool illuminations.

The problem with being on the radio is you can't possibly have any idea who is listening, if anyone at all. Oh yes, they are listening alright.

You begin to take the phone calls for me, chatting to the listeners, and the first is a guy from Bartons Bakers in North London who tells you he's left a custard slice with the security guard downstairs. We declare him the winner and still the phone flashes like some kind of nutcase. You run down the stairs and grab the custard slice and we have half each, even though my slice should be bigger as I'm the presenter!

After about ten minutes or so there is a knock on the door of tiny Studio 4 and it's the security guard holding numerous cake boxes and bags in his arms. He looks bemused. London by night has gone totally bonkers in a small way. He obviously isn't listening to the radio whilst on duty so he has no idea what the hell is going on. I explain about the London Bakery Grand Prix and he shrugs his shoulders as if I have a screw loose. We take the cakes and I tell him that if any more turn up it's best that he leaves them in reception and I'll pick them up at the end of the show. We still fail to bring a smile to his weary face.

On air I'm consumed with reading out the names of the drivers and the bakers they are delivering to between the records. You scribble more names down and pass them to me and it's relentless. It's free advertising after all and it has really caught their imaginations. Ha-ha, you are now a Production Assistant at Capital Radio, the biggest commercial radio station in Britain, with your very own designated job of making a list of the calls and callers for me to mention on air. It's so much fun and great to have a kind of physical contact with people we will never know, with someone beside me for a change too.

By 4am the foyer looks like a patisserie according to Phillip Schofield who is taking over the reins when I come off air. As is always the case Phil brings me a cup of tea and realising you are with me he nips off to make you one too. It was the first time we had tea and cakes instead of just a cup of tea. The three of us laugh our heads off like naughty little children. All in one night you've become a production assistant and met Phillip Schofield who is all set to become one of the country's top television presenters.

The show ends and the administration takes place before I can leave the building and head for home. We list the music played on PRS forms, it wasn't done online back then, to ensure the musicians get their radio royalties before putting the records back in the racks for another week. We make our way down the sweeping staircase to where the security guard is sitting, surrounded by a sea of cakes and pastries, Phillip was absolutely right. I guess around 80 or 100 varieties in all and the foyer smells like bread and fresh cream. We say our goodbyes to the security guard and he grunts as usual, not even bothering to look up from his morning paper first edition. Don't take it personally, he's only ever grunted one or twice to me the whole time I've been doing Midnight Special, let alone talk.

We both go our separate ways as dawn flickers in the sky whilst London wakes up, and I watch you head off with various cakes and a Capital Radio tee-shirt to remember the event. You look more than happy with your night in London with me and I'm so glad you enjoyed yourself. Maybe you ponder as you watch the cars in Euston Road and beyond. Do they have their radios on? Have they been listening to The London Bakery Grand Prix from that little cupboard where you were sitting? The answer is probably yes they were. You want to shout out at the top of your voice that it was you who took the calls from the delivery drivers but it's pointless, but you have gained an insight into the world of radio.

The lonely presenter, plus one, linking with the lonely van driver or the lonely person in their bedsit. Somehow it came together and the job was done. I think back now on how many lonely people rely on that personal interaction with the radio. Back to back music like so many modern radio stations play today as a modern format doesn't really provide that. There are still many lonely people around, times don't change that much. I wonder if you remember that night we brought London to life and had a good laugh.

I thought that would be the best way to describe my odd time at Capital, to actually take you back there. I hope it worked.

One can only assume that the number of lonely people multiplied during lockdown and that the radio presenters did their jobs assuring them they were not alone.

As a footnote, I ran The Grand Prix for a couple of weeks before the novelty of it all ran dry. After a couple of weeks a few baker's vans used to be waiting outside the studios when I went on air to make sure they were winners of the race. They say little things please little minds but it was more than that because a radio presenter and a few delivery drivers joined together to ease the boredom of working through the night whilst others slept peacefully in their beds, totally oblivious of the fun that was going on in the hours of darkness. I reckon I put on quite a bit of stomach weight during that time, what with all those cream cakes.

I remember on another occasion I announced I'd run out of cigarettes and I had an equally successful result, leaving the studio with a good few dozen packets of fags from passers-by. Yes, everyone smoked back then and smoking in the studio was allowed and the odd fag helped me stay awake through those long and lonely hours talking to that photograph that Kenny Everett had suggested.

I left Capital Radio in 1984 but I took some amazing memories with me. I hope it was an amazing memory for you too. Before you and I return to these modern times we're enduring right now, I'd love you to stay by my side a little longer as I take you back to an event just down the road from the Capital Radio studios. I love my history and London is full of it and as I sit here in the remote Wiltshire countryside I try to re-live one of my favourite historical trips when living in the capital. Let's go.

The Great Fire of London began on 2nd September 1666 and it raged until the 6th. It was a hell of a fire by all accounts, destroying 13,200 houses and 87 churches including the original St Paul's Cathedral. The population of London at the time was 80,000, less than the capacity of Wembley Stadium, and 70,000 of those were rendered homeless after the blaze. Amazingly only 6 people lost their lives, even though most lost their wooden homes.

I feel it's appropriate to take myself back after the Capital Radio experience because The Great Fire of London began in a baker's shop in Pudding Lane. I doubt if they made custard slices in those days but, hey, you never know.

Being born and brought up in London it's history became of great interest to me. At school I wasn't bothered in the slightest to be honest. A school trip to The Tower of London was like watching paint dry, queuing up to see the Crown Jewels, what was that all about? Having jewellery for the rich being rammed down my throat did nothing for me and I laughed at those Beefeater chaps in their silly hats and bright orange socks along with shoes with buckles. Soldiers? I would have taken them on any day looking like that.

One of my passions, as I grew a little older, was to take myself off to various parts of the city of London on my bike and try to feel its history, all on my own. More than that, I loved to discover stories that few others had bothered to find out about. Of course, there are endless sights to see in such a big place as London, but I had my favourite, as it really sparked my imagination.

These days The Monument is difficult to find as it is surrounded, let's say engulfed, by large modern buildings. Yet it never used to be like that. So what exactly is The Monument? Yes it is the very spot where The Great Fire of London began but it's also a beautiful work of art that has become lost in the crowd, like we all feel at times, and I feel it's time to re-light its fire and try to restore it to its former levels of glory, strange glory of course, and importance.

It's actually situated on the junction of Monument and Fish Street Hill and it's exactly 61 metres from Pudding Lane, where the fire apparently began. Oh my god, I've just realised I sound like those two dodgy Russian tourists that came to Salisbury on a 2,000 mile day trip.

It now hides behind by tall clusters of offices, nameless and faceless offices that look cold and forbidding. When I first visited The Monument on my bike it stood high and proud, but sadly no longer. It's a shame because it was built with incredible flair and imagination. Well of course it was, it was designed by Sir Christopher Wren, the clever man of the time. Now this chap really did get through some pencils as he also designed St Paul's Cathedral, plus Hampton Court Palace, The Royal Naval College at Greenwich and The Royal Hospital in Chelsea.

I loved to stare up at his smallest and yet most incredible works of architecture. Oh such a brilliant and creative man. He had help from a man by the name of Robert Hooke as you shall hear, but right now I recall climbing those 311 spiral steps, more Russian tourist facts, that took me to the top, two-hundred plus feet above London. There was a pure gold urn with flames protruding to remind one and all of why it was there. I used to look down and feel dizzy, imagining Pudding Lane as it used to be, the wooden shops all huddled together with as many stray animals roaming around as bare-footed children.

By all accounts, Thomas Farriner set fire to oddments close to his oven and smoke began to bellow from the baker's shop and then London was on fire. We all know about the fire but to stand above the very spot where it all began used to stir my imagination and it made my bike-ride to London worthwhile. They built a small laboratory at the base of The Monument, and that was Robert Hooke showing his worth.

The Monument was not just built as a statue of remembrance, but it was also London's first telescope, a little-known fact. Just imagine the eyes that looked up to view the stars and planets overhead, trying to work out all the facts that were discovered years later. It was such an important symbol of both the past and the future and yet so very few people are bothered about it these days, such a shame. I have always been totally obsessed with this tiny monument, tiny by modern-day standards at least, and now you see why. So, back to the music.

So many of Britain's top folk musicians came to my house to record, including Richard Thompson, Ashley Hutchings, Martin Carthy, Martin Simpson, John Kirkpatrick and Dougie MacLean. Me and my new family were having a wonderful time until a bombshell fell from out of the sky. My life evolved around recording at the time, having also been involved with much radio documentary work.

I'd been involved with numerous radio documentaries. That particular facet began with a BBC Radio 4 documentary about Sir Rowland Hill, the creator of the Penny Post. One of the songs I wrote still stays in my memory as its title 'Rowland's Over The Hill' which was one of the corniest I was able to boast. I then teamed up with Ralph Bernard. Allow me to tell you about Ralph.

He was an East End journalist, working on my local paper, The Stratford Express, and we became friends after he interviewed me. He even acted as my driver on a folk club tour of The Lake District. He went on to LBC, a news radio station, as a newsreader, and from there to Radio Hallam, an independent radio station in Sheffield. At Hallam we made three radio documentaries together, Dying For A Drink, Down To Earth and Can Buy Me Love and all three won Independent Radio Awards. I went on to provide incidental music for The BBC, Saatchi and Saatchi and the world's biggest selling travel author, Bill Bryson while Ralph became boss, ironically, of Capital Radio, Chief Executive of The Royal Albert Hall and creator of Classic FM, whilst picking up a CBE along the way for his troubles. On the downside he supported Leyton Orient for which, in my humble opinion, he should have been stripped of his royal ribbon. For a while we did hospital radio shows together at Moorfields Eye Hospital in London. Our helpers at that time were two ladies, Lisa who Ralph went on to marry, and Jenny Dawson, who was a wonderful lady whom I should have married too but I forgot to ask her. Well, I was busy and it slipped my mind. We went out for a while and then she dumped me for a lorry driver, telling me what a lovely guy he was and how articulated he was. An articulated lorry driver and she didn't even realise the joke.

We enjoyed a great reunion a few years back when Ralph booked the Newtown Theatre in Edinburgh as part of the Fringe Festival. It was the old Masonic Hall in George Street and a perfect venue. I did 32 shows through the festival period and my boast was that no show would be the same, a boast I managed to achieve. You may not know but all shows at The Edinburgh Festival are an hour long, so it's a bit of a cattle market. I followed radio presenter Johnnie Walker and I was followed by a Burlesque show. In the mornings I presented a children's show, The War of The Worms, with my daughter Rosie for which Rosie received an amazing review in The Stage.

So back to the Essex plot, our home was sold in the wake of the development of Stansted Airport and people from the BAA came knocking on our door. We didn't want to move, had never thought about moving, but we realised it wasn't a bad idea when they trialled the first Concorde flight over the village rooftops. Sheep genuinely died of heart attacks, cows ran about like little kittens and chimneys wobbled like jellies.

Polly hadn't started school so it wouldn't be a major disruption to her. Like everyone else I'd always wanted to live by the sea and so that's what we decided to do. However, I didn't fancy the windy Essex coast too much and in my head the warmer south coast seemed far more appealing. So on a day of extreme madness I got in my car and headed south-west to Dorset, stopping off for a cup of tea in Lyme Regis. I was about to travel on to Devon maybe but I didn't need to travel any further as I fell in love with the place the minute I arrived. I'd never been to Lyme Regis before but something told me it was calling me. It was old England personified, full of history, my favourite subject.

It was therefore with a certain amount of sadness and reticence that Appletree Cottage was sold and we moved from Essex to our new home overlooking the sea at Lyme Bay. I thought it would be my family's final move but I didn't allow for the uncertainties of my profession. Things happen, times change and being in the entertainment industry is all about following your hunches and doing what you think is right at the time. It's a precarious job that often goes wrong many times before it corrects itself. It was a massive transition period for me and my job would take an unexpected turn that didn't quite fit where I lived.

Chapter Six - Lyme Regis

There is no prettier town in England than Lyme Regis on the Jurassic Coast of Dorset. Those who live there are amongst the luckiest people in the world. Our new home in Clappentail Lane overlooked Lyme Bay and I could go fishing whenever I wanted. I lived in Lyme for eight years, Polly started school there and Rosie started her life there too, being born in Exeter. It all seemed idyllic, but life is never quite that easy is it?

Stumbling blocks I hadn't foreseen were heading my way at a rate of knots. Whilst still in Essex I went to The Middle East with comedian Jim Davidson as his support act, along with his manager Laurie Mansfield, a man I admired tremendously. He was the boss of International Artists, one of the country's top agencies and all of a sudden I was plunged into the world of television when I joined his company upon our return from Dubai. Shortly after joining I was in The Falkland Islands entertaining the troops down there and my world of performance changed drastically. When I got back Laurie secured my first TV special with Thames Television. I never saw it coming, I have to say, but suddenly International Artists had changed my life. I was doing summer seasons as opposed to tour dates, I was making endless appearances on TV and my days at Capital had drawn to a close as they didn't like my TV involvement much. They'd had a similar problem with Kenny Everett and Michael Aspel and they'd started getting quite demanding and forthright. I loved radio, I'd been brought up with radio, but all of a sudden I knew that phase of my life had ended and my romance with radio had kind of ended too, at least for a while whilst I concentrated on other things that would enhance my career.

As a young kid we'd listen to Journey into Space on the radio or The Navy Lark. My life has evolved around radio broadcasts since I was knee high to a grasshopper. It all began I suppose when it was the only entertainment I knew as a kid, good old radio, so it's no real surprise that I hold that particular medium so close to my heart. I began my entertainment career in hospital radio too and my audience were in stitches, particularly in A&E. How ironic then that I write at a time when hospitals are bursting at the seams and when the NHS is struggling to cope with yet another spike. Hospitals are busier than ever before, but dear old hospital radio has sadly become a prehistoric thing of the past, give or take the very odd exception. A very interesting word is prehistoric because it makes me ask myself if there was something pre-historic then when did history actually end? Surely history encompasses all years and ages, but were that the case then there have been no prehistoric if you get what I mean. I thought I would just throw that thought in, but now it's time to throw it out again.

There was sadly no antidote or vaccine for hospital radio, it had more or less died of old age. Every hospital used to have its own radio station, manned by trusty volunteers who gave up their evenings to be amateur presenters, but now they're as rare as rocking horse poo.

In the old days hospital radio was vital for patient morale. People like me would walk around the wards with a pen and notepad taking requests from patients in the hope of cheering up those in great pain, a dubious claim as I think back.

I'd done a fair bit of it myself, being president of Camelot Hospital Radio in Yeovil and Goodmayes Hospital in Essex as well as serving time on the turntables at Moorfields Eye Hospital in London and East Ham Memorial Hospital, where it all began just down the road from where I lived with my parents in the East End of London.

Nowadays it's obviously different. Patients have mobile phones, iPads, laptops and TV sets, so the need for hospital radio had sadly disappeared with the women pushing trolleys full of sweets and magazines around the same wards. Strangers strolling around wards had become a thing of the past. Can you imagine that happening today? Good heavens, I'm old enough to remember when the only people who wore masks were bank robbers or the Lone Ranger. The only time I ever saw a mask in real life was one odd week when the London smog engulfed us as if a chimneysweep had cleaned the clouds overhead. Suddenly the whole world was wearing masks.

I remember when most hospital cases were cured with a bottle of Lucozade and a bunch of grapes as opposed to a phenomenal vaccine they came up with in an Oxford laboratory. We didn't know the word cancer back then because most people died of old age. At my own age of 72 as I write this I can't help wondering about the years you needed to have been around to have a death certificate stating you'd popped your clogs due to old age. A scary thought for me.

Actually, my earliest recollection of radio was before then, before I dabbled in hospital radio, as I listened to Radio Luxemburg under the sheets late at night in a bedroom I shared with my brother. The signal was rubbish, barely audible, but it was an exciting thing to do, listening until the batteries on our tiny transistor radios gave up and died. They had a guy on there by the name of Horace Bachelor who used to tell me and my brother how to win the football pools and become millionaires. I sense his success rate was zero, it certainly didn't help us two. Imagine being a millionaire at seven and a half years of age, all the new bikes I could have bought. The problem was that the aforementioned signal faded in and out, what with Luxemburg, I presume, being so far away, so I struggled to get a grip of his astonishing advice, even though he broadcast from Keynsham in Bristol. I know what you're thinking, Bristol? Luxemburg? I have no idea either. It was all so long ago and I have no explanation to offer, but hey it was called Radio Luxemburg.

For those of you not old enough to have hear of this naughty audio escape under the bedclothes, the station began in 1933, the first ever commercial radio station in fact, and it closed down in 1992. That's really all I know. Because of that technical hiccup of a dodgy signal I never won the football pools and became a millionaire. Confusing? Not half. My whole life was confusing as I tried to find a genre of music that took my fancy. I eventually found folk music but that was many years later and it was a genre of music they never played on Radio Luxemburg anyway. My learning curve was one hell of an arc let me tell you.

One thing that has been on my mind since those early days was, if Horace Bachelor really knew how to win the football pools and make a fortune, why on earth would he have shared his master plan with a reprobate like me? Of course he wouldn't, you're absolutely right. He would have retired and lived a life of complete, splendorous luxury by a swimming-pool in Barbados while I went about doing my paper-round for my local newsagent. As if he'd want to share such an amazing secret with me. He obviously didn't, but I have no problem sharing my modern media journey with your good self. Be warned though, I can't make you a millionaire either! No, I never promised my listeners they would win the football pools. Come to think of it, whatever happened to football pools? Come to think of it whatever happened to football? Games are still drawn. It's only just occurred to me that football coupons don't seem to be around anymore. A relevance of a no-score draw is long gone, as too my passion for football I hasten to add.

Suddenly, Lyme Regis wasn't so wonderfully idyllic as I drove three or four times a week to London, clocking up as many miles as a long-distance lorry driver. I would look in the mirror each morning and see the face of my Dad. My marriage was on the rocks and there was no sign of a lighthouse to help save the day.

The travelling backwards and forwards to London, a five- hour journey, was seriously taking its toll on me and, although my family were enjoying life by the seaside, I was becoming totally exhausted, driving backwards and forwards. There were days when I got home from rehearsals at two or three in the morning before getting up to see Polly before she went off to school and then driving back across to London, writing material in the car on a portable recorder. I had made myself rather unwell. In my defence, I never knew my career change was about to happen when we moved to Lyme Regis, or I wouldn't have even considered the idea, it being too far away from where my new job direction would take me.

The other issue with Lyme is that you never are considered a local unless your previous generations were born there. I was appearing more and more on television and I was being branded the gobby Londoner who'd moved into their town and they didn't quite get me. I knew I would never be regarded as a local. The issue raised its head when, one day, driving Polly home from school, I asked why she hadn't been invited to any birthday parties by her classmates and she told me it was because we lived at the top of the hill where the posh people lived when they moved into the area. I felt gutted and I didn't want Polly being brought up in a place that bore such class grudges.

Oh I nearly forgot, I was also banned for three weeks and fined £100 for driving through Lyme Regis at 1.00am at 37mph, a scary 7mph over the limit in the middle of the night. Do you share the feeling that they had something against me? When you drive through the night with nothing else on the road you're bound to speed as you can't wait to get home. If you're shaking your head saying no, then you haven't shared my lifestyle and hours of work. So my final memory of Lyme Regis, where I lived for six years, is funny in the extreme. I'd only been there a week and I was done for not having a dog licence and I'd been banned from driving.

The first week was spent unpacking and also ensuring the garden was safe for a young Polly to run around in. I was up a ladder, tending to a threatening, overhanging branch when Sergeant Brown drove in.

'Excuse me, are you the owner of the house or the gardener?'

'I'm both, can I help you?'

He pointed to my two dogs, Russell and Sheba, who were wagging their tails at him as a means of a friendly introduction. They both thought it best to befriend him just in case they met up with some snappy Alsatian with an attitude problem.

'Are these your dogs?'

'Yes.'

'Well, they nearly caused a car pile-up in the road. Do you have dog licences?'

Now then, have you ever er been to Lyme Regis? Multi-pile-ups are highly unlikely in the extreme, certainly more unlikely than London of the M25.

I explained to the police officer that we'd only just moved in and we were still unpacking boxes. I told him we had two licences but I didn't have a clue where they were until we had fully unpacked. He demanded I produced them at the police station the following day, an impossible request, but to keep the peace and smooth things over I went and bought two more licenses, took them down the station and apologised. The police were having none of it. I received a summons from Dorchester Magistrate Court and I decided to appear and plead not guilty regarding the 74p breaking of the law, even though I had the licences anyway, it's just that they couldn't be found in time. I conjured up a plan. I decided to request the case was taken to the High Court, even The Old Bailey if necessary. It made the local papers. What was my plan?

I decided to employ barristers to fight my cause in London's highest court. My plan was to ridicule the police officer who had done me. His name was Sergeant Brown and he obviously had nothing better to do than bear a grudge about this new Lyme Regis resident. I have always respected the police and the tough jobs they undergo but this was the exception.

I rang Bob Voice at International Artists and he helped me secure the services of Jim Davidson, Chas and Dave and my mates Hale and Pace. I joined International Artists the same time as Gareth Hale and Norman Pace and our shows were screened the same weekends. The plan was to book The Royal Albert Hall, raise tons of money, pay the double 37p dog licence fee and donate the remainder to the RSPCA.

When we requested this at Dorchester Court they decided to drop the charges and Sergeant Brown was the laughing stock of Lyme Regis. My dogs were not shipped to Australia and I got away with not being hung from the gallows. He moved to Retford, near Nottingham, and Lyme's dog population relaxed.

Lyme is a beautiful part of the country but I never really felt comfortable living there, or more correctly they didn't feel too comfortable me living there. They never really embraced the TV celebrity thing with me, even though Peter Cook was born there, football commentator Peter Brackley lived two houses away from me and Jane Austen spent a lot of time there in her day. Perhaps it was just me they didn't take a liking to.

All things considered, particularly for the sake of my marriage, things had to be resolved regarding the distance I was having to drive every day. I worked out the mileage halfway back to London as a kind of geographical compromise and it resulted in a house-hunting campaign in The New Forest area of Hampshire.

The only real connection I had with the area was my good friend Robin Smith. Robin played cricket for Hampshire and England and it was a phone call from him that got me into my car to view a house that had just come on the market. It would cut my travelling time to the TV studios by half and The New Forest was a delightful area to bring up a family. With Rosie still a tiny baby we uprooted once more and moved to the Hampshire village of Sherfield English, just outside the town of Romsey.

Chapter Seven - Life in Hampshire

The family moved to Hampshire at the height of my television career which I found a little disconcerting. As I've already admitted, I wouldn't say for one minute they all liked me, but most residents of Lyme Regis were used to seeing me in the shops or running Polly to school in nearby Charmouth and thus didn't bother me too much. They nodded occasionally but never stood gaping with their mouths wide open. It would be a new experience for me to live in a goldfish bowl in a brand-new area, but I have to say it wasn't anywhere near as bad as I feared. There were people living close by, far more famous than little old me and so it was nothing new to the area. There was Sir David Frost, David Gower, Kevin Keegan, oh and they made the Inspector Wexford TV series there, so no it wasn't anything unusual to see a familiar face from the small screen or a TV film crew wandering about the place. I felt far more comfortable the day we moved.

Far more interesting is the fact that the Rev Wilbert Awdry was born and raised there and his Thomas The Tank Engine series of books were launched at The White Hart, just off the market square.

Sherfield English is still I place I visit often as my friends Liz and Linnie run the pub there, The Hatchet. It remains the only pub gig I do these days and we all have a great time. We fitted in nicely and quickly at Sandy Close Farm and my travelling backwards and forwards to The London Studios was far more bearable. The girls settled into their school and I built a new recording studio in the barn. Just down the road was a music pub, The Shoe where I went most Sunday nights when I wasn't performing myself and so I was in my element. They used to have more lock-ins there than Dartmoor Prison and although I promised not to namedrop too much I have to tell you of the spectacular nights we had in The Hatchet. I remember the time Rick Wakeman stayed at the house and we lugged a piano from my house down the road to the pub and he did a session on the old Johanna. One of the locals was so pissed he thought Rick was a girl, due to his long blonde hair, and his words still ring loud and clear in my ear.

'Excuse me love, do you mind if I accompany you on the spoons?'

It was a circle fully turned for me because I first became friends with Rick when I used to sing in my early days at the Plough pub in Ilford, Essex and Rick was the lounge pianist in the other bar. We've known each other all the way through our professional lives and done charity shows for each other from time to time.

Back at The Hatchet, Joe Pasquale became a waiter for an hour at the peak of his career and the diners couldn't believe their eyes when he walked around the tables with a white tea-towel draped over his arm.

Chris deBurgh popped in on one occasion and the landlady thought he looked a bit suspect in his full-length leather coat and so she considered slinging him out.

Apart from mates I took down there when they stayed at the house, including Duncan Preston and Susie Dent, there were famous locals too, particularly Sir Edward Heath who loved to sit quietly and down a few whiskeys. We always knew when he was there because armed security guards sat outside in their red jaguar. They rarely spoke to anyone for obvious reasons, except for Keith who came from East Ham and went to a school I used to play football against so we always had lots to talk about while he waited to drive his boss home to Salisbury. The reason he popped in so often was because the pub was on the A36 Southampton road, the route that took him down to The Solent where he kept his yacht.

My new home was actually featured on Through The Keyhole, presented by Sir David Frost who lived just down the road. I remember Lloyd Grossman sitting and doing nothing but reading the newspapers all day during filming and then springing into action when he had to do his walkabout. I made more friends in a week there than I did in a year in Lyme Regis. It was a sharp backdrop difference from the house with sea views over Lyme Bay to the beautiful New Forest and I'd consider them both equally spectacular in different ways.

The day we moved in Robin and Cathy Smith, who lived in neighbouring Whiteparish, had left a carrier bag on the door handle full of goodies to get us through the first hectic day of moving. Needless to say I became a regular visitor to Hampshire's cricket matches at the old ground before they moved on to the Rose Bowl as it was originally named. I was always made welcome and in return I did my bit for all the players as their testimonial years arrived.

Polly attended what was then called Embley Park School, a building steeped in amazing history. Embley Park, a converted stately home, was the family home of Florence Nightingale, the lady who founded nursing as we know it during The Crimean War. It seemed bizarre that the 200th anniversary of her birth coincided with the 2020 lockdown when nurses and other front-line workers were put to the test in the most horrendous way possible. Florence, the first lady of nursing, is buried at St Margaret's Church, just down the road from Polly's school, having declined a state funeral and a final resting place in Westminster Abbey.

Rosie went to the same school, but being younger than Polly, the school had been re-named Hampshire Collegiate by the time she went there. Both the girls did well at school and both went on to university, Polly to Winchester and then Aberystwyth and Rosie to Bath Spa. The only thing that marred my time in Sherfield English was my divorce. I had hoped the move from Lyme would solve such a domestic issue but, unfortunately, it didn't. I choose to not air such personals in this book but it meant the wonderful house had to be sold. I used to joke that my wife got the inside and I got the outside. It was a time of endless court appearances and I genuinely am a little hazy as to what went on because I rid my brain of such events many years ago. However, Polly loved being so close to The New Forest, being horse mad, to the extent she gained a degree in equine science.

Many of my close friends still live in the village of Sherfield English and I still consider The Hatchet as my local. We've had some great nights in the village hall, including a memorable evening with my close chums Chas and Dave, Chas Hodges and Dave Peacock, who loved The Hatchet so much it was a tussle to get them out of the pub and walk to the hall to perform.

Friends are forever
Friends always stay together
Friends are forever
Through good times and through bad
A true good friend
Will be there to the end
Through happy times and sad

As I complete this chapter I genuinely ask myself how the hell did I end up in Hampshire? I was born in a part of the East End of London that had been bombed a few years before, spent months trekking around the country in a VW Camper Van, moved backwards and forwards to Mum and Dads more times than was healthy and yet I ended up buying a house in a most beautiful part of England. Me buying a farm? When I started out there wasn't even any chance of buying a sewage farm, but that's exactly what I did, via Reading, Debden, Thaxted and Lyme Regis.

Chapter Eight - Ampfield

Ampfield is a leafy suburb of Romsey and it has to be mentioned in passing as a remarkably short chapter in this book because it became the stop-off house for me as I got my life back into some kind of order after the obvious. I knew I wouldn't be there long but my duration was cut short for a few good reasons. The house on The Avenue, and I can't even remember the name of the place, backed onto a lake, which seemed like heaven to an angler such as myself, but heaven it was not.

I'd only been there a couple of days when I realised the whole garden was absolutely sodden and infested with bloody crayfish wandering about all over the place. They strolled in the kitchen and then through the lounge. Most disturbing. I hated those bloody creepy-crawlies, but not as much as spindly trees that were twice as high as they should have been. I applied to have them topped but they declined my request.

My friends, Nick and Helen Curtis who now run The New Forest Folk Festival, helped me to move there and it was a day that would be difficult to forget as it was the 11th September, 2001. Nick had set up the TV as we began unpacking boxes and as Helen flicked through the channels we suddenly witnessed the terrorist attack in New York that killed nearly three-thousand people. It should have been quite an exciting day, moving to pastures new, but events soured the proceedings. We couldn't believe what we were watching, the world had gone completely crazy. I'd experienced a bit of a rough time domestically but it was nothing compared to what was going on across the pond.

As the winter of 2001 set in I thought about knocking down a few of those very high trees that were swaying around like pissed dancers. I knew they were protected, even though they were dangerous and likely to make my roof collapse at any given moment. Yeah, their crashing down would frighten off the crayfish but I didn't fancy being in the house when it happened. It was definitely time to move on. I sold the place as quickly as I could and got out of town, leaving the crayfish to wander around the living-room in peace.

Although having to leave Sandy Close Farm, the place hadn't actually been sold and so we moved back for a while. Circumstances had tarnished the atmosphere of the house a little but there were so many smiles around as we returned to the house where the girls had grown up. I tried to re-buy the house with my part of the divorce settlement but, and how stupid when you think about it, I couldn't afford to buy my own house off myself. While the house had sat empty, thieves had broken into the barn and nicked all the garden equipment and tools and the house looked a sad and sorry sight as we moved back in. I tried so hard to sort the finances but it just wasn't working out in my favour so I knew my days were numbered, a hard pill to swallow.

It had been a mistake to move to Ampfield, I knew that, but at least Sandy Close Farm was there waiting to help me get out of a situation that I just didn't like. The Avenue is a very swish part of Romsey, but, just like Lyme Regis, it didn't happen to suit me and I was glad to get out of the place. I wanted privacy.

To that end, my nomad existence continued as I had to move on when Sandy Close Farm was finally sold. I fell in love with Salisbury the first time I went there, a bit like Lyme Regis, and so my next move would be eight miles from Sherfield English to the city in the countryside as it is known. I was sick to death of house-hunting and so I didn't hang around. The day I began my search there were only three places on the market that suited my pocket and I decided by the end of that one day I would have decided on which one and made an offer. Estate agent, Jamie Armstrong, took me to all three houses in the afternoon and by the evening I had decided which one to buy. No messing, pay the asking price, no haggling, Sandy Close Farm had been sold and I had to get out a bit pronto. My god, it was all such a far cry from 39 Blaney Crescent.

I came to say a last goodbye
It's breaking my heart but I don't know why
It was only a pile of bricks and a creaking door
Yes it was only bricks and mortar
Some windows let in water
But we all go a little downhill as time goes by
It was only bricks and mortar
The roof let in water
But I still had to come to say a last goodbye

Chapter Nine - Salisbury

I'd been to Salisbury many times in my life and loved the place, especially on Tuesday market days, but never thought I would live there, but it was one of my most delightful moves. Just in case you never heard the press conference by the two Russian tourists who popped over for the day from Moscow on 4th March 2018, it has the tallest cathedral spire in Britain. No wonder that they just had to fly two thousand miles to take a look for themselves before buggering off back home the next day. The River Avon meanders through the main streets and to the right of the Market Square and it's a place of true beauty.

It provided an opportunity for my daughters, Polly and Rosie and myself to enjoy a little peace and quiet, a little respite from what had gone on before as we settled into our new country retreat in the middle of nowhere, just a couple of miles from Stonehenge. It made sense as Polly studied at Winchester and Rosie began college at Eastleigh, near Southampton, so basically we were equidistant.

My tour manager at the time, Matt Hampton, along with his wife Lucy, stepped up to the plate, along with my PA Tracey Hollis, and helped me considerably when we moved there. I had various recording commissions and soundtrack work in the diary and so we built a large shed in the garden as quickly as we could in which I would piece together my new recording studio. It sounds easy enough but recording had moved on hugely since the days when I built my first one in

Essex and the time had come to get rid of all the old kit, the huge mixing desk and tape machines, and go digital.

My early home studio productions were made on quarter-inch Ampex reel to reel tape and I no longer had my sacred Revox B77 editing machine. Of course, it was sophisticated for its time, but when you look back, it was basic alright, and yet the quality of the content still shines through and that's what's important. Sir Winston Churchill's wartime speeches weren't exactly of the highest technical quality and yet they remain a perfect example of recordings of great value and importance. Richard Burton's War Of The Worlds makes him sound like he had a stinking cold during the recording session, but what an epic example of enthralling storytelling. Technical quality isn't everything but it certainly helps.

I'll never forget reading about how record-producer George Martin recorded The Beatles first two albums, Please Please Me and With The Beatles, on a two-track BTR machine. Yes, a two-track machine for heaven's sake. The Beatles were responsible, long before Pink Floyd and others, for developing the art of multi-tracking as it's known today.

Sgt Pepper, one of the most famous albums of all time by anyone, was recorded using two Studer four track recording machines. It's difficult for younger people than myself to realise just how innovative and forward thinking The Beatles were. They may not know much beyond Paul McCartney bashing out Hey Jude yet again at various national celebrations, but they changed the face of music and dare I say the whole world to a certain degree. They certainly moved recording techniques forward at the famous Abbey Road Studios in London, which at the time was just as basic as all the other recording studios in town. One could still argue that the pedestrian crossing outside is still better known the studio itself.

The amazing George Martin had to devise a tracking technique to create his unique productions and that's exactly what he did. Just think about that, a simple two-track machine to record a drummer, two guitarists, a bass guitar, numerous vocals, plus harmonies, and additional keyboard ideas that George thought up and played himself. Pure masterstrokes all the way, just like a stick of rock. No wonder he was given a knighthood. It was he who came up with the idea of linking two machines together in series and with the advent of the four-track machine the genius got to work in a way that can only be admired.

George Martin's technique was innovative to say the least. In actual fact, he used two Studer four-track machines, so when all four tracks had been used up on one machine he literally bounced them across to just one track on a second machine, leaving three more tracks available on that second machine for overdubs and that's exactly how multi-tracking came to be. Having bounced the tracks from the first machine to the second he was then free to go back and re-record over the four tracks from the first machine, and so on. When you listen to Sgt Pepper it makes you realise what a genius the man was. He had to be aware of degeneration as the more you bounced tracks around back before the days of digital recording the more quality you lost. George Martin was a genius, a true genius. I realise I've used that word a lot in the last couple of paragraphs but he really was and so I make no apology.

Sgt Pepper was voted the greatest album of all time by Rolling Stone Magazine, something I cannot possibly argue with, and when it was released it went straight to number one in the album charts and stayed in the album charts for an incredible three years, and all on two four-track tape recorders. You can't really argue with that either.

George Martin died in 2016 but his memory will live on forever and people like me will be forever thankful that he had pioneered such an inspiring studio technique. What a brilliant man! Coincidentally, on Platform Fifty I would feature an interview with former Fairport Convention drummer, Dave Mattacks, who worked with the great man, Sir George Martin, when he drummed for Paul McCartney.

Bearing Mr Martin's amazing achievements in mind my very own recording techniques weren't as archaic as maybe I first thought, even if they weren't suitable for my new recording techniques in Salisbury. Back then I'd bought myself a portable recorder, a UHER 4000, identical to the machine used by roving radio reporters, which I kind of was I suppose at the time, and it was on this very machine that I did so many interviews and festival clips that I've mentioned throughout these pages. The microphone it came with I swapped for a Sure SM58 to improve the quality before I began mixing in the studio. It was all above and beyond the studio work I did at Capital, but it gave me a chance to get out there and meet up with various friends at their convenience and not mine and they are great interviews to own. The UHER, with its leather case and shoulder strap, used small plastic tape spools that I would then convert onto the more professional AMPEX 456 quarter-inch tape on metal spools that I used in my own recording studio back home. I would spend hours editing and enhancing those field recordings, as they are known, and then, being producer of my own folk programme, I inserted them into my broadcasts. It was an arduous transition at times, but I loved every minute and it allowed me to have interviews that would have otherwise been too difficult logistically to happen. Hello all you spiders in the attic, now where are my old tapes hiding?

I can't speak highly enough of the UHER portable recorder and the technique is a great one for anyone starting out recording for the first time. These days Phillips and Sony make a basic recording machine for as little as £30, Zoom and Roland offer more expensive alternatives, but I recommend spending a little more and investing in one that offers a mixing facility. A friend of mine uses a Tascam DP006 and gets great results from it and you can pick them up for less than £130. It makes it easier to enhance your recording.

All that said, the digital age of recording had arrived and the days of analog recording on reel to reel machines and huge mixing desks had disappeared forever, and so the time had come for me to get up to date. My musical productions needed to be of the best quality if I was to continue with my recording duties but, unfortunately, I knew nothing about digital recording. It meant that Matt and myself spent literally days studying the manual that came with my new machine. It was all very third party for me because I didn't understand a word of it. Matt read and understood each page, being much younger and brainier than myself, and he relayed to me what we had to do to get the machine working. So, it wasn't just the new shed that Matt, Lucy and Tracey helped me to build, but he also educated me and pushed me into the new world of digital recording and mastering. It worked, it took a while but it worked.

My first recording equipment way back when I lived with Mum and Dad was a Grundig tape recorder that I think we bought from a catalogue, I really don't remember. I recorded my early demos on it and sent the tapes around the folk clubs to try and get work. I have to say the idea worked and it did help me get gigs further afield than where I lived, indeed that's how I got my first tour of Wales that I told you about earlier. From there I moved on to a TEAC four-track recorder, a tape machine that allowed you to record four different tracks and mix them down to two, left and right stereo if you like. That may sound quite old and antiquated but that's how, as I explained earlier, George Martin recorded Sgt Pepper, the legendary Beatles album. That amazing album recorded on just four tracks is still way beyond my comprehension but it's absolutely true, that's all he had at his disposal and he did it.

Things were feeling good as we all overflowed with contentment. We had a new house, a new recording studio, Polly and Rosie were doing really well with their studies and all the grief was finally behind us. During the transition between Hampshire and Salisbury I hadn't been in a position to tour as much as I would have liked and so I was delighted to get back on the road and do the only thing I was any good at, performing. Having said that, I'd worked hard at my art, my most engrossing hobby, and that was coming along nicely too. I had looked at my paintings as nothing more than a delightful pastime when I wasn't fishing, never thinking they would play such an important part in my 2020 survival when theatres closed and my world collapsed around my ears, or should I say when our world collapsed around our ears? Suddenly, they were a source of income.

I had gone all methodical and placed my various forms of work into categories and Salisbury became more and more sensible by the day. I certainly live my life around the strangest of hours. When I started out I was just glad to be on the road and enjoyed roaming around the country looking for work. I lived half my life in my camper van and the other half with Mum and Dad in East Ham. I hovered between a rebel without a cause to a rebel without a bank account. All these years on it's so different, it has to be at my age. There are so many different aspects to my job these days, on stage and behind the scenes, that I self-manage along with Tracey Hollis who has been working by my side for nearly a quarter of a century. There is no one person could ever take care of everything, so I do it myself with Tracey taking care of the paperwork. Shows, books, documentaries, speech writing, studio recording, I have to try and fit it all in but it has to be carefully managed or it would all collide and crash. Luckily it never does. The time I end one day controls what time my next day begins.

The various things I do don't allow any facet to be controlled by an agent. One may be good at booking live dates but unable to put together an art exhibition or book out my recording studio. A media agent couldn't get involved with my live performances and so on. I'm sure you understand why, to keep things simple, it's so much easier to do it all myself with Tracey overseeing the paperwork. What kind of paperwork you may well ask. Well, there's email enquiries, contracts, royalty logging, technical specifications, documentary scheduling, accounts, publicity in the shape of flyers and posters, marketing and so on. Tracey takes care of it all while I get on with the only thing I'm any good at.

Most shows finish around 10.30pm or 11.00pm and my journey home can be anything between an hour and six hours obviously depending upon the venue's location. Either way, I'm always home in the early hours. The average trip home is three hours when sensible people with sensible lifestyles are tucked up in their beds, sound asleep. Once indoors I have to have a cup of tea before bed. Whatever time I get home I never get up late, even if it's just a few hours sleep. Then my routine begins. As soon as my eyes open it's a cold drink with my vitamin D and cod liver oil tablets, a cup of tea, a daily tablet for my dodgy stomach and then a bowl of porridge before I go about my day. This brings on its problems as I'm fairly nocturnal and yet I like my daytimes too. After fifty years you do tend to have routines.

Let's take a day when I have a gig in the evening. After breakfast I have the morning off. A bath at lunchtime while I do The Daily Telegraph Crossword and then a small snack, full of goodness, before hitting the road late morning as I don't like sitting in rush-hours. Why would you if you don't have to? Anyway, most gig days are like that in some shape or other.

On a non-gig day I wake up and get up early and mess about, often doing a bit of gardening. I love going to Salisbury Market before lunchtime on a Tuesday and depending on the time of the year I make chutneys and jams from stuff that shoots up in my garden. Hey, that's rock and roll for you. The Telegraph crossword is pushed back to 6.00pm, Tracey stops working and goes home and that's the end of the working day. After 50 years of doing this I need to relax and try to switch my brain off every so often. The other side of me, the documentary work and incidental music, operates in business hours too so it can all meld into one gigantic, sleepless mess if I'm not careful.

Touring the country is compounded by the fact I still hate big, sterile, over-priced hotels. Is that weird? No, not really. I'd never stayed in a hotel in my life until I went on tour with Steeleye Span in 1974 at the age of 25, not even on holiday. I used to love the sitting up late with the band in the bar but it also caused a certain amount of embarrassment as I couldn't afford a round of drinks too often at such highly inflated prices. I was earning ok by this time, I was paid well by Steeleye, but after agent's fees, travel and food I was still having to watch my step financially. That's when my routine of going home every night began I suppose.

I find hotels impersonal places, checking in and out is a chore, parking a nightmare, bar prices extortionate, so to be honest I'd rather just get in the car and drive home. If I've come across as a workaholic, then nothing can be further from the truth. I work hard, I have to, but it isn't an obsession like it was when I started out. For instance, I never have the radio on in my car. I use travel time to think of ideas and write new songs. I spend hours in my car, 75,000 miles a year, and it's dead time for me listening to Steve Wright in the afternoon telling me how so many people love his show, though not quite as much as he himself loves his show. I rarely work up ideas at home. If I'm writing a new song, poem or working on a documentary then most of the groundwork would have been done in the car. I purposefully don't have a CD player in my car either as other music may influence my own new stuff to the point I would end up nicking it. No, once in the car I get to work mentally and use what would otherwise be that dead time as I weave my way home. Having done that I don't have to work so hard the next day, if I'm off, and it frees up time to paint pictures or go down the pub for lunch.

As I made my way through the 1970s I watched how some of the big names toured. When I toured with Supertramp for instance, the Breakfast in America tour, the team travelled in motor homes or caravans, parking them by loading bays or by stage doors. They travelled with their families and I really admired them. To me it was an extension of the days in my Volkswagen camper, hanging around at a venue until the next morning in self-contained fashion. They were remarkably friendly guys and it wasn't really like being on the road at all, more like being party of a travelling family.

Another point to remember is that, as a support act, I would never be off stage any later than 8.45pm so I could get on the road early. Failing that, when a band as massive as Supertramp toured they often did two or three nights in the same venue, in which case I would stay with various friends dotted around the country or find myself a late-night appearance at a local folk club. I loved working with Supertramp, you couldn't have met a nicer bunch.

Elkie Brooks, with whom I toured for nearly four years, travelled in a classy tour bus supplied by Len Wright Travel and she insisted I travelled in it too. Elkie had been there and bought the tee-shirt, she even supported The Beatles. I was with her for so long I became part of Elkie's family too, often staying at their delightful Devon house. Elkie had a class-less policy whereby everyone on the tour was equal, from the stage riggers to the star of the show. She paid for everything, even the drinks bill when we checked out of hotels and the bus always stopped for lunch somewhere along the road. I never spent a penny and it was Elkie's generosity that allowed me to find some kind of financial stability at the time. Her musicians were great too and we were all great friends, so much so that we recorded Nellie The Elephant together, a track on my Live at the Fairfield Halls album. I'd never worked on stage with such amazing musicians before. Tim Hinkley played keyboards with The Rolling Stones for a while. Geoff Whitehorn on lead guitar, he who played on my next two albums, came from Roger Chapman's Family, and later Procol Harum. Matthew the drummer is now with Status Quo. That's quite a formidable line-up to sing a silly song about an elephant, but we did it. My days, or should I say my four years, with Elkie Brooks were memorable, the period culminating in a Christmas concert at The Royal Albert Hall, another ambition fulfilled for me.

One night, after a gig at Liverpool Empire, we were in the bar of The Adelphi Hotel and Elkie had ordered the largest pile of sandwiches I'd ever seen. You needed a Sherpa to reach the top one. We were all rather drunk so we decided to have a sandwich regatta in the hotel swimming pool so we all spent ages building our yachts with cocktail sticks, bits of cucumber and sails made of cheese and onion crisps. We even used polo mints as the rubber tyres you see on the side of boats. We sneaked down to the hotel swimming pool only to find some fit bloke swimming up and down the pool like a dolphin. Such an obstacle wouldn't deter Elkie and her team, especially Tim Hinkley.

The regatta took place and it was so funny as this bloke collided with our sailing ships, him swimming lengths and our boats doing widths. There simply had to be a collision. Seriously pissed off, he complained to the hotel manager. There he stood, dripping wet, in only a bath towel and dressing gown, at the hotel reception. The poo was about to hit the fan so Tim Hinkley suggested, if the manager gave him the man's room key, he would put a bottle of champagne in the man's room as an apology. So while he stood ranting and raving at reception Tim and Hugh, a roadie, went to the man's room. Instead of a bottle of champagne they totally emptied his room, bed and everything. The disgruntled man eventually went to his room only to find nothing in it. He re-appeared frothing at the mouth telling the hotel manager what had happened while we all sat quietly in the lounge. What he didn't know was while he'd retuned downstairs Tim and Hugh had put it all back, so when the hotel manager went to look at the damage there was no damage. Finally, the bloke came down and joined us in the bar and we all got pissed. You never mess with a rock band on the road.

The next night, while Elkie sang Lilac Wine at Sheffield City Hall, Tim placed a little sailing dinghy on top of his piano. The whole band stopped playing, creased with laughter, and Elkie, being the trooper she was, carried on singing unaccompanied with a straight face. She didn't crack.

Before every show me and Elkie's husband Trevor Jordan were the only ones invited into her dressing-room. We had a glass of brandy before every show, medicinal purposes you understand. We sat quietly before I went off and started the show and Elkie always stood on the side of the stage while Trevor did my sound.

Touring in your own in a car isn't the same as what we got up to in the 70s and 80s, but times change and sadly we all mature. Maybe that's another reason why I prefer to go home after a show. I'm also a bit of a cottage industry so there is always work to be done the next day.

As I mentioned before, there's an awful lot of paperwork in getting on stage. There's contracts, technical riders, accommodation, parking permits, PRS royalty forms to complete, local paper and radio interviews to arrange, public liability forms, directions to theatres, stage-clothes to be washed and ironed, guitar strings to change, merchandise to record and produce and a car to load and un-load after every show. It may look simple when I stroll out on stage but there's tons of preparation before anyone buys a ticket. Tracey works office hours and sometimes attends shows to sell the merchandise. Just the two of us have made the wheels go round for a long time now and we like to think we know what we're doing. Of course there are agents and promoters who book me, but all goes through my tiny office at home. Tracey is the admin side of Richard Digance and we work well together. I've known her for twenty years now and I think of her more as my younger sister protecting her older brother from boring paperwork. She's a brilliant artist too and she designed and drew the artwork of my Letter From Afghanistan album. It's getting on for a quarter of a century ago when Tracey turned up at my house with a rucksack and set of golf clubs, don't ask, and asked for a job as she'd left home.

Although I've been on the road for fifty years I've met very few theatre managers. Don't forget I turn up at around 5.30pm by which time their theatre office has closed for the day and they've gone home. There are very few theatre managers who hang around to say hello to a visiting act, very few indeed. If I said I could count them on two hands, all around the country, I wouldn't be lying. It's a case of never the twain shall meet. Tracey speaks to them more than I do. There are the odd managers that have become personal friends but very few.

Although my world may seem a bit topsy-turvy I think it works ok. Long drives and concerts on gig days or mornings and the odd evening when I'm at home with afternoons off to re-charge the batteries.

Being one myself, I watch all the antique programmes, particularly the ones that have used my music in the background. I don't watch much evening television as I think so much of it is rubbish. University Challenge is a must as is Only Connect. Do I watch Countdown? No, haven't seen it for years. I have my memories of that programme and that's enough for me. There's a comedy version of it too now and I hate it. I shudder to think what dear old Richard Whiteley would have made of it. I have a fair idea but bollocks is only eight letters. But there are fond memories of my 20 years of doing the show.

I mentioned Richard Whiteley earlier but I knew the whole team well. Susie Dent in Dictionary Corner remains a friend, I did the reading at her wedding in Oxford. It was a poem titled 'How to get rid of a Dent.' Susie and I, along with Carol Vorderman, ran The Great North Run together twice in aid of The Marie Curie Trust in memory of Richard. I ran the first one with a nasty hangover after driving from a gig in Lincoln the night before and the second time I improved my personal best, even though I stopped off for a couple of sneaky fags along the way. Oh, and the numbers lady Rachel Riley's brother went to school with my daughter Polly. As far as Countdown goes that's about it really. Susie and I went to Richard's grave after his funeral in East Witton, Yorkshire, and we knew it would never be the same again. I visited the grave on my own just a couple of years ago and his headstone had tilted slightly. Knowing daft Richard as I did I wasn't in the least bit surprised. Great bloke with great memories of him stored in my brain.

I tried my best when the late Des O'Connor took over presenting the show and again when Jeff Stelling, nice guy, and then Nick Ewer took the reins but it just wasn't the same for me. Richard wasn't there and we used to have such fun together, drinking the night before or going to the York Races. In my opinion he left a huge void that cannot possibly be filled. The arrival of Anne Robinson to the fold meant I felt even further away from the good old Countdown days. I returned in 2021 and took my guitar but I can't really see myself being a regular like I used to be.

How do I shut off? We always have a jigsaw on the go in the kitchen and I love to go fishing. It's not always to catch fish, I just love the solitude of sitting by a lake or a river and Wiltshire has an abundance of beautiful, serene locations. I love to sit by The Kennet and Avon Canal near Devizes and watch the narrow boats chug by.

My current projects involve intense documentary work, requiring hours of concentration getting it right and so it's good to chill at times by the water's edge. There's no room for mistakes if you want to be top of your trade. Travel-time is non-existent so I'm always fresh when I turn the machines on by late morning. There is always a project in the making and recently I've made a couple of albums for some friends to keep my hand in at the more multi-track style of digital recording while lockdown kept us all homebound.

In 2015 I was invited to compose some music for Bill Bryson, the world's biggest selling travel author. His new book 'The Road To Little Dribbling' was released in the October as an audio book and I composed and recorded the incidental music and songs for the release. It was a pleasure which took me ages to do. I've always been a huge fan of Bryson and never believed for one moment I would ever work in conjunction with him, but I did. It involved a few songs and 38 pieces of instrumental music on just my guitar with no embellishments.

Penguin, the publishers, were pretty demanding but they had every right to be. It was their flagship publication of the year and they wanted it to be something special. Just one song was re-written six times before they were happy with the lyrics. Bill Bryson was delighted with the final product and I felt proud to have been able to deliver what was wanted by one of the world's top authors.

That said, I still find it totally bizarre that all that music came from a shed in my garden. That's the great thing about music of course, it can be played anywhere and these days it can be recorded anywhere too. Young writers have recorded stuff in garages, slung it up on YouTube and become massive stars. That's the way it is these days, yet it isn't unlike what I did years ago. Rather than pay the extortionate rates of a London recording studio, to say nothing of the time, the travel and the cost of getting there, I built my own studio. On the few occasions I've moved house I've had to build yet another studio and get it in working order as quickly as possible. It's a necessity more than a luxury for me. All that stuff for Bill Bryson was the result of a huge learning curve I went on for about forty of my fifty years on the road and I'm proud and delighted it paid dividends.

I'd written for people before, from ghost-writing autobiographies, to after-dinner speeches and even wedding and best man speeches. Once you get known for writing after-dinner speeches in particular the floodgates open and everyone gets in touch. I wrote one for Chelsea and former England footballer Peter Osgood, based on how he slept with the FA Cup, and through that one speech I ended up scribbling stuff for his Chelsea team-mate Bobby Tambling and the greatest of them all, George Best. Come to think of it, George Best never paid me. I wonder what he spent that money on? Answers on a postcard please.

I helped out with West Ham players Tony Gale and Alvin Martin and helped write Chris Kamara's autobiography. I'd already helped with his speech and we'd co-written a football trivia book called Footynotes so I was more than pleased to help out with his amazing life story. Kammy is a real laugh but the opening chapters on how he was picked on as a black kid in Middlesbrough was quite compelling.

I could easily have made a living as a ghost-writer for others but it wasn't that satisfying for me. It wasn't an ego thing, more the fact of sitting at a keyboard for hour after hour just didn't appeal. I still loved being on the road, doing my live shows and both were equally time-consuming so one had to go. It was the writing for others that went. Bill Bryson was different, I was writing music and lyrics for him and it was great fun as I'd been such a fan in the past.

The Bill Bryson project was amazing for me and yes I was proud, yet a song I wrote in 2016 made me feel just as proud I have to say. It came about because of the closure of West Ham's football ground, Upton Park. It was time for my football team to move to The Olympic Stadium or whatever it is called now and I was invited by West Ham Supporters Club to do the final performance at the club. I was honoured to be asked, really honoured to be asked, and I knew it was never going to be just another gig. The memories of going there as a young lad with my Dad, my cousin John, John Cooper and Roger, were uppermost in my mind as I took to the stage, full knowing nobody would ever stand there again. It felt weird, a bit like going to a funeral. There just had to be a special song. I think the last time I actually gulped when I wrote was when I composed Letter From Afghanistan but I had the same feeling as I started to put pen to paper.

Passing time has made its mark
the floodlights have gone dark
the time has come to wave a last goodbye to Upton Park.
No magic anymore
from the heroes that we saw
just ninety minute memories back to 1904.
I don't get it though I've tried
will it work I can't decide
but my dreams like the bubbles have faded now and died.

The Supporters Club fell silent, the last league game against Swansea had been played and there wasn't a dry eye in the house. These were the people who started out in life similar to myself and each and every one of them could have written those words themselves. The players gave me a last game shirt signed by them all. You rarely find yourself in a position on stage whereby you know every person there, young or old, is hanging on your every word. In fact, I don't think that's ever happened before in the entire fifty-odd years on the road. It was such a moving experience as I kept my nerve and sang the song with all the pride I could muster.

It's all about the money
or so sang Jesse J
but you cannot take a hundred years and sling it all away
as though it didn't happen
although it wasn't there
and make a famous football team go and play elsewhere

It was the last song ever sung at West Ham Supporters Club, the place where I went with Dad from the age of five. Enough said.

We raised a fair bit of money that night in May 2016 and every penny went to The RSPCA as I'm President of the East London Branch. For many years I'd been doing shows at the football ground in aid of building a cattery for the numerous stray animals that roam around the East End, discarded and unloved. That final concert at West Ham was the final raising of the funds needed to build the home. They wanted to name the place after me but I wasn't interested in

that, a bit too glory-seeking for me I'm afraid, so they named it after my beloved dog Jess who sadly died just before Christmas 2015. It's a lasting memory for me of a wonderful four-legged friend who I'd rescued from a dog's home after she'd been given a week to live. She was with me for nearly nine years so what a result. We were best friends and we both relied on each other in equal amounts.
I was presented with a plaque which sits proudly in the study where I do my writing. It reads as follows;

'Thank you, Richard Digance, for supporting The RSPCA's vital welfare work and for holding the concert marking the opening of our new cattery. Named in the memory of your beloved German Shepherd Dog Jess with the inscription 'She spent her life chasing cats and now she will be looking after them.'

I don't have any of my various awards and achievements on show in my house, they're all hanging proudly in my recording studio down in the garden, but Jess has to be here with me. Mind you, I bet she would have preferred to have been in the garden!
Sometimes money just isn't important is it? That's what I was trying to say at West Ham football club that very night. The Upton Park ground held so many memories for me and I didn't want them to bring in the bulldozers and flatten it. But they did, and that's progress for you. Dear old Jess never lived in the East End like me, she had acres of garden to run around in and enjoy a wonderful life in the country. Now she will be remembered forever in the place where I was born and raised.

No, sometimes money isn't important at all. Unless, of course, you're a footballer.

Now you see the importance of me doing that last ever concert at West Ham Supporters Club. I had to do it and would have travelled half-way across the world if I'd had to. It was about the closing of a couple of chapters of my life.

Goodbye Upton Park
Thanks for all the fun
I'm really going to miss you
And I'm not the only one
Time moves on, it doesn't wait for no man
Time moves on it never turns the other way
Time moves on, we can't turn back the hours
Maybe I was wrong, I think it turned today

Chapter Ten - Festivals

Festivals are a major part of my job. For the folk scene where I learnt my trade they are a vital ingredient of the well-being and future survival of a scene that began in the 60s and is in danger of disappearing unless more young musicians are encouraged to play at folk clubs.

All festivals disappeared in 2020 and 2021 but they are a shop window for new acts on the scene, an important shop window, and they offer a chance for the older musicians and the younger breed to come together which doesn't really happen in the folk clubs that have survived to this day. I've seen so many new acts over the years appearing on a major stage and building their names. Having said that, small clubs need to survive too, the folk scene isn't only about performing in front of thousands on a summer's day, it's about keeping our musical heritage alive, to sing the songs that were collected hundreds of years ago, to sing the shanties our sailors bellowed out when pulling up anchors. That's really what it's all about.

My own first festival appearance was at The Cambridge Folk Festival in 1974 and it worked for me too. Oddly enough, top of the bill was Arlo Guthrie, the cause, or should I say inspiration, of my VW Camper Van purchase. If it hadn't been for him that girl in stiletto heels in the back of my van would never have punctured the water carrier my Mum had bought me. By the way, I never explained that accident to Mum and I never saw the girl again.

I shudder to think how many festival appearances I've made since 1974 but that weekend still stands out as a gem. I was determined to make a mark so my plan was to write a song that I could get the whole field singing along to. That song, Working Class Millionaire, worked for me and became a bit of a folk club favourite at the time with other singers performing their own versions of it. It must have worked ok because they booked me back the following year. The Cambridge Folk Festival was the one to do at the time, the one that elevated you to the top of the folk scene if you went down well. Unlike today, most of the crowd were folk club members and all the organisers were there too so you could fill your diary in one afternoon. These days not many festival goers attend folk clubs. It's all changed so much and The Cambridge Folk Festival no longer has the clout it had back in the 60s and 70s.

Since that festival debut I've done many of the big ones, the biggest being Knebworth in 1980. Like most festivals it pissed down with rain and the field was a quagmire. The line-up was amazing; The Beach Boys, Santana, Elkie Brooks, Mike Oldfield and right at the bottom was Richard Digance. Things didn't quite turn out as you'd imagine as the heaven's opened, causing huge logistical problems, the main one being electricity not being a big friend of water. Things were in my favour when Mike Oldfield refused to go on. I didn't care, there were a quarter of a million people there and I couldn't waste such an opportunity. I volunteered and on I wandered. The audience weren't struck at first, preferring Tubular Bells to some East End folkie, but one chorus of Singing In The Rain and I'd won them over. When the rain ceased my job was done. Mike

Oldfield went on and I'll tell you what, he's one of the most under-rated guitar players I've ever seen.

A couple of hours later the rains came once more and proceedings were halted once again. Imagine my surprise when a quarter of a million people started chanting my name. It grew louder and louder until the organisers demanded I went back on, which I did. I suppose I'd become a bit of a watery hero, if I dare say so myself, and I ended up making five appearances, culminating in a few songs before The Beach Boys performed. I sat on a flight case on the side of the stage and watched them from just a few feet away. It was a sparkling experience. Carl Wilson shook my hand as he took a break between songs. I moved over and he joined me on the flight case, a bloody Beach Boy no less. I didn't even have a dressing room and so, just like Cambridge, I passed the time sitting in my car when I wasn't on stage. I didn't care, I'd sat and chatted to a Beach Boy.

Then along came Fairport Convention's Cropredy Festival, the most prestigious on the folk calendar as far as I am concerned, although some would argue the fact. I've played there every year for so long I can't actually remember how many times. I love Cropredy as much as the crowd, it's become a real home from home for me and without doubt my favourite festival anywhere in the world. Fairport are big friends of mine, each and every one of them, past and present members. I've spent many social hours with them and that's all part of the festival. Fiddle players Ric Sanders and Chris Leslie are huge comedy fans by the way, particularly Tony Hancock.

I first met Dave Pegg when he was a member of The Ian Campbell Folk Group in Birmingham just after The Crimean War ended. We've always got on really well. We rarely talk music as he's too busy telling me his dozen latest jokes. My claim to fame with Peggy is that I helped to get him the gig with Jethro Tull. He still owes me a beer for that. In actual fact he's owed me that beer for a good many years and it's a bit of a standing joke that it's never arrived, nor shall it I fear.

Tull's bass player, John Glascock died in November 1979 at the age of 28. He was a truly great guy. My first gig with Tull was at Bristol Colston Hall and he was the first member of the band I met. Despite me being a lowly support act and him a bill-topper he introduced himself and immediately made me a cup of tea, even though they had a catering company on board. I never knew at the time he too had been a Jethro Tull support act as a member of the band Carmen and so he must have known only too well the nerves that were welling up inside. We became mates and he invited me to his house, beneath the shadows of Twickenham Rugby Ground, on a few occasions. He once turned up at my gig at The Winning Post Folk Club in Twickers, he being a true rock icon, yet he sat right in the front with his girlfriend and sang his heart out and laughed his head off. John died from a heart defect. They gave him a pig's valve but sadly it didn't pay off. Shortly after John Glascock's death Barry was sitting in my living room, we were watching Fairport Convention on a BBC2 In Concert. I told Barry what a great player Peggy was, he agreed and immediately rang Ian Anderson, telling him to put the telly on. Dave Pegg became the replacement for John Glascock in Tull and he stayed with the band for fifteen years.

It was all part of the Reading era I told you about. When we weren't recording in Barrie's garden we were swimming in

Barry's pool, canoeing along the Thames or getting drunk at his local, The Baskerville Arms. It took a week to make the album and one night I agreed to do a gig at the pub in return for them letting us drink late there after long recording sessions.

We were having a brilliant time when in walked Beatle George Harrison who lived just down the road towards Henley on Thames. He sat down and listened intently, at least until like an idiot I decided to sing Here Comes The Sun, at which point he got up and walked out. Whoops. Hey, no big deal, we both saw each other perform just the once, a good thirty years apart but that's not important. Whilst he stood in the other bar I went and apologised for being so stupid. He laughed and told me not to worry, explaining that the reason he'd walked out was because he feared I would drag him up to play with me and he wasn't sure if he would remember the words!

That time was ridiculous beyond words for lowly me. We needed an electric lead guitarist on one track so Barry made a call and Alvin Lee of Ten Years After turned up, out of the blue, and cleared out my eardrums playing lovely stuff on a song I'd written about Jimmy Greaves. That may sound impressive but it takes second place to what happened the following day.

Many years ago I'd heard John Kirkpatrick sing A Nightingale Sang in Berkley Square at The Sidmouth Folk Festival, so as John was at the recording I decided to record it. I'd always loved the song and he sang it perfectly. John could only stay for a day so unfortunately couldn't play the track with me as we ran out of time, a bit of a bummer as I couldn't play the middle bit on the guitar as it was too difficult for someone like me who couldn't read music. I still wanted to record it.

Barry had the answer. He rang rock legend Jon Lord of Deep Purple. He would know the middle part, he was a keyboard genius, second to none. Not content with trying to explain it to me over the phone he drove over and played it for me on the album. The budget was small and I was embarrassed, scared of what sort of money he would want for the session. The most famous keyboard player in the world charged me a bottle of vodka. The song was released as a single by Chrysalis and although it didn't chart, it remains a wonderful memory. It was also played at my Mum's funeral at St Mary's Church, East Ham in 1985, because it was her favourite song too.

Everyone wants to play Cropredy and I feel honoured I do it every year. They never send me a contract, there's no need. Tracey once rang Festival Director Gareth and asked why I hadn't received a contract, he told her there was no need as I'd been booked for life. Yes, I do indeed feel very honoured. My annual appearance on the Saturday lunchtime was called the Graveyard Slot when I first took it on as the field wasn't very full, maybe just 300 or 400. As the years have passed we've built the slot up to a capacity of 23,000 and we have a great time. I just love it. It certainly isn't The Graveyard Slot anymore, it belongs to me and the Cropredy crowd, it's our slot and doesn't need a put-down name.

Cropredy has very little backstage facilities, intentionally. It has no backstage bar for instance and the reason is so the artists mix with the festival goers at the one and only bar of the festival. Some artists don't like that very much but I thoroughly enjoy it. I've watched big names walk off stage after their gig, get straight in their cars and go. Not me, I have so many good friends at Cropredy, artists and audience members alike so I wouldn't dream of just turning up and treating it as a gig. I'm aware what it means to the crowd to be there and it means an awful lot to me too.

Life on the road is a solitary existence and so all artists use festivals to meet up with other performers they don't get a chance to meet up with the rest of the year. It's a time to discuss health, good gigs, bad gigs, recording sessions, anything really, and for some it's more personal. I always meet Ralph McTell at Cropredy and we have a good old natter about things in general including the old times when I followed him around like a limpet. It came as a body blow to us all when circumstances meant the festival wouldn't take place in 2020.

In 2015 I met up with ace musician Joe Brown. We hadn't seen each other for so long and it was wonderful. He gave me a huge man-hug and said 'hey, mate, we're still here.' Two Plaistow boys who both thought we never stood much of a chance in life, yet we'd done it against the odds. The music scene is like that, a very friendly bunch of chancers who didn't fancy getting a normal job. In that respect it's nothing like the show business world that I entered with Jim Davidson back in the 80s. That dog eat dog world I found difficult and I don't keep in touch with many TV celebs I met along the way.

If I had to sum things up, the music business is as sincere as it gets and show-business is as insincere as it gets. They are both classed as part of the entertainment industry, but there the similarities end.

Festivals disappeared from the calendar for health reasons and our annual re-unions were put on hold. It's sad to think that many of the smaller festivals, folk clubs and theatres will never recover from the dreaded virus, such a great shame.

It was like an entertainment cull that none of us saw coming our way and it left a fair few number of casualties in its wake. I doubt if there wasn't a musician in the land who had financial difficulties.

There are small festivals all around the country, indeed all around the world. Basically, there are two categories of artist on such weekends, those whose names help to sell tickets and those lesser names that need the exposure a festival offers. That has to be taken into account when organisers are planning their budgets that have to incorporate a few dozen acts and their demands. Firstly, they have to consider the fee and then there are the hidden extras such as hotel accommodation. A band, for example, will require three or four hotel rooms with a breakfast thrown in. That alone could amount to £400-£500 pounds in extras. They are also fed and watered on site. The extras of one band alone can easily equal the fees of names that will fill out the line-up and make the festival more attractive. That's where the local acts come in I suppose as they have no expenses and are usually lesser names not known around the country and therefore willing to perform at all costs. It's all a juggling act that determines the success or failure of any festival.

I know some acts protest that festivals, taking money over the gate, lure lesser names at no cost. I personally think it's quite reasonable as I did endless gigs free of charge when I began, just to get my name around. It's something you have to do in my job. The big names draw in the crowds that are hopefully impressed by the new names they may have never seen before. That's how our tiny folk scene will survive and long may it do so. I see it all a bit like a pond with big fish that have staked their claim and loads of little fish that are struggling for survival. Somehow, all the fish get by, along with a few casualties, and it makes the pond healthy. It's just like any other job where the newcomers want promotion and have to work hard to achieve it. Agents may not always see it that way but that's the way it is. Get the exposure and the money will follow. I'm well aware I have repeated myself a few times in this book as flashbacks occur and I scribble them down but it hasn't particularly bothered me. I do know I've already written of my disdain for agents who drop you like a red hot poker when they feel like it and I make no apologies for repeating that fact either. Anyway, fancy coming on a cruise?

Chapter Eleven - Cruising

I've done my fair share of cruises for P&O and would probably do more if they could understand that what they put performers through in finding the cheapest possible routes home is close to unacceptable, depending upon how badly you need the work and what you're prepared to tolerate when times are hard.

In case you didn't know, performers don't stay on a cruise for the whole trip, especially a world cruise. They get you on and off as quickly as they can to make room for another performer. That way they don't use up so many cabins that could be making them money if sold to passengers.

The final straw was when I sat in Los Angeles Airport with Clem Curtis of The Foundations. Now listen to this, bearing in mind we were staring through the glass at a Virgin plane about to take off on a direct flight to Heathrow. We had already flown from Tahiti to Los Angeles in a plane resembling an Airfix kit with propellers that spun on elastic bands and we'd spent nearly four hours in LA Terminal due to their scary security checks. They look menacing and they are menacing. P&O flew us from Tahiti to LA to Frankfurt, with an overnight hotel before flying back to Heathrow the next day. Remember there was a direct Virgin flight just taking off. Our journey home was just over two days after leaving the ship. Would you bother? Truth is I wouldn't and haven't. Job done, off you go, we need your cabin. No thanks. The shows on the ships were always great and for a few years I had the highest marks of appreciation among British entertainers which was fine but the travelling to and from each ship was totally unbearable.

How about this for an intro from the cruise director to the audience on Artemis, my first P&O cruise; 'Ladies and Gentlemen, please welcome someone who walks in the shadow of Jasper Carrott, Richard Digance.' I didn't go on. This silly woman, a former Eastenders bit-part actress called Sally Sago, came backstage to see what was wrong. I took her arm and marched her back on stage and made her apologise. She said she thought it was funny, but it wasn't as funny as me dragging her on stage to apologise in front of the audience. They wet themselves and she never spoke to me again even though I did two other cruises on Artemis with her after that. But you put up with it until the breaking point.

It's all very much an us and them situation, the hopping on and off entertainer and the band and dancers that are on the entire cruise. Passing ships in the night haha. Band members and dancers have their own area for relaxation and their own bar so you barely meet up with them, especially me as I didn't use a band anyway. I remember one member of the resident band telling me how he'd heard I was a fair guitar player so I asked him if he watched the show to which he replied he didn't because me not using the band had given him the day off.

You mustn't eat before the passengers, that's a serious no no. If you're at the bar you must step back and let passengers buy their drinks, then you wait to disembark to leave the ship or going sightseeing, you mustn't go in the casino, not that I would anyway, and then it takes you over two days to get home when it could take seven hours. No wonder I don't fancy it anymore, but hey I saw the world a bit and thoroughly enjoyed the shows, but enough was enough.

Cruise companies think it's a great honour to work for them. A pleasure maybe but an honour, no. I have friends who spend the whole year jumping around on different cruise ships and it's a steady stream of work, I respect that, but I found it all a bit of a cattle market. Give me my own theatres with my own audience any day.

What was my favourite cruise? An easy answer. Forget The Caribbean and a trip round Australia, my favourite was a short jaunt to Belgium when my tour manager, Matt Hampton, and I visited the war graves of World War One. To stand at the Menin Gate in Ypres and see all the names carved in stone is a moving experience and one I wouldn't have missed for the world. They were great cruise passengers too. Many of them were searching for distant relatives through the record books or on the marked graves. It was that kind of cruise, full of respect, which gave me the chance to sing more meaningful songs that evening and that made me feel far more at home when I got on stage in front of strangers.

What always confused me with cruise work were the playing times due to restaurant sittings. On the bigger ships they have three different sittings to fit everyone in and feed them, which means three different shows throughout the course of the evening. That's bloody hard work, especially as they want the same show three times so the cruise crew know what you're doing. They insist on it. Doing those three same shows in one night is brain-bashing as you can't remember what stories you told or if you had told the same story twice. It needed full concentration. Under normal circumstances if was doing three shows a night they would be three different shows and that wouldn't be so bad. They didn't want that. Blimey, I didn't even go to grammar school so it was a big ask.

As an entertainer you were expected, every time the ship left a foreign port, to be on deck waving a Union Jack and singing Rule Britannia at the top of your voice, led by a couple of very young cruise entertainment staff who really should have been baby-sitting at a holiday camp. I used to cringe. No wonder there was a mutiny on The Bounty. Then it was flag semaphore while we sang We Are Sailing. I bet every place was glad to see the back of us red, white and blue merchants. Once at sea the passengers went back to their jigsaws, water-colour painting and cribbage afternoons after they'd hidden the flags in their suitcases. Cruise companies still celebrate the days of The British Empire when our navy was the most dominant in the world.

On the subject of The Mutiny on The Bounty, for my last cruise but one I sailed from Chile across to The Pitcairn Islands, the last British Overseas Territory in The Pacific Ocean. It's only two miles across, not The Pacific Ocean but the Pitcairn Islands, so small that Captain Cook sailed straight past it in the 1770s. It was in 1789 that Fletcher Christian led the Mutiny against Captain Bligh and sailed the ship to Pitcairn. Nine of them set fire to the ship and jumped ashore. The wreck of The Bounty can still be seen in Bounty Bay and a cruise ship moors up right next to it. Nobody gets off but locals row out in rickety boats to flog local souvenirs most of which were made in China. I did laugh.

They set out their goods on tables around the ship's swimming pool, the most popular being pictured envelopes that can be stamped and posted from the islands for a few quid. They then introduced this huge bloke that looked like a New Zealand rugby player who they claimed to be a direct descendent of Fletcher Christian himself. The cost of the envelope quadrupled if he signed your envelope. Really? A distant relation? Yeah ok. The queue stretched around the swimming pool while he scribbled away and then they were gone. Through it all I sat alone staring at the water where The Bounty had gone down. On some days it can be seen. I was unlucky but I took it all in and soaked it all up. I certainly didn't buy an envelope from some geezer without a birth certificate.

All that said, I got on well with the other visiting entertainers as we crossed paths while we waited to get on and off while cabins were reappointed. Roy Walker was a hell of a nice guy, as was the late Tom O'Connor. I'm still great friends with Jimmy Nairn. Jimmy and I were on many cruises together and I remember in Madeira we jumped ship and went drinking on a yacht once owned by The Beatles. We went there a few times over a few years and we loved each other's mad company, as was the case with Clem Curtis, whom I mentioned earlier.

So there you have it, my cruise career wrapped up in just a few pages. Hey, I gave it a go, saw the world a bit and survived. 31 cruises in all, that was hell of a lot of Jack Daniels and ginger, but on a cruise you are just one of the many acts offered to an audience that could easily OD on entertainment.

Now you understand why I love turning up to a theatre, club or arts centre that have sold tickets to people who want to hear my songs and stories. It's sheer bliss for me. The alternatives previously mentioned I've known only too well for so many years. Of course I'm a hypocrite. I admit that. I didn't have to do that sort of work but, be honest, if you were being paid to go to The Caribbean you'd think about it wouldn't you? I did and I did.

They say variety is the spice of life and all that corny stuff, but I feel safer and far more comfortable with my own friendly audience. Some of them have followed me for years and I know many of them personally. I never care about the numbers, probably because of my tiny folk club beginnings, so long as they have a good time. I never forget every single person has had a long day, rushed down their dinner and got showered to come out to see me. Anyone who forgets that shouldn't be in the entertainment business. Empty seats mean nothing to me. As I always say, I didn't build the theatre. Indeed, you have to work harder to a smaller crowd, particularly if you want them to sing along with you. It always works though and I love it as much today as I did when I turned up to a pub in my VW camper van. I never thought for one minute I would meet the brother of Fletcher Christian, or whoever it was he claimed to be, when I sang my first song at The Bus Folk Club in Stratford.

Living reasonably close to Southampton I often drive past the cruise terminal and wonder where the big white beast is bound and which entertainers are suffering interminable queues as they wait to get on board. There's no VIP treatment no matter how many times you've been on TV. At least in Southampton there's every chance your cabin is ready. It isn't always the same if you pick up the ship in another country. Another entertainer is due to vacate their cabin but their flight home is later that evening and so they don't exactly get their skates on. I've literally sat for hours after a long flight waiting for my cabin to be ready for my occupancy, and I do mean hours. There's nothing showbiz about passengers staring at you as you sit on an outer deck with a suitcase, guitar, coat and a shoulder bag you could take into the aeroplane cabin. You look and feel distraught, like some homeless individual in a shop doorway. If you think post office queues are a pain in the arse then try and be an entertainer on a cruise ship.

Chapter Twelve - Heroes

Sadly, these days, I seem to reflect more on friends who have left us more than those who are still around. The folk scene has its losses the same as the rock and show biz scenes. They don't make the national headlines like the big rock stars but we miss them just as much. Genuine mates have gone in recent times, starting of course with my student pal John Martyn and Sandy Denny as previously mentioned. I've said goodbye to Fred Wedlock, the oldest swinger in town, Johnny Silvo, John Renbourn, Cliff Aungier, blues guitarist and football chum, Johnny Jones our folk football manager, Bob Williamson, the list grows ever longer as the years pass by. New names to that list are met with great sadness but little surprise, fact of life, and that's why the younger names are vital to keep the scene we created in the 60s alive today and for years that follow. The standard of musicianship these days is stunning way beyond my own capabilities and so I assume the folk scene is in good hands.

Changing the subject, but not really changing the subject, I loved Richard Whiteley, presenter of Countdown. I know I've already mentioned Countdown earlier but another story has popped into my head. He was nothing like you probably imagine. We got on so well and I used to look forward to driving up to Leeds so much to do the show for Channel 4. I appeared on Countdown nearly two hundred times and I loved every show. I even got on It'll Be Alright On The Night. It had something to do with the word 'swanked' and I shall leave that to your imagination.

On 26th June 2005 I was driving up to Leeds to take over presenting the show due to his serious illness. We were about to start filming the next morning with me in Richard's chair. TV Executive Claire Peasie offered me the job and I was really excited. I'd reached Nottingham from Salisbury when she rang me to tell me Richard had died. I couldn't believe my ears. She said 'turn your car around and go home, we're not recording tomorrow,' which I totally understood. I pulled into the services and cried my eyes out. Susie Dent from Dictionary Corner rang me and I drove to her house in Oxford where we polished off a bottle of wine in memory of a great friend.

So, do I like everybody? Did I like everybody? Of course not. Life isn't that wonderfully simple is it? I know it sounds like I do, but I don't. Are all musicians wonderful people? Certainly not. I worked with my total and utter hero James Taylor at The London Palladium and he totally blanked me backstage when I introduced myself. I still adore the man's music but I wouldn't have him round for a cup of tea and crumpets, not that he would come anyway. Never meet your heroes. I'm also a great fan of Ry Cooder.

I was following Ry Cooder at The Cambridge Folk Festival and he wouldn't allow anyone near the backstage area until he had done his bit and gone. I explained I was on next and I was told in no uncertain way to get on my bike, not a strange thing in Cambridge as it happens, and let's just say I was gently helped on my way. I never heard his set because I had to sit in my car. I still love Ry Cooder's music but I wouldn't invite him round for a cup of tea and crumpets either.

I did a British Tour with Tom Jones over three months and never met him until the final night at The Royal Albert Hall. He asked how the merchandise had gone! Yes, he thought I was the merchandise seller. When we finally met he thought I was the guy selling his stuff in the foyer. Unreal. But hey, I once tuned Roy Orbison's guitar, also at The London Palladium, so it isn't all bad. I did warn you about the name dropping, didn't I?

Touring America I had my fair share of highs and lows. Working with Steve Martin and playing Duelling Banjos or Foggy Mountain Breakdown with him every night was a total joy, one of the highlights of my life. I was warned about his encore where he took the audience out into the street and showed them how to steal a car so I was very surprised when I met such a gracious gentleman.

The story that probably beats them all was all about Billy Swann. Remember him? He had a Number One hit record here with I Can Help. I'd finished a gig supporting The Allman Brothers and joined him for a week at The Great South Music Hall in Atlanta, Georgia. I never spoke to him all week. We were on the same record label over there, Mercury, and so they put us together in concert but we still never spoke. It was my last week of touring America and I couldn't wait to get back home as the audiences didn't really take to me over there most of the time to be honest.

I got on the plane with great relief in Atlanta, prepared for a long flight home, back to my friends and family. Who was sitting next to me? Yes, Billy Swann. Sitting right next to me he was on the same bloody plane because Mercury Records had bought the tickets for us, from America to Heathrow, and he didn't say a single word to me on the plane either. We were three inches apart and I'd been on the same show as him for a week. Awkward or what? The one thing about my chosen occupation is that it's never been dull.

I went back to America to play the notorious Bottom Line club in New York, supporting Tom Rush. It was a daunting place to play and let me explain why. The steps up on to the stage from the backstage area were centre stage and as you approached them you faced a wall signed by all the big names that had climbed the very same steps. There they were, my Dad's mate Bob Dylan, Springsteen, Joni Mitchell and so on. It makes your legs wobble let me tell you. It went well, I didn't get booed off anyway, and from there I flew to a festival in Denver that The Nitty Gritty Dirt Band headlined. They were big mates with Steve Martin, thus the connection. They did the most spine-chilling version of The Battle of New Orleans that I've ever heard. I actually shivered.

I flew home and that was the last time I tried my hand with American audiences. They couldn't really get used to my London accent and I can't remember the times I was asked if I knew Michael Cain. If I had to give myself a mark out of ten for my American experience I think it would be a six and a half, no hang on, call that a four.

Working with Steve Martin, the master performer, has to go down as one of my most inspirational times, so much so that, when I returned to England, at my first concert at The Fairfield Halls in Croydon I had a slight American twang embellishing my London accent. I was saying 'man' at the end of every sentence and everything was 'far out' but I soon returned to normality when I spotted the confused faces in the audience. They'd come to see Richard Digance and not some American smoothie.

I watched Steve perform every night and his timing, his pauses and his dangerous antics were a marvel to behold. He sucked a grand piano through a drinking straw into his lungs, well at least he tried to and failed, he showed his audience the art of cat-juggling and made bizarre balloon animals that didn't resemble any animal on our planet, mainly because most of the time he didn't blow them up. Much of his act I saw in his movie 'The Jerk' and I've laughed myself stupid the many times I've watched it. Shortly after my dates with Steve he had a massive American hit record with King Tut and he was on his way to becoming the huge mega-star he deserved to be. I couldn't have worked with a nicer guy, a discerning and modest chap who exploded into a wild and crazy guy the minute he set foot on stage.

So who did I work with in America? I really have to rack my brains on this one. Obviously Steve and The Allman Brothers, Tome Rush and The Nitty Gritty Dirt Band, but I also supported Esther Phillips, the legend, in Denver, Colorado and Livingston Taylor, brother of James if I recall correctly, at The Cellar Door in Washington. The last name I recall is a certain John Hartford and he is certainly worthy of a mention, mainly because he played fiddle and clog-danced at the same time. It was real hillbilly, Cajun stuff and mighty skilful. There was something else about John Hartford that may just raise your eyebrows because the chances are you've probably never heard of him.

. Not only was he a musician inspired by the traditional music of America but he also happened to be the guy who wrote Gentle On My Mind in 1967, a song covered by both Elvis Presley and Glen Campbell, so I doubt if Mr Hartford was short of a few bob. I supported him in Philadelphia and it was so refreshing to see a guy who had written such a monster hit simply being himself, enjoying playing the music he loved to play. I see him now, white collarless shirt, waistcoat, ragged trousers and wooden clogs on his feet. I'm sure Elvis Presley never walked onto the stage looking like that.

Chapter Thirteen - As An Author

I became a member of The Institute of Contemporary Arts in 1969 and I loved mixing with other writers, every single one of them my superior. I learned so much from those who knew what they were doing, unlike myself. Actually, that may be a tad unfair on myself as I'd studied Crabbe, Keats and Patten during my English Literature lessons at East Ham Technical College.

However, it was through working with The BBC I gained my first book publishing contract with Michael Joseph Publishers and Puffin Books in November 1980. They serialised my Animal Alphabet poems, narrated by Hannah Gordon and Windsor Davis, and Michael Joseph Publishers put it in print while Puffin Books bought the paperback rights. They published a second volume, Another Animal Alphabet in 1982.

The poems are now used around the world as English teaching aids. The University of British Columbia, Vancouver; Fearon Teaching Aids, Illinois, USA; Australian Education Syllabus; Swaziland; The West Indies; India and The Oxford University Press. Not bad for a lad who left school with just four GCEs, thankfully one of them being English Language. How embarrassing that would have been? It all sounds very impressive but I sure ain't one of the most published poets in the world. I might be in the top ten thousand like an English tennis player. I'm possibly the most published poet in Salisbury where I live and that's good enough for me but that isn't exactly the entire world.

I remember being invited to the Michael Joseph Publishers Christmas Luncheon at their plush offices just off Gower Street in London, close to The British Museum. The room was full of men wearing hacking jackets and Harris Tweed socks beneath their sandals. The women wore flowing, flowery dresses from Harvey Nicholls and they all spoke rather posh. I felt a complete and utter fish out of water. I didn't know who anyone was and I questioned myself as to why I was there. It was a buffet lunch with classy wine. It was in bottles and not cans, that's how posh it was. My book had sold well, they'd sold the paperback rights to Puffin and the BBC had serialised it so I had loads to boast about, given the chance.

As people nattered about literary agents and their latest novels I edged my way to the buffet table, not really knowing what to say to anyone. To be completely honest I felt totally inadequate. I stuffed my face with a giant sausage roll and as I did so I was joined by another gentleman who nodded and also stuffed a sausage roll in his mouth. He introduced himself as Alf White and I muttered my name back with a kind of self-effacing embarrassment. He asked me where I was from and when I replied West Ham he asked if I liked football. At last I had found someone with a common interest, someone who certainly didn't talk down to me. We got on like a house on fire. It turns out this gent felt equally out of place and was grateful to find someone to talk to. He wrote under a pseudonym and he chose to name himself after a Birmingham City goalkeeper who he idolised. That goalkeeper was Jim Herriot and the man I'd befriended was none other than James Herriot, author of All Creatures Great and Small and It Shouldn't Happen to a Vet. My Mum couldn't believe it when I told her, she never missed an episode. If my Mum had known he was going to be there she would have taken our dog who was suffering from arthritis in the back legs.

The following year I left Michael Joseph for MacMillan Press, following my editor Alan Samson, who published my first two novels, Backwater and Run Out In The Country. I have to admit the two novels didn't do anywhere near as well as Alphabet but even so, I was as proud as a peacock to have been published by two of London's leading publishing houses.

My next book Today Chardock Tomorrow The World was published by TW Books in Somerset. I co-wrote it with football commentator Peter Brackley and the foreword was written by my friend and cricketer, David Gower. Having sold so many books at my concerts I wondered why on earth I was having others publishing my books and giving nearly half the income away, so I decided to publish my books myself. I've really enjoyed going down that path many times, starting with an empty notebook and ending up with a finished manuscript and artwork. I remember when my Backwater novel was spellchecked at MacMillan Press there were more crossings outs and corrections that there were words that had survived the graphite attack. I didn't get it, I wrote with a style as me and I definitely didn't claim to be some literary genius. I wrote as I spoke, as did Spike Milligan for example, and the stuffing was kicked out of the book due to the onslaught of the spellchecker. Publishing my own books I was answerable to no-one and I wrote as I chose, which I found refreshing. The only time I wrote for a publisher was when they contacted myself and Chris Kamara with a request to publish our football trivia book Footynotes. Kammy and I travelled miles around the country doing signings at bookshops north and south and we both realised we were far too busy to be at the beck and call of the publisher. I also helped Kammy write his autobiography Unbelievable and we had a great time piecing it all together. If Kammy was commentating at Southampton he would stay at my place overnight, we'd chat through things and then he was off to face the TV cameras. Kammy didn't and still doesn't ever stop working.

Animal Alphabet came back to life in 2015, 35 years after it was first broadcast by The BBC, when I licenced it to actress Nicky Kemp as a kids' theatre show. She did a brilliant job, bringing it back to life around the theatres. I think I've written 18 books in all and it's due to my daily routine more than my desire to be a workaholic.

When I get up in the morning, something I became far more disciplined about during lockdown, I write for an hour. I do that every single morning before I have my breakfast. An hour on the screen and then a bowl of porridge with a couple of cups of tea before I set about whatever else I have planned for the day. During lockdown I spent more time than usual in my recording studio. I made an album and dithered around recording incidental music just for something to do really. I knew my soundtrack income had dried up as no new television shows were being produced but it didn't really matter, it was a chance to swell my catalogue with new material for when the good times returned, whenever that would be. It was better than staring at four walls going mental.

My normal working, creative day, when I'm not doing shows, ends at 6pm when I throw myself into a hot bath where I sit and take on The Daily Telegraph cryptic crossword. My evenings are my own until I go to bed, the point at which I meditate for fifteen minutes. It's what I call having a ponder as opposed to meditating and during that quarter of an hour I make plans related to the following day and ponder upon the day that is drawing to a close. The buzz word is now mindfulness but I've been doing it for years and find it a brilliant therapy and a means of closing down the brain and getting a good night's sleep. Every single night without fail it's my ritual. During lockdown my body-clock had gone completely haywire as you can imagine. Without shows and travelling I began going to bed earlier and enjoying sunrises I rarely see.

Chapter Fourteen - Always Football

I kept in touch with my friends on the folk scene by playing football for the Folk All Stars team in south London. We played in the BBC Inter-Department League at a ground in Raynes Park and we played every Sunday morning. We were called The Blue Moon All-Stars, named after the most famous folk club in London, The Half Moon, Putney. There was myself, Ralph McTell, Cliff Aungier, songwriter Roger Brooks and Melody Maker editor Colin Irwin amongst others. None of us ever missed a game, regardless of where we were working the night before. We'd all have Sunday lunch together and then return to our respective musical worlds. I absolutely loved it and it kept me fit, apart from the two pints of lager and a fag at half-time.

The team was managed by Johnny Jones who used to look after Fairport Convention and we all loved those Sunday games of football so much I can't tell you. My first ever football injury came whilst playing for that team, when I fell and broke my collarbone. Colin Irwin rushed me to Wimbledon Hospital in his blue VW Beetle and it was a nasty break as I was about to discover.

They decided to put me under as they re-positioned my shoulder and they began preparing me by cutting off my football shirt with a pair of surgical scissors. As I lay there, in marched Johnny Jones demanding the shirt as they only had ten and a goalkeeper's jumper. Unfortunately, they'd cut it to ribbons to get at the injury and Johnny went mental. I remember going to the game the next Sunday as a spectator, my arm in a sling, and I saw my replacement running around in a white tee-shirt. He didn't have a great game and Jonesy blamed it on me ripping the shirt. He said nobody passed to the lad because he had a white tee-shirt on and nobody knew he was in our team. We still laugh about that to this day, me, Colin Irwin and Ralph McTell, every time we meet up. With one shirt missing we weren't going to last long in the league and we finally disbanded the following season. I still remember Johnny Jones saying there was no point signing up for the following season with just nine shirts. Who said there's money in football?

I got injured again when The Capital Radio All Stars, whom I also played for, played the Showbiz Eleven at Walton and Hersham's ground in Surrey in 1982. Mick Brown and I were the only presenters in the Capital team and we tried to take our football seriously, kind of. In goal for the Showbiz team was Jess Conrad, a pop singer of yesteryear who was still deeply in love with himself. He had a hit way back with a song called Cherry Pie.

I went forward when we won a corner kick hoping I could get the ball into the net. Over it came and as I jumped to head the thing Jess Conrad joined me and punched me straight in the face, knocking me clean out. I met up with Jess at Dave Lee's Golf Day some years later. He introduced himself and the conversation went as follows. Stand by because this is funny;

'Hello Richard, I'm pleased to meet you. I've always admired your work. I'm Jess Conrad.'

'Yes I know Jess, we've met before.'

'No we haven't, I've always wanted to meet you.'
'We've met before Jess.'
'Really love?'
'Yes, I'll jog your memory. Walton and Hersham football ground. You were in goal for The Showbiz Eleven. You ran out to punch a corner kick away but you missed the ball and punched me instead and knocked me unconscious.'
'Really love? What was I wearing?'

Two classic stories that typify the difference between showbiz people and musicians. We've met tons of times since then, Jess and I, and every time we do he pretends to punch me in the face. One day I know he's going to push it too far, but for the moment I remain uninjured and unharmed.

A game of football has always been just around the corner in my life. Any excuse to run around, kicking a ball, and I'm there without question. When I lived in Lyme Regis during the mid-1980s I heard they wanted to build a medical centre and so I organised all sorts of concerts in the town plus a football match on the Saturday afternoon to raise funds. It was Lyme Regis Town v Richard Digance All-Stars and was probably one of the most ludicrous games of football that have ever taken place. Is that so? Oh yes. If I told you Brian Conly went in goal, sitting in his Dad's car so Lyme Regis couldn't score against us. My team consisted of comedians Jim Davidson and Mike Osman, England captain at the time Gerry Francis, West Ham and England goalkeeper Phil Parkes, Arsenal and England's Stevie Williams, with Elkie Brooks kicking off. We raised £34,000, an awful lot of money in the 80s. I moved from Lyme Regis the following year to be closer to London as you've already read and when they opened the medical centre I never even got invited. Oh well, good deed done by loads of good friends and that's all that matters. Oh yes, and I played for folk All-Stars team at The Epping Folk Festival, a game we won easily because six of the opposition were morris dancers in full regalia. Bells were ringing everywhere as they ran around like headless chickens.

Chapter Fifteen - Looking Back

Having come this far with my story, and reading back on what I have already written, apologies for repeating myself by the way, it has occurred to me how much I leaned on other guitar players at various times until I finally had the confidence to really go it alone. I'm known as being a solo act and I always wanted to be one yet it's interesting how many false-starts I had before I kicked on and realised I could do it all on my own. I wonder if other solo acts had to rely on others on stage to build their reserve. It's something I've never discussed with other solo performers but I have a funny feeling that many of them needed propping up like me as they forged their directions and their careers. It probably worked that way around more than band members deciding to go solo.

Once in a rock band or whatever it must be difficult to decide you can do it all on your own without any help, especially if you're a drummer or a bass player I suppose. But I really have to publicly thank those who were by my side at those early stages of my job. I didn't realise until I read back how insecure I was about my own abilities. Maybe we all need to hang out with others to learn more about ourselves, maybe in more ways than one. I most certainly did.

Being alone on stage can be a very lonely job at times, particularly when you're dying on your arse at Butlins which I seemed to do with alarming regularity to pay the bills after my divorce. Luckily, I never played a working man's club in my life so I never got frightened, but I do remember feeling a few tingles when I'd made it on television and nightclubs were requiring my services. The first time I played one, The Circus Tavern in Essex, I'd never been in a night club in my life so I didn't really know what happened. I remember turning up there in my usual wardrobe of jeans and tee-shirt and not being allowed in until I'd gone to the car and changed into my stage clothes. People chatted in night clubs while I was on, I'd never experienced that before so it was something I had to get used to. You couldn't tell a table-full of party-revellers to shut their mouths while you sang a song about a couple of trainspotters.

Television had changed my perspectives so much as I moved away from the comfort, security and friendliness of the folk scene where I had learnt my trade. I was on television four times a week at one point, so every nightclub gig sold out but not many of the punters quite got what I was all about. It didn't matter, I had loads of chorus songs to cheer them up while they belched their way through a chicken in the basket and bottles of house wine.

In my television hey-day, I think in 1991, I had the busiest Christmas period ever. I did 42 gigs in a month, lunchtime celebrations included, and none of them were theatres where I felt at home. They were nearly all company Christmas parties or lunchtime bashes in the City. I had to learn odd material like White Christmas and Rudolph the Red Nosed Bloody Reindeer, thank you Johnny Marks, to keep them all happy. That was when I wrote my alternative version to The Twelve Days of Christmas, the one that was nicked by someone far more famous than me, not that I cared, it had served its purpose. Yes, I also had one song that seemed to work.

Mince pies, Morecambe and Wise
Going to sleep without closing your eyes
Giving a card to someone at school
Not getting one back and you felt such a fool

Being a shepherd in the school play
Bubble and squeak on Boxing Day
Eating a layer of Cadbury's Milk Tray
And spitting the coffee cream out

And so it went on

It was tough but I was hanging out with music mates who didn't have any work at all so I just counted my blessings and got on with it. Those damn streamer things used to get on my nerves as did the office juniors who couldn't hold their drink as they tried to pull a secretary, but I got through it all using the experiences I'd learnt from playing in the folk clubs. The money was great and I'd spent so long being skint I didn't mind singing a song about a famous reindeer to keep my very tolerant bank manager happy.

John Banks of Lloyds Bank, East Ham was my bank manager when I was a struggling teenager and I feel I should mention him because he once gave me an overdraft at a time when I really stood more chance of selling a fridge to an Eskimo. My guitar had been stolen and had it not been for John I would had to have given up playing the guitar long ago due to lack of funds, so I thank him so much for that. At least he prevented me pulling up more sticks of rhubarb with Margaret Duly as my partner in crime.

However, enduring those lucrative Christmas parties never came close to that five weeks running up to Christmas in Sweden. Nothing could have ever been worse than that and I suppose that's why I was happy to get out there and bash out songs that others would never have dreamed of playing. It really didn't matter to me.

After those four false-starts as a solo performer I'd made it so I had no problem cashing in on my name. After all, it had taken me long-enough to get there. By Christmas Day I was sick to death of turkey and mince pies, to say nothing of stupid hats from cheap Christmas crackers, but the new bank manager was happy and I always had a month's break in January, a real treat to myself for what I'd had to endure. I would take my family to nice warm places on the other side of the world before getting back on the road in February. For about ten years that was my routine.

I knew as much about the entertainment industry as you did when I made my debut on television. It created a strange paradox whereby I enjoyed the success but hated being recognised in the street, particularly if my daughters were with me. I was more interested in being a Dad than a circus freak and so I never sat comfortably with that side of things.

Before I made it on to TV with my own series in the 1980s I was busy living the life of a jobbing musician through the 1970s. Although I've mentioned some of them before, here's the full list. I supported Steeleye Span, Supertramp, Steve Martin, Cher and The Allman Brothers, and Billy Swann in America, David Essex, Elkie Brooks, Tom Jones, Cat Stevens, Joan Armatrading and then a second tour with Jethro Tull. I literally lived on the road and loved every minute. I remember in 1978 I did 252 supports in just that one year. Things would begin to change in 1979, that's when my multi-media career really began.

Life on the road changed dramatically once I'd entered the world of show business. I'd grown used to one-nighters, driving up and down the country through the night, mostly on my own, so my first summer season, in glorious Torquay down in Devon, was to be enjoyed, which I did. Twelve weeks of not going anywhere except to the beach or messing about learning to play golf on a pitch and putt course. I'd never done anything like it before, like I did with the big music stars in the 70s, doing my best to go down well with people who had never heard of me, I played all the biggest British theatres to thousands of people as a support once again, I'd more or less gone full circle. Jim Davidson was a big name then, with his weekly shows such as Big Break and Generation Game. Two summer seasons in Great Yarmouth and four years of touring around the world until my shows with Jim ceased when I got my own TV show. With that I could fill the theatres myself so we went our separate ways, my finding fellow folkie Colin Reece to take my place, only to re-unite for a tour in 2014/15 during Jim's horrendous time with Operation Yewtree. He needed a shoulder to lean on and I was happy to oblige. I owed him that. He lives just down the road from me and yet I haven't seen him for a couple of years.

His Operation Yewtree arrest was a joke. It involved a dancer in The Falklands, a 1983 tour where Jim and I shared a portacabin in Port Stanley. It was so bloody cold we slept in thermals and layers of clothing we never took off. We were more like onions than people and all we did was drive around in a land rover doing gigs and then sleep. I made my statement to Scotland Yard and wasn't the slightest bit surprised when all charges were dropped. Jim felt at the time the damage had been done through the national press so it was only right to stand by him and get back on the road, which I did. He went and won Big Brother half-way through the tour and suddenly he was back filling the big theatres once again. Job done. Love or hate his style of humour the treatment he endured was grossly unfair so it was the done thing to be by his side at such a time of need.

During my early British tours, I kept my loyalty with the folk scene where I had learnt my trade way back, starting with the double-decker bus. My support acts included Scottish folk band Silly Wizard featuring Pete Cunningham, a master fiddler, Sally Barker, now Sandy Denny's replacement in Fotheringay and my show on ITV included Paul Brady and Buffy Saint Marie, and Doug Morter joined me on a song or two for old time's sake. I enjoyed my TV work at that time but in my heart I remained a musician, it was, after all, all I ever wanted to be. Paul Brady and I did a duet of his great song I Will Be There, backed by The Burton on Trent Silver Band, a truly wonderful moment of my life. Paul came into the studio at Capital one night to plug his new album and he stayed on-air with me for the whole four hours as did Dean Friedman once. I love Paul Brady's music and could talk to him all night about songwriting. Well, that night I did. He's a musical genius and my London audience thought so too judging by the reaction.

I'd done quite a bit of work on BBC Radio 2, including eleven years of my own show. I'd started out with Bernard Braden way back and so a few people had heard of me although perhaps they didn't know what I looked like, a blessing many would say. Producer Andy Aliffe took one series, Digance Does It Locally, on the road, where I felt most comfortable. We recorded shows in village halls all over the country, including Quaker settlements in Yorkshire, potteries in Stoke, even a post office outside Dartmoor Prison. It was a huge success, my best radio ratings ever. The first on-location BBC radio series since Down Your Way some thirty years before.

What the public don't really understand is, in that game, your career is always at the whim of the TV and radio executives. They come and go like you wouldn't believe and it's the luck of the dice if they like you or not. Of course, as you get older the less the young, trendy executives want you around, and I was a victim along with everyone else. Luckily I had my music and theatre career so it didn't really bother me. I've always shrugged my shoulders and moved on as it is the best job in the world so you have to take the knocks.

Alan Nixon was my big ally at the BBC until he went off to become Programme Controller at Channel 5 and his departure was the warning signs my radio career at the BBC was probably about to end, even with the arrival of my Capital Radio show it would probably end anyway. I'd done Braden's World, 26 shows; Stop The World with Francis Matthews, 39 shows; Animal Alphabet with Hannah Gordon, 12 shows; Digance Indulgence, 12 shows; Digance Does it Locally, 6 shows; Richard Digance and Friends, 24 shows. So there you have it, 99 shows for the BBC.

You can't feel sorry for yourself when things and trends change, there's no point, much better to think you were given the opportunity in the first place and many would have loved the chance. It worked for me as even to this day it all helps to sell tickets to my shows.

The same thing happened at Capital Radio. Four years of folk programmes, 190 shows; Midnight Special, 212 shows; Sunday Funday, 24 shows; R2D2 school quiz, 12 shows, all going well until Aiden Day, who found me in the spaghetti house, moved on to pastures new and a woman called Jo Sandilands took over. She didn't like specialist music and that was the end of that stint. I was about to make my move with Jim Davidson anyway but that wasn't the point. Then it happened again years later on television.

My ITV career, eleven years of TV Specials came to a halt when Nigel Lythgoe ceased the shows without warning or reason. One minute I was with London Weekend Television and the next I wasn't. There was no phone call, no explanation, Lythgoe just didn't rate the show and I was out. I have a funny feeling I may have spelt his name wrong but hey, he'll get over it. I never realised at the time he and his ego was all about being a television personality himself. Once again, no complaints, that stint at LWT built my name way beyond the height I could ever have imagined and Nigel and I had something in common, we couldn't bloody stand each other. I still think he could have told me my stint with LWT was over. Ha, all's fair in love and showbiz.

Despite his opinion that show was a huge success, got me a BAFTA Nomination for Television Entertainer of The Year in 1988 and gave me the chance to perform with superstar musicians. A guitar duet with Brian May who played an acoustic guitar his Dad made, I joined Status Quo to do an acoustic version of the song Address Book, I played with The Moody Blues, sang The Lonely Goatherd with Elkie Brooks, her dressed in Swiss National Costume. I played with Susie Quatro, flamenco guitarist Juan Martin, while Chris deBurgh and I duetted 'That's What Friends Are For.' I was joined by Rick Wakeman, Paul Brady, and finally Marc Cohn. Can you imagine what a huge thrill it was for me to do all this stuff?

Marc was relatively unknown when he came on my show, certainly in Britain. He'd written a song called Walking in Memphis and he sang it that night. By Monday morning it was in the top twenty and the song became a total classic, recorded by Cher amongst many others. Marc sent me a silver disc as a thank you. The only other silver disc I've owned was sent to me by Chas Hodges of Chas and Dave. I once told him I would never win one for record sales and so he sent me one of his through the post wrapped in wallpaper with stamps on.

The late Chas Hodges, a diamond geezer and right good china. His partner in crime, Dave Peacock, came to my house when I lived in Debden. There he stood in The Plough pub, number one in the charts at the time, wearing a brown pin-striped suit, braces, Doc Martens boots and a collar-less shirt. He just had to be one of Chas and Dave. He said to me, dressed as described, 'the trouble is I can't go anywhere without being recognised.' When Dave and his late wife Sue returned the compliment I struggled to find their remote house near Enfield. Eventually I saw the tell-tale sign, a pair of tracksuit bottoms on the washing line with a pair of braces attached to them. It just had to be their house, and it was. Chas and I did a show with Alvin Stardust just before he died and we last met up at Dave Lee's, our mutual friend's, funeral. That's what happens as you get older, fewer weddings and more funerals. As I always say, same suit, different tie.

As far as radio is concerned I tried my hand again as recent as 2012/13 when I presented the folk programme for BBC Radio Devon, a bit of a weekly commute from Salisbury to Plymouth but I went every Tuesday because I really enjoyed it. Who was my first guest? Ralph McTell of course. Exactly 60 shows plus sitting in to present The Morning Show when the presenter, Judy Spiers, went on holiday. I was paid £100 per week, £60 of which went on petrol and £10 on my lunch. They didn't have any folk music library so I bought all my own CDs, so as you can imagine I was miles out of pocket. The plan was to try it for a year and if it worked they would pay me a sensible fee. It worked well. Then the BBC offered me another contract on the same deal, a nett sum of £30 per week. No ifs or buts, no discussions or negotiations, just take it or leave it. I left it.

My days at BBC Radio Devon were over in a similar fashion to BBC Radio Two, Capital and ITV. I wasn't surprised having been there a few times before. It's the way of the industry but still a shame because I enjoyed making that folk programme. I had some wonderful guests including Ralph and Ade Edmondson, but there's no loyalty in that dog eat dog world. Did I enjoy it? Of course. I loved making programmes but it has to be considered a short-term gig until some new boss turns up and makes life difficult. I don't do difficult so I up and go. I've always been like that. That's assuming, of course, they hadn't already dumped me. In most of the instances mentioned I was dumped. Best to own up. Yes, it hurt at the time, it dents your ego and you worry for a while as we're all self-employed, yet somehow it all comes out in the wash.

To summarise, I made 671 radio shows across the board under my own name and numerous other appearances on other people's shows, but when your time's up, your time's up. I loved radio. There's something about radio I adore, perhaps because you're teasing the imaginations of the listeners and that's quite exciting. I still often think about going back into local radio. It's just finding the time, plus the fact I think I spend enough time in a studio as it is.

I kept my hand in with documentary work, making three for Radio Hallam in Sheffield, Dying For A Drink, Down To Earth with Arthur Scargill and The Grimethorpe Colliery Band and Can Buy Me Love. I won my first Local Radio Award for my music for Dying For a Drink. I did Over The Hill, the history of The Post Office, for Radio 4 and a few others followed.

Radio has changed so much now. Most FM stations are full-on music and The BBC aren't as interested as they were in spending money on anything, least of all me it would seem. It's hardly surprising they're short of cash when you see how much they pay their TV presenters. Four million pounds a year? Blimey, I missed out there folks. I could easily present a football show for that figure.

Not one to be beaten I set up my own music production company and my incidental music is used from time to time around the world. I've done ads for Weetabix, Lux Soap, Tennent's Lager, KP Nuts and probably a few others that have slipped from my mind. They're all recorded in my shed by the kitchen door, I make a mug of tea and in I go.

Through all the ups and downs, my steadying factor through it all was the live theatre shows that I never stopped doing. It's the one thing I've always loved doing more than anything else in the whole wide world. It's not really a job, it's an enjoyable passion. Whatever went on in my strange world of radio and television I continued to tour regardless. I saw my audiences and their demographics change and doctored the show accordingly. Those who had seen me on TV expected a slightly different act to those who had seen me come through the folk clubs or supporting rock bands. They enjoyed the funny poems and a good old sing-song and my job was to please. I had to learn to read audiences quickly because it all changed when I turned my back on TV to concentrate more on my first love, my music.

I remember one elderly lady came up to me after a show at The Princes Theatre, Clacton and admitted she didn't even know I played the guitar. She'd only ever seen me making up nine-letter words on Countdown. I mentioned Jerusalem Artichoke and Sheffield Wednesday but she didn't really get it. Joking aside, that woman made me think very seriously about my direction and what I was doing. I thought really hard about what she said, that fact that she didn't know I even played the guitar. I knew I'd got something wrong and I decided to do something about it. For example, it was as a singer/guitarist that I performed to our men and women in the armed forces. They wanted a bloody good sing-song, not my comedic anecdotes. Stand-up comedians were and still are far more suitable than me in that respect.

I entertained the troops all over the world; The Falklands, did a live TV show from The Berlin Wall on Christmas Eve 1984. Then there was Cyprus, The Yemen, Hong Kong, Belize, Beirut with the UN, Germany and probably a few others I can't recall. I played on many ships too plus the submarine

Torbay. There was HMS ships Brazen, Exeter, Andromeda, Ark Royal, but my favourite has to be HMS Glamorgan.

Glamorgan is responsible for one of the funniest troop entertainment stories ever in the history of CSE, Combined Services Entertainment. Apparently, a good few years ago, Glamorgan wanted a theatrical play instead of the usual comedians and singers. CSE reluctantly agreed and the play they were sent boasts to be the shortest play in the history of the theatre. They were sent The Diary of Anne Frank. The story goes that a German soldier walked onto the stage and as he did so one of the sailors in the audience shouted out that she was in the attic. The German soldier thanked him very much and walked off stage, end of drama. I think it's the only play that has ever been sent out to our serving men and women, so it wasn't considered a smart move or a roaring success.

I went to The Falkland Islands twice and I still have a soft spot for the place. Sitting up front with the pilot of a Hercules Transporter plane, Peter Harbourne from RAF Lyneham, I still see the islands in the distance, way off on the horizon, a tiny little speck in the sea that underwent such bitter fighting and political disagreement. Even as it draws near it still doesn't look much of a place size-wise. When I first went in 1984 Jim Davidson and I were invited to Government House by Sir Rex Hunt and his wife Lady Mavis. We were driven there from the barracks in Port Stanley in a London taxi. I was more than surprised to discover Lady Mavis came from Ilford, not too far from East Ham. She poured us gin and tonics all day and invited us to stay for lunch, which we did.

FIBS, the Falkland Island Broadcasting Service, went off air when Argentinian soldiers took the islands. I am proud to say I was there when it went back on air after the war. There I sat with my headphones, as proud as any broadcaster could be. The studio was small, the kit was ancient, but somehow it was strong, representing the backbone and the resilience of a place bullied by a larger force. It's the furthest distance from home I have done a radio show. My training at Elstree Radio School proved to be useful.

So what's my take on The Falklands? Well, to be perfectly honest I didn't even know where The Falkland Islands were until the conflict began. Yes, without wishing to seem hypocritical I think it's a little odd that we have a British independent land as a kind of left-over from the days of The British Empire when he roamed the world attacking and taking over various landmasses with gay abandon. Imagine Argentina having control of The Isle of Wight and that may confirm why I do consider it all rather odd. The Empire disappeared with the sunset and there's no need anymore for The Empire to strike back. Yes, I went a couple of times, but as an entertainer with no political take on the subject.

On the way back home from The Falklands it's compulsory to do a show for the American troops on Ascension Island. Bearing in mind my luke-warm response when I played in America it was a gig I wasn't really looking forward to. I wasn't wrong. And yet it got worse. You'd struggle to find a more disinterested or a ruder crowd than American Marines in a military bar, standing around at the back, refusing to sit down.

What seemed even more daunting was the demand that we did a concert for an audience that spoke little or no English. Please allow me to explain.

The domestic helpers on Ascension Island were flown in from St Helena and they were given their own show. How on earth would I do such a show to those who wouldn't understand? I had no need to worry as they all appeared in their colourful shirts as though they were heading for a Bob Marley concert. No, no need to worry at all. They were politest of people and enjoyed every song I sang. When I performed my song Poor Poor Jane they all got up and danced and it was a sight to behold. They loved every minute and I loved every one of them as much as I disliked the swanky American Marines. I shook the hands and hugged every single one of them when the concert ended.

Next morning, when the Hercules plane took off on the next part of my journey it circled Ascension Island and tipped its wings to those below. I looked out the window and much to my surprise the St Helenians were waving goodbye and dancing as we disappeared in the distance. The Marines were probably sleeping off hangovers. So there you are, the nicest and the most undesirable audiences both entertained on the same evening. Military shows were always a mix of pleasure and displeasure.

Whilst doing a show in Hong Kong on the land-based HMS Vernon I expressed a desire to visit China, somewhere I'd always wanted to see. It was near and yet so far. I was told there was a British military base in Sek Kong and those in the know could arrange a visa if I was happy to do a show there. I agreed immediately and within an hour I had permission to enter one of the most secretive of places. I couldn't believe my luck, a dream come true. A few bumpy hours later in a knackered land-rover I'd reached the remote base beyond the eternal strips of rice-fields. It would be an open-air show beneath the stars set in the most beautiful, gardened area. I went for a bite to eat while the soldiers took their places.

I was introduced by my CSE representative and there was loud applause. I walked on stage to find the entire audience was made up of Gurkhas. Two hundred Gurkhas and not one of them spoke or understood English. That's when you realise you're really up against it. I played some Scottish jigs and invited them to clap along, which they did once they'd been given the all clear to participate. Strangely they loved the blues so I managed to save the first half of the show by belting out some blues songs I learnt during my early days in Scotland. 'The Midnight Special' 'Cocaine All Around My Brain' 'Hesitation Blues' Luckily I remembered the words to them all and the show went well up until the interval, with the politest applause any performer would ever have had the pleasure to receive after a performance.

As I sat beneath the stars wondering what the hell I was going to do in the second-half a young soldier approached with a guitar-case. He smiled and we shook hands after politely saluting as Gurkhas do. I gestured for him to open the case and as he did so I saw the most beautiful Gibson guitar, a pure gem of an instrument. I didn't have a clue how he came to own it on his wages and he couldn't tell me as he didn't speak English. It was nothing to do with me anyway. He began to play and he was good, far better than me, and then he started singing, he was good at that too, also far better than me which wasn't that difficult.

He had adapted country and western songs into his native language. I knew the tunes and so my second half was sorted. We went on together and brought the house down. Well, we didn't actually because it was open-air but you know what I mean. A wonderful musical moment that still stays with me to this day.

After all I've just told you about travelling to distant lands to perform, it's nice to get back home to a more usual existence of life on the road here. Touring is an expensive business if you're not careful. Successful bands used to tour breaking even knowing they would be boosting their album sales. It all changed in the 1990s but that's the way it was when I started out in British theatres as a support act. That was my transition, from folk clubs to concert support act.

Sometimes I want to get home
Spend a few hours on my own
With you that's true
You're the best friend that I ever knew

I was always treated well by the top acts, well most of the time anyway, and I vowed I would treat my team the same if I ever managed to do a headline theatre tour of my own. That came to be in the late 1970s in the smaller theatres and then things accelerated in the 80s as my ugly face appeared on more and more TV shows. Tell you what, despite all the success, take me back to my camper van days as soon as you like. They were the really fun days when success meant having the money to stop off at a transport café with a return gig slung in the diary. You couldn't ask for anything more.

Yes, it was amazing to travel the country in my VW Camper Van back in the early 1970s but times change. Roads weren't as busy as they are now, boy-racers were few, probably non-existent, parking was easier at venues and life was altogether much slower. Yet it all seemed so exciting, to the extent I loved the journey as much as the show. Toodling around Wales or The Lake District used to be sheer bliss.

I still see the odd Volkswagen Camper van on the road, a reminder of those wonderful days when the sun shone brightly and the Moon watched over us who travelled through the night listening to our favourite cassettes until the tape broke. They look different now, curious pieces of nostalgia on four wheels, and more to the point they cost a bloody fortune. You can't get for £799 today what I got for £799 in 1969. What did I get? Freedom, excitement and liberation, not a bad investment and it was worth every penny.

Sadly, I have no idea where my camper van ended up. The last time I saw it the engine bellowed smoke out the back as though it were undertaking its own cremation, its own final farewell up the A1 just north of Peterborough, a fitting place for it to die as I had done the same thing on stage on a few occasions in the same area. I once played in a theatre in Peterborough, The Broadway before it closed down, and the St John's Ambulance crew were treating people for loneliness.

Driving one now would scare the living daylights out of me as I happily toodle along in the slow lane, glad to be alive, only to be awakened by some steaming great truck hurtling up behind at a rate of knots that could endanger my life. Truckers own the slow lane these days and they're determined to let you know too. Some are British, others have raced over from Poland, Rumania and other countries I only used to know of through the various football teams each of them had. It's like some international Truck Grand Prix. They have more lights than a Christmas tree and if you look carefully there's every chance you'll see the driver mucking about on his mobile phone as he approaches your rear end. I'm not tarring with the same brush but some are right cowboys.

Most of today's truckers would know very little about those halcyon days of bliss and constant sunshine. Let's face it, most of them probably weren't even born when I drove for a whole day to my first distant gig at the Merthyr Tydfil factory, as happy as Larry. I still remember that first tour date as though it were yesterday. I remember the sleep-over too. Did I manage to entice anyone into my new exotic accommodation on wheels? Don't be ridiculous, of course I didn't. I wore pink, flared corduroy trousers and a tye-dye tee-shirt. Of course nobody wanted to join me. I looked like something you'd buy in a sweet-shop. Hang on a minute, of course I did. You know darn well I did.

These days I hate daytime travelling to work, particularly on the motorways on a Friday afternoon. It's a total pain, not enjoyable in any way. Driving home at night I'm fine, when it's quieter. If nothing else you need a tour manager who can share the driving and put up with the miserable person on the Satnav. That's a miniMum, as I say, but sometimes a full team is behind a show. Having said all of that I have been known to drive to a show on my own, do an entire tour on my own, particularly if I'm working on a project and need thinking time in the car. That's possible because most venues have their own sound systems so I don't have to lug too much gear around. Let me try to take you behind the scenes so you have some idea what my working life is all about.

It all begins when you are booked in the first place. In all my fifty years I have never hustled for work, I only perform where people want me, I never ask, I never have. I've always hated the thought of rejection. Lots of people suggest venues to me, particularly on social media, but if the venue doesn't get in touch there isn't much chance of me performing there. It comes from performing floor-spots in folk clubs. I used to turn up and sing in the hope they would book me but I never asked, either they offered or I went home to try again in the next folk club on my list. None of us want to be where we're not welcome do we?

Let's forget about the old days now and run you through the logistics of today that end up with me walking onto a stage somewhere or other. These days I will be contacted by email, or occasionally by phone from an agent or promoter, and so begins the routine. It may be an individual or a venue contacting me direct, but it's the same procedure either way.

First point of contact is my PA, Tracey Hollis. She doesn't work for me, I prefer to say she works with me and has done since January, 2000. She knows her job inside out, knows what I would do and wouldn't do. From that point, the date is pencilled in her diary and when confirmed the publicity is sent out. If an agent or promoter is involved it still all goes through Tracey so we know there's no double-booking. The date goes on her wall-chart and when everything is confirmed and sent out it will be coloured with a blue marker pen. Her next job is to then send what we call 'press kits' to local newspapers and radio stations around the country. Sometimes they use it and sometimes they don't, we don't have any say, but they get it nonetheless. We have to be careful not to book near another theatre over a period of time, usually about six weeks. Smaller gigs sometimes like to use a local act as a support. I never object to that but I'm not keen if they happen to be a guitar player who sings funny songs. You wouldn't believe the number of times that has happened over the years. As if I need that before I go on.

Some of the enquiries you just wouldn't believe. There's a Richard Digance Appreciation Society in Spain, who all sing my songs. They're obviously ex-pats and therefore like the nostalgia that many of my songs offer. They tried to get me over there last year for just the one show, via Portsmouth and Bilbao, and I was considering it when they sent another email telling us the show would need to be in Spanish. Spanish? Yes, some smartie over there takes my songs and converts them into a different language. That's all very well but it was a bit strong to ask me to do the same to perform for them don't you think? Needless to say I didn't take them up on their offer.

There are numerous odd enquiries, even singing at funerals, so you need a Tracey to sift through them all before your head explodes.

A lady once emailed me to tell me she had a terminal illness and was planning her funeral and wanted to know how much I would charge to perform. How much I would charge??? I'd never met the woman but I promised her I would be there at her farewell at no charge. She died literally three weeks later and her husband sent me the funeral details, a church in Bramshaw, Hampshire.

I was touring in Devon at the time. I did the show at The Watermark, Ivybridge, drove to Hampshire very early the next morning, read a personalised poem at her funeral before getting back in the car and driving back down to Tavistock, the other side of Dartmoor. It had to be done and I never let her down. The strange thing was her husband wondered why she emailed me as he'd never heard of me. Charming, you need a put-down like that when you've done a three-hundred-mile round trip. As I say, it goes with the job, when you're in the public eye people can say what they want to you, full knowing you cannot respond without getting your name in the papers.

I arrive at a theatre around 5.00pm and the first thing is to unload the car and make myself a cup of tea. Sometimes a kind stage-hand will make one for me but I usually end up making one for myself. I then walk the theatre, particularly backstage so I know how to reach the foyer to sell merchandise without walking through the audience, which isn't very classy. I check the ticket sales as it helps me decide what kind of lighting we will have for the show, intimate or full-on full stage. Then it's nice to sit down and relax for half an hour, particularly after an arduous drive of a good few hours. I sound check at 6.00pm and it takes the same format wherever I am, big or small venue.

Once plugged in and raring to go I start with my guitar sound. There are two sounds to work on, the house sound for the audience and the monitor sound on stage for me, the performer whose ears have had a serious bashing over the years. I always start with my guitar sound on stage. When I'm happy we get to work on the theatre sound. In my case it doesn't usually take longer than 15 to 20 minutes. Then it's exactly the same routine for vocals. My stage sound is the total opposite to what an audience hear as I like my guitar louder than my voice. This helps me sing in tune, hopefully, with the guitar blaring in my ears, something that works on most occasions.

Then it's time to sort out the lighting. We can't see much from up on the stage but I hate the lights being so bright I can't see a bloody thing, especially when I'm up there for two and a half hours.

The usherettes arrive and take up their places while I place a bottle of water by my monitor speakers and we're all systems go. Suddenly the venue comes alive for both artist and audience.

We're together for the evening
Together me and you
That's what performers and audiences do
Isn't it peculiar your days nearly done
Mine is the opposite
Mine has just begun

Once the show is over an entertainer doesn't have the time to relax and enjoy the memory of what had gone on just a short while before, not for a while anyway. It's a weird time for any performer when you have changed from your stage-clothes back into your civvies and you walk back onto the stage to make sure you haven't left anything behind. It's so empty the silence is deafening as you stare at the empty seats. Just a few moments ago they were cheering and applauding as you left the stage and now nothing, absolutely sod all. The audience have emptied out quicker than the water from that broken plastic carrier in the back of my camper van. You have shared a few hours together and now you're a million miles apart as they get on with their lives and you get on with yours. There's no admiring fans hanging around like there used to be, they've all upped and gone, in more ways than one sadly. Then it's time to get back on the road, first job being to find a garage as not all of them are open all-night. The carpark is as empty as the theatre so nothing holds you up. Your job is done. You have made many friends and yet no friends at all.

I remember the first time I experienced a garage that made me pay before filling up. It wasn't that long ago either, but long gone are the days when a nice man welcomed you to a garage and gleefully filled your tank for you and presented you with a strip of Green Shield Stamps while he asked you if you were having a pleasant trip. All those nice chaps will be dead and buried by now and I have to say I miss the passing of each and every one of them.

The garage was a blaze of coloured lights with goods ranging from firewood kindling to sumps for a second-hand Ford Cortina. There were shelves and shelves stacked with stuff I wouldn't dream of buying in an ordinary shop. You want an example? Where else would I buy a circular tin of sweets, covered in self-raising flour or whatever it is, for five quid?

I recall how, from the outside by the pumps, my eyes squinted at the brightness of it all. It was just like a fairground spectacle full of fun and desire until I came across the sales assistant who had finally decided to press a button that allowed me to fill my car with diesel. Yes, it must be quite a thankless task on cold and rainy nights but their choice of occupation was hardly my fault I remember thinking to myself. Is it just me that thinks they wait longer to activate your pump when it's pouring down with rain? I'd hate to think they're that sadistic. Of course they're not.

So there I stood, petrol pump thingy in hand, awaiting the clattering noise that allowed me to press the nozzle and fill up. The anticipation was electric, a bit like the feeling of Lewis Hamilton as he waits to roar off at The British Grand Prix at Silverstone after a four-second pit-stop, I don't think. I remember so well how the mood changed abruptly and a voice from somewhere or other in the distance told me I needed to pay up before filling the car. That night I realised trust and honesty had left Great Britain forever. It was long before Brexit. Try and think of any other shopping expedition where you pay before you buy the goods.

For those of you who don't travel at night that's what lots of garages do these days when it's getting late. This garage was between Swindon and Marlborough and I don't know why but I still see the face of the guy behind the bullet-proof glass. I'd put the nozzle back and trudged off through the puddles full of Arabian rainbows to pay for my fuel. Like a crocodile snapping at an antelope he grabbed my hard-earned cash and I had the all-clear to get on with the job in hand. Fifty years on the road and I was suddenly having to learn an entirely new protocol where I was at the mercy of some bloke who didn't want to be working the night shift in the first place. Oh yes, as I said, I still see his face alright. The diesel went in and I remember wanting refreshments to get me through the last part of my journey back home to Salisbury. There was food and drink everywhere, but the place was locked and bolted. I could see but I couldn't touch.

It all reminded me of a dimly-lit street by an Amsterdam canal which I once visited, where the window-shopping was interesting. My VW camper van was so embarrassed I seem to recall it turned its own headlights off.

Meanwhile, back somewhere between Swindon and Marlborough, the sadistic fun began. It was well worth adding another fifteen minutes to my journey to enjoy myself.

He looked at me through the kiosk window and I looked back at him. He reminded me of a Barcelona footballer whose name I couldn't remember. I asked what flavour sandwiches were available but his look didn't change. Not so much as a flicker. I think that footballer was a central defender, but I still can't name him. I decided upon chicken, just like a fox would in the middle of the night, and I watched as he scraped his feet across to the refrigerated section before returning with the aforementioned. I couldn't touch the goods until they were paid for so they remained his side of the glass panel. This was all so new to me, a stand-off of cowboy film proportions.

Ah yes, it wasn't Barcelona it was Real Madrid but I still couldn't remember his name.

We continued to stare at each other, as though they were playing our respective National Anthems before a game, until I broke the silence with a request for a packet of cheese and onion crisps. He sauntered off again like some wounded roadside badger. There they were behind the glass, my sandwich and packet of crisps. Sod it, I fancied a bar of chocolate to restore energy for the remainder of my horrendous journey. For the third time he set off, slower than the last time. He hated me and I didn't particularly like him. To be honest I'm not that wild about Cadbury's Fruit and Nut but it just had to be done. Every time I see a bar of the stuff I sing that annoying song from the TV ad and see that bloke's face. I'm a Cadbury's fruit and nutcase. It went with a tune very similar to R.White's Lemonade, I'm a secret lemonade drinker, apparently sung by Elvis Costello's Dad. Now there was a guy from the folk scene who did rather well for himself once Oliver's Army had arrived.

I nodded at a man waiting behind me in the rain and I apologised for the time it had all taken, but he totally ignored me, sniffing as raindrops fell from his nose whilst he carried on texting his mate.

I settled up, the hatch opened and I collected my goods feeling rather proud of myself. I checked there was no message in a bottle from the man barricaded from the world by the glass window. He'd chosen not to bare his soul to me, for which I felt eternally grateful.

Why he left Real Madrid I had no idea.

Having collected my change I set off back to the car, nodding once again at the waiting customer who once again chose to ignore my gesture. When my journey began fifty years ago it was nothing like that, I didn't want it to be anything like that thank you very much. I often stopped at the same garage time after time and I got to know some of the petrol-pump attendants. It was like some kind of a reunion.

The car door closed behind me and I was safe once again, all set to continue my night on the road with a new-found gusto from the bar of chocolate. The chicken sandwich tasted crap, soggy and laced in pepper. I slung it to the voles in the hedgerow before heading back onto the main road. I opened the crisps in the darkness and spilt half the contents between my legs. It was all par for the course, it had happened so many times before. My crotch has often stunk of cheese and onion, but in a nice way. I saved half the chocolate for later, it was the safer option as you know if you've ever tried getting chocolate off your trousers, and I didn't really want it anyway. I was simply making an awkward statement. Everyone's a fruit and nutcase.

In the good old days of my camper van I would have sat at the table in the back, placed the chocolate on a plate and eaten it with a knife and fork, then washed my hands. With a bit of luck I would have shared it with an attractive woman, he said jokingly yet sadly. Mind you, I did have my moments in that old van, it's just that sharing a bar of chocolate with someone wasn't one of them.

As I pass into the greener areas of our nation I'm always on the lookout for four-legged creatures that know nothing about The Highway Code. Many's the unfortunate badger that can be seen at the side of the road having pushed things a little too far and the same can be said of pheasants, pigeons, foxes, voles and even the odd stoat. Without question the beast that scares me the most is the deer, the leaping, idiotic deer. For starters they're always racing about in pairs, so there's a double chance of a collision. They run alongside each other like swans, magpies or Siamese children and two of them flying through the air at ninety degrees to your vehicle is a frightening experience.

I remember how excited it used to be to see a deer hopping about, strange as it may seem there weren't as many around when I started off in 1967.

That Pythagoras chappie, a Latin name that translates to 'my homework is too difficult,' has an awful lot to answer for. Deer flying at right angles didn't exist until he came along with his ridiculous theorem that none of us have had to use since we left school. The world was a much safer place until he invented the geometry set some time before 1967. That one tin divided us, rubbed us out, sent us round in circles and taught deer how to jump into the road in a perfect semi-circle or at right-angles to a vehicle. I bet the Ancient Greeks didn't smash their cars up by hitting a fallow deer on route to the Hippodrome in their chariots. Pythagoras should have taken up golf. Oh, and there wouldn't have been any road signs if he hadn't invented the triangle. Yes, he has a lot to answer for.

By the way, seeing as I mentioned emails earlier when a theatre first makes contact, the most common email these days is for CDs or books for charity auctions, as opposed to someone wishing to book me, and we obviously do our best to oblige. Last year we sent out well over 100 packages of signed stuff and guess how many emails of thanks we received? None. Not one. Once you've sent the stuff they move on to the next, bigger celebrity. I find it all very rude and impersonal but it would never stop us doing our bit. It isn't the charity's fault. I will say again that celebrities are there to often be used and abused. Not all the time of course but, believe me, it goes on. At least it keeps your feet on the ground.

Speaking of which, the day after my very first major TV appearance on The Old Grey Whistle Test I walked around Romford Market in the hope I would be recognised. Hey, I'd been on TV the night before and my head had swollen to twice its normal size. I looked the part with my long curly hair and full- length leather coat as I swanned around waiting for someone to come up to me for an autograph. I didn't have to wait long as this keen young lady rang across to me with a piece of paper and a pen. I almost grabbed them out of her hands, she didn't need to ask if I minded. I signed my name and she smiled as she looked down at my signature. The facial expression quickly changed when she saw my name, causing her to look back and apologise to me for wasting my time as she thought I was Leo Sayer. I wasn't bothered, I still signed an autograph after my first TV appearance and that's all that I needed to satisfy my ego. Leo Sayer? I'm 6 feet 2 inches tall for heaven's sake. At least she didn't think I was Cilla Black. Nice lady Cilla, very down to earth and a sad loss but I didn't look anything like her.

The smashing up of all motorways would not be such a sad loss. They should all be turned into rockeries. As the years passed I watched the A3 lose its status as the M3 pushed its way into our road atlases. I used to enjoy a slow run down to the south coast to do a gig but the M3 changed that. Don't forget I know them all and that M3 has more constant roadworks than almost all the others put together. It's always been a hazard to musicians and I quote;

'In the early morning of 25 April 1999, the drum and bass DJ and record producer known as Kemistry was killed on the M3 near Winchester by the steel body of a cat's eye which had been dislodged by a van and flew through the windscreen of the following car in which she was a passenger. The Coroner recorded a verdict of accidental death. Accidental death? A question was asked in the House of Lords about the safety of cat's eyes in light of the highly unusual incident, and Highways

England conducted an investigation into the long-term integrity and performance of various types of road stud.'

It didn't make any difference, the poor lass from my industry had become a motorway statistic.

The only motorway that can possibly rival the M3 for mess and mass destruction is the M25. What a circular dump that is, Pythagoras again. The original idea of an orbital road around the capital was first mentioned in 1937 in The Highways Development Survey. They put it off for forty years, that's how sure they knew it would be a raging success. Those of us who use it know they shouldn't have bloody bothered in the first place. By simple maths one can assume all those involved with the making of this race circuit are now six feet under and therefore have no idea of the total nightmare they created. When I say six feet under I don't mean under the motorway, more a reference to a graveyard, although come to think of it .

It is 117 miles of chaos and frustration all the way round, the slowest 117-mile journey you can make in Britain, that can sometimes take up to three and a half days. It's packed solid during the London rush-hour and its half closed during the hours before and after work. Most of Britain's roads are hundreds of years old and yet this relatively young thirty-year-old member of the road network that should be fitter and healthier than its older relations is now the most worked on and the one in need of the most attention, more so than the M3. What, I wonder, did they build it out of then, marshmallows?

A fair few musicians have lost their lives on our roads, travelling through the night. The first I recall was Martin Lamble the drummer of Fairport Convention, followed by Adge Cutler, vocalist of Somerset folk group The Wurzels. My old friend Nic Jones was seriously injured when he collided with a truck in the middle of the night. Some pop singers have met the same fate.

We all leave a gig with adrenalin flowing but it soon disappears and the tiredness sets in quickly as you clock up the miles. For a solo performer such as myself it can be much harder to stay awake. I always carry tubes of fruit pastilles in the car. As soon as the eyes start drooping I eat a whole tube in one go, not just one but, yes as I say, a whole packet of fruit pastilles all in one go. My eyes open so wide I could take to a night-club dancefloor or spot a mouse from two hundred yards like an owl.

I suppose that's how things have changed the most over the fifty years. Staying over at someone's house after a folk-club gig and guzzling home-made wine along with lumps of cheddar and sharing a cigarette in the back garden with some girl you fancied was all part of the job when I began. Then it was on to hotels when I made it on to television and carried a bigger team around with me, drinking all night and acting like children, setting off the next day with a violent self-inflicted headache. These days, it's home whenever I can make it or a simple guest house or bed and breakfast. I don't need the big restaurants for a fry-up breakfast anymore. Poached eggs on toast or porridge is fine these days with a nice cup of tea before I set off on the next part of my fifty-year trip. My show is simple, a two-and-a-half-hour bash, so I don't need a crew alongside me like I did in my TV days.

Why don't I stay in hotels? Because they now sling you out at 10.00am and I don't want to be slung out at 10.00am. Who does? Oh and I don't want to listen to chambermaids shouting at each other about their troublesome boyfriends outside my door either. Ok, you've had your sleep in our beds now piss off. That's more or less the attitude of most British hotels. We've got your money, off you go. They wouldn't get away with it in America. Mind you, I didn't really get away with it in America with my job either. I much prefer Bed and Breakfast but even then it can be a pain. Some owners are wonderful and very friendly; others have watched too many episodes of Fawlty Towers. Some object if you're getting in late. Hang on, I'm doing a show down the road and I don't come off stage until 10.30pm 'Make sure you don't make a noise when you come in, we have to think of the other guests.'

Oh yes I'm going to walk in playing the bagpipes whilst accompanied by some stranger I met on a park bench who happens to have a set of dustbin-lids he can use as drums. Maybe I'm being harsh because bed and breakfast establishments have my vote and the breakfasts are much nice than warm serve-yourself fry-ups that have been festering for an hour under lights. I'm not one for full-English breakfasts anyway. I used to call them train smashes in the old days, everything piled onto a plate and covered in tomato ketchup, or Tommy K as my daughter lovingly calls the stuff. I'm a cup of tea and a bowl of porridge or a couple of boiled eggs. I don't need all the objects that have been sitting under sunlamps for an hour or two.

The cost of staying over anywhere also has to be taken into account, especially nowadays when money is much thinner on the ground.

In a working year it isn't difficult to spend ten or fifteen grand on hotels if you're not careful. Just think, you can buy a vintage VW camper van for that and live the dream all over again for a second time. It's a lovely idea but I don't think my poor old back would be too struck on that one. Multiply that by fifty years on the road and you can imagine how much money you can waste by staying in a bed only to be woken by those two chambermaids in the corridor discussing their love-lives and what they did the night before as I choose to mention twice because it annoys me so much. No thanks. In three years, you could spend the same amount of money on a nice, plush motor home with all the facilities you need in the back. Now that sounds a bit more like it. You can get up when you feel like it and have a good scratch in private. You can laze around and not have to keep looking at your watch in case you have outstayed your welcome.

What do you do from ten in the morning when you're slung out until five o'clock when you arrive at a gig to do your sound-check? That's seven hours a day of wasted time. Some of you may suggest visiting places of interest to kill the time. I agree that seems ok on paper but when you've been on the road for half a century it isn't quite as exciting in real life as it sounds. I've seen most places of interest. At my age the most interesting place for me is my own bed. The other point is that most tours are done during the winter months. It's got to be a hell of a place of interest to walk off in a hurricane or a snowstorm. I obviously have my favourite places where I do take the time to wander around. I love the Industrial Revolution history around Ironbridge and Telford, all the museums there are well up my street. I love the fishing spots of Lincolnshire and of course there's always the natural beauty of Devon and

Cornwall. It's a beautiful island we live on but as I say I've seen most of it twice over.

Here's an interesting one. I recently did four socially-distanced gigs at The Apex, Bury St Edmunds. The show had sold out over a year before but due to obvious reasons hadn't gone ahead. It was decided to split the sell-out into four smaller shows over two days. The theatre very kindly booked me into a hotel on the edge of the town, The Dragonfly. The theatre staff were lovely, the audiences were equally lovely, but now we come to the theatre.

The first show was on the Saturday at 3pm and the second at 7.30pm. It made sense to check into the hotel before I did my 12.30pm soundcheck. Thus, my first conversation with the hotel receptionist ensued;

'Hello, I've been booked in by The Apex, where I'm playing for two days.'

'Have you checked in your car registration number of you will be fined £100?'

'No I haven't.'

I never remember my registration number and so I walked back out to the carpark, took a photo of the number plate and returned. I registered the car so I wouldn't get fined. Job done, or so I thought.

'I'm sorry but check-in time is anytime after 2.00pm.'

'I won't be here at 2.00pm, I'll be in the theatre.'

'I'm sorry, we can't check you in any earlier.'

I walked back to my car and found somewhere to have a coffee. After both shows were done I returned to the exceedingly friendly Dragonfly Hotel to book in and get my head down.

'Breakfast begins at 7.30 until 10, the bar is open between 1.00pm and 9.00pm and will you be eating later in the restaurant?'

'No, if you recall I told you earlier I'm working at The Apex so it's all irrelevant.'

'Check-out is 11.00am.'

'But I'm staying for two nights.'

'Have you registered your car?'

'Yes, I did it earlier.'

'If you drove out the carpark you will need to register again, oh and I need to take a £25 charge from a credit card.'

'Why? The room is paid for by the theatre.'

'It's company policy and, anyway, you're only booked in for bed and breakfast so you may want to use the restaurant or bar.'

'Listen, I get up, have my breakfast and leave for the theatre before the bar is open. When I get back the bar and the restaurant will be closed, so I can't spend any money here, even if I wanted to.'

'We refund the £25 five days later.'

'So why charge it in the first place then?'

'It's company policy and I can't give you your room key until you have paid £25.'

Wouldn't you think, after nearly a year and a half of laying idle, they would have welcomed customers with a smile and a certain amount of understanding? No chance. Ah yes, The Dragonfly Hotel in Bury St Edmunds, the classic example of why I prefer to drive home to my own bed after a show. Rude people and stupid, nonsensical rules.

I feel sorry for hotel receptionists in those big chains of hotels. Sadly, they're not allowed to use any common-sense whatsoever. They have defined sentences to quote to you and even if you interrupt and tell them you will not be using their facilities, they totally ignore you and finish their statement as drafted by the management. Isn't it sad the personal touch has disappeared, never ever to return? They even give the carpark control over to one of those money-grabbing companies that take you to court if you stay over two hours. We've all had enough of it all and yet there is nothing we can do about it. Hey, stop the world I want to get off.

Chapter Sixteen - Where Now?

The title of this chapter is a difficult question to answer. We are all as confused and uncertain as each other since the unwelcome visitor of 2020 totally messed things up. I think most of us are just happy to still be around to continue our journey through life. The one thing lockdown did was make us all hark back to days that weren't as frightening, that's for sure. In my lifetime nothing has been more frightening than what we have experienced recently. But, as they say, the show must go on, albeit in a different way than we had all expected. I was born to perform in front of an audience and that had happened for a while so I didn't know how my years ahead would fan out. So much depended on the nervousness of the public and the various confusing announcements that were coming from Downing Street. I realised I wasn't much good at anything else, writing songs and performing them to an attentive crowd. That's what performers and audiences do.

We are together for the evening, together me and you
Cos that's what performers and audiences do
Isn't it peculiar that your day's nearly done
Me I'm quite the opposite, mine has just begun
Yet here we are together to share an hour or two
Cos that's what performers and audiences do

You look at me and I look at you
Cos that's what performers and audiences do

We watch from here and you all sit down there
Judging if our skills are in a state of disrepair
Some of you will clap and some of you will boo
Cos that's what performers and audiences do

Up here we do one man shows, musicals or plays
Then performers and audiences go their separate ways
We get on the road again after every show
Cos after each performance that's where performers go
Motorways at midnight through the dark to somewhere new
Cos after each performance that's what performers do

With the truckers and the traders the motorways are ours
It's all part of the job driving through the early hours
Coffee at the services home at half past two
After each performance that's what performers do
That all happens later, right now it's me and you
Cos that's what performers and audiences do

I was lucky enough to find music in my life although I would have found it much sooner if I'd not wanted to be a professional footballer. To that end, as my story draws to a close I must mention a nice lady I never saw as a serious figure in my life, although she may well have been. She was my piano teacher, a lady both upright and grand, when I had no real interest in playing the piano and I have saved her mention to the end as a kind of apology to her. Her lessons were the very start of my musical life and so it's fitting to bring her in here as we all consider where we move on to in such difficult times.

Mrs Meacher, dear Mrs Meacher lived in one of the terraced houses in Charlemont Road, East Ham, luckily only a few doors down from Colletts sweetshop so it was never a wasted journey to her house. She was over two hundred years old, and my sister and I had fortnightly piano lessons in her front room that stank of damp digestive biscuits, as did Mrs Meacher strangely enough. Once again, there was no clue at that early time of my life that music would be my life as I busked my way through my lessons, never bothering to learn to read music like my sister did. I still cannot read music, not a note. Still to this day I know nothing about blackbirds sitting on telegraph lines.

Needless to say reading music was a major part of my piano lessons but it was also my first opportunity to learn to play by ear, making up stuff as I went along. Dad got hold of a piano, I can't remember where from, but it seemed to take up most of the living-room. It was painfully out of tune and before you say anything, yes it probably does account for my vocal style. I only ever played it the evening before going to my piano lesson. My sister would play what I was supposed to have learnt, I would watch and memorise and I thought that would be good enough. Mrs Meacher rumbled me as a chancer early doors, but I suppose she was getting paid by my Mum so she wasn't that bothered if I tried to read music or not. I really wish I had been more dedicated. Many of my jobs have involved producing manuscripts and for years I've had to get help from someone who can read and write the dots.

I had piano lessons for two years, until football took up more of my time when I gained a place in the East Ham Schools district team. I was a goalkeeper too don't forget, not great for delicate musical fingers. At that time, I would have put money on me following in the footsteps of local hero Bobby Moore rather than my early musical inspirations. At that point I'd never picked up a guitar, let alone played one. They were things played by early rock and roll groups, oh and my schoolfriend and Blaney neighbour Kevin Sullivan, but not me. The only thing I played was truant from school.

Thinking back makes me feel both genuinely bad and very guilty to boot because Mum was broke and she took extra evening jobs to pay for us to go to Mrs Meacher and I just wasn't interested. If only I could say sorry, I would say it a thousand times. In my defence maybe those piano lessons gave me a hint as to what music was all about. If that was the case, there is no need to apologise to my dear Mum after all.

Phew, talked my way out of that awkward moment. In my defence though it wasn't just piano lessons my Mum worked extra hours to finance. My brother needed money to go to Goldsmiths College in London, to say nothing of art materials and a pair of very tight jeans. Mum also went to woodwork lessons once a month and that needed to be paid for along with my sister's riding lessons. Ah, I really don't feel so guilty now I've cleared my mental decks.

The same could be said for Mr McDonald, my English teacher. He had to be the most boring teacher in the northern hemisphere and it took all my energies to stay awake as he made one of the class recite from the most boring books in the northern hemisphere, With The Eagles. If I'd paid more attention to him then I wouldn't have had to fork out for evening classes to get myself to college. Let's just call it a rather costly ignorance.

My final credit has to go to my cousin Margaret's husband, Mick. Mick Cook just happened to play the guitar. He'd even had classical lessons no less and he could finger pick a little which was very impressive. I was fascinated and so it was he who taught me my first three chords of A, D and E. Everyone begins with those three simple chords, the three that give you your first blisters on the end of your fingers, but hey I learnt three classical music chords, still A,D and E but classical because his guitar had nylon strings like Andre Segovia's. I was on my way to playing Johann Sebastian Bach.

I just had to get a guitar of my own. I didn't know how but it had to be done, end of.

The odd thing is that man, Mick Cook, who taught my first chords on the guitar and who was in some way related to me as he married cousin Margaret, has never ever seen me perform on stage. If you're asking why, I can't answer that question. He's just never been interested. I've only bumped into him twice since then, both times at funerals. The first was Auntie May's. It was such a sad day as Margaret's Mum was very special to me as we spent all our summer holidays at her rather posh house in Upminster, Essex. We also spent every Christmas there too, so yes she was very special. It certainly wasn't the time to talk about guitar playing when we met up after so many years. My family never had a Christmas at home, it was always off to Auntie May and Uncle Harry's house and I so looked forward to the journey there. Not having a car it was a bit of a trial, a long walk to the Barking by-pass to get a 175 bus to Barking station, then an underground train to Upminster Bridge and then an eternal walk up Bridge Avenue weighed down with Christmas presents and spare clothes.

The memory still sat firmly in my brain when Christmas 2020 arrived. It had been a hard year for us all let's face it and I spent the festive period at my daughter Polly's place in Wiltshire. My granddaughters Whizz and Ellie re-lived the magic that I recalled as they unwrapped what Father Christmas had left them. I felt Auntie May was watching over us and smiling. I hoped 2021 would be a new beginning for all of us, yourself included, never thinking for one minute the damn enemy would hang around for best part of another year.

So what happens now? It's one of those kind of questions that are so difficult to answer. I had a master plan a year ago to undertake one last huge tour and call it a day. I could have paid up my taxes and sat at home painting pictures and having friends round. It all seemed so idyllic but it was never to be. The lack of work for so long had just about drained my savings and I knew I would need to postpone my pending retirement until I was in a better position with my bank manager. Hang on, bank manager? I don't think I have one. I have a bank that you can't ring unless you fancy an international call to India, I speak to a different person every time, not knowing who they are, and they care about my financial position about as much as I care about The Eurovision Song Contest. I just thank my lucky stars I came out the other end unscathed.

I don't have too many regrets though, in fact, I'm struggling to think of any. I suppose I should have got out of the television industry and the world of pushy managers and agents long before I did. I'd made my name so I should have returned to my little inoffensive world of music earlier. It was a major misjudgement on my part. I hated being bossed around by people who had about as much creativity as a cold sausage sandwich and I only have myself to blame. In truth, I wouldn't have survived in the modern world of television anyway, the whole industry had changed with the appearance of so many crap channels and endless options for the public. After appearing at The London Palladium show on a Sunday night I couldn't walk down the street the following day without being stopped a hundred times by those who enjoyed my performance. Nowadays I doubt if anyone would even notice if they bumped into me at Tesco's. As I mentioned before I made very few friends in that world because I don't think they quite got me. It was a wonderful way to build my name, of course it was, but I didn't enter the world to build friendships because I had my own circle of friends. Strange as it may seem I made lasting friendships with the studio warm-up acts more than I did the stars on screen, Dave Lee and Bobby Bragg in particular. Just before Bobby died he told me he was drinking morphine with ice and a slice of lemon. Most warm-up comedians were better than those who were on the shows.

I remember on one occasion I appeared on 321 with magician Wayne Dobson. It was hosted by Ted Rodgers, a great guy and real prankster, so Wayne and I decided to get our revenge. It was filmed at Yorkshire Television in Leeds and there was a lot of hanging around so we went to the snooker club next door and got totally pissed, not a great thing to do before a TV show. We both had clues written on cards which helped contestants win a prize but Wayne and I swapped cards and poor old Ted, following his script, didn't have a clue what was going on but he ad-libbed his way out beautifully. After the show the three of us laughed all night at the hotel and shared a bottle of Scotch.

I'm often asked who was the nicest person I met during my days in television and one stands out way beyond all the others, Bob Monkhouse. Every time my show went out Bob would call me the next morning and go through the show with me, telling me the bits he thought worked really well. I so respected his opinion, such a kind man. Yes, Bob Monkhouse was top of my league and Jim Bowen of Bullseye took second place.

As I sit here now I'm proud of myself for always wanting to try something new. Leaving BBC Radio 2 to join Capital Radio, a smart move that qualified me as a radio producer, a move that gave me the skills to work my own recording studio. Giving up television to return to the music industry where I really belonged and rebuilding my association with the folk world. Ralph McTell has been a lifelong friend along with members of Fairport Conventions and our reunions are always joyous.

In truth I'd love to be back in the world of radio. It's where I started as a presenter at East Ham Hospital Radio, but I suppose the chances are slim. I had a brief stint at BBC Radio Devon and Essex too, which I both enjoyed immensely, hands-on with the public, but things change, times change and we all get older. There's nothing wrong with looking back and re-living days gone by, we all do it, the problem I've had with this book was getting things in the right order. Some events are hazy and others stand out like a beacon but that doesn't matter because they have all been part of my life.

Having said all of that my greatest memories are off-stage and I refer to the births of my two daughters Polly and Rosie. Polly was born in Cambridge in 1983 and when my wife went into labour I was presenting Midnight Special on Capital Radio. Disc jockey Phil Allen took over and I sped up the M11 in thick fog and got there just in time for Polly's arrival. I remember, as Polly's head appeared, the midwife asked if I could get her a couple of tickets for a Genesis concert in London. Let's just say I had my mind of far more important things at the time. Polly has been both a daughter and a close friend through the highs and lows of my life, a very special person.

Rosie was born in 1992 in Exeter and again I was performing on stage, this time at an Allied Dunbar conference at The Royal Lancaster Hotel in London. Sadly, very sadly, I missed Rosie's birth, even though I almost broke the sound-barrier driving from London to Exeter after my gig, but I'm glad to say that Rosie has inherited my bad timekeeping skills so all was not lost.

Polly is now very high up in the scientific world at Porton Down and has more letter behind her name than a postman with a hole in his sack. Rosie, an equal academic success, began her teaching career during lockdown, a dreadful time to learn a trade, but she stuck with it, on-line teaching and one to ones with special need kids, along with nervous parents, and I'm so very proud of them both.

We all want the best for our children and as far as my girls are concerned all I ever wanted them to do was marry multi-millionaires and give me half for bringing them into the world. Is that too much to ask? Apparently the answer is yes.

Who would ever have known that all of our lives would suffer such a monumental setback. Lives and jobs lost, dreams shattered and future uncertain. All I can say is I am a very lucky man to have been wedged between the Second War and The Third World War. In my opinion I lived through the best years this planet of ours could offer and I made the most of every day.

It's the little things in life that mean so much
The little things I can no longer touch
A gentle hug and kiss yes that is what I miss
I can't believe my life and times are playing out like this
As my days grow ever dark and long
I can't believe such little things have gone

Shaking hands is something of the past
Shaking heads now, how long will this last?
Just an empty room to emphasise such gloom
I have no-one to talk to other than the Moon
I hope my new friend sees me through the night
At the end of this dark tunnel it's my light

Respite I seek with each new day
A return to where the little children play
Where people laugh and sing and Sunday church-bells ring
The smiles on the faces that conversations bring
I wonder is this all too much to ask?
Is my smile forever hidden by a mask?

It's the little things we have to keep alive

The little things in life that must survive
The bustling arcade the celebratory parade
Students in the lecture hall trying to make the grade
In this time of darkness and despair
Words seem to be the one thing we can share

It's made me realise that words are strong
They help us all to right things that are wrong
The time is to believe that words will never leave
Words are always here to send or to receive
Words are always here to keep us strong
When all the little things in life have gone

Our lives were in the laps of gods so we are here against the odds
Our lives torn apart and petrified
Blessings we have counted now, we're still here and we don't know how
We're the survivors who reached the other side

The day the Third World War came
Things would never be the same
Friends we'll never see again
Lost in The Third World War

To us all the army came, no uniform no shape or name
Trillions upon trillions came to take our lives one day
An enemy we never saw brought to us The Third World War
It took us by surprise and took so many lives away

The day the Third World War came
Things would never be the same
Friends we'll never see again
Lost in The Third World War

It picked the sickly of our fold then turned attentions to the old
Those who never had the strength to fight
As they joined old soldiers in the sky with not a chance to say goodbye
Leaving us survivors the ones held on tight

The day the Third World War came
Things would never be the same
Friends we'll never see again
Lost in The Third World War

Memories of those we lost those who sadly paid the cost
Memories of those we hold most dear
Now just photographs staring back and smiling
Whispering they wish that they were here

The day the Third World War came
Things would never be the same
Friends we'll never see again
Lost in The Third World War

If you've ever heard my Two Hundred Remembers song you will recall how I once tried to encompass my entire years of growing up in verses, lots of verses, that I sang almost every night I performed. Apart from the previous paragraph regarding my daughters you could have listened to those words and they alone would have summed up y early days growing up in London., then you would never had had to waste your time reading the rest of this book. I think the words say it all and are therefore a fitting finale to my story.

It's a weird full circle that I came into this world a scared little nipper and as I reach the twilight years of my life I am, surprisingly and through no fault of my own, equally scared about what the future holds for us all, but this was the life I enjoyed between those two scary things. I don't think the book turned out too bad to be honest. You start these things and you never know how they are going to turn out, a bit like my life really.

Fruit salads, black jacks, marshmallow shrimps
Jubblies, bazookas and spangles and imps.
The kid in the class who spoke with a lisp
Boxes of Brocks on November 5th
The Saturday classified pink with the scores
Dad checking his homes his aways and his draws
Knock down ginger banging on doors
Does anyone remember love hearts?

Tortoises sleeping in cupboards for months
Catching the chicken pox measles and Mumps
Dennis The Menace and Korky The Cat
Desperate Dan in his ten gallon hat
Pineapple chunks, strawberry pips
Kissing a girl who you love on the lips
Bottles Of Tizer all taking sips

And washing up bowls full of tadpoles

Danger Man was terribly hip
Like 77 Sunset Strip
No Hiding Place, Dixon too
Captain Pugwash and Mr Magoo
Remember how his sight was short?
Here's an insignificant thought
How come the fugitive never got caught
After all those years on the run

So that the barber could cut your hair
You sat on a plank on the arms of a chair
The barber said to the grown up men
Is there something you need for the coming weekend?
A packet of three they usually said
Which went completely over my head
Til I got a girl called Jenny in bed
And I could have done with one them

One potato two potato
Three potato four
Five potato six potato
Seven potato more
Palm toffees, scoobedoos,
Reginald Bosenquet reading the news
The Animals House Of The Rising Sun
A five minute single at number one
Palma Violets, jamboree bags

Round the bike sheds puffing at fags
Flashy cars like e type jags
Though we only had a Cortina

Down to the Army and Navy store
For things worn in the second world war
Duffle bags, duffle coats
Idiot mittens with string round our throats
Sooty and Sweep, Beyond our Ken
The Michelin Man and Bill and Ben
Do you remember conkers when you
Made them hard in the oven
Flying saucers and liquorice wood
William Tell and Robin Hood
The Dandy the Beano The Beezer as well
Bing Crosby going well on shell

Putting a tiger in your tank
Watching tales of the riverbank
Rin Tin Tin, Lassie and Hank
Parker and Lady Penelope
Esso key rings, packets of Tide
Where you were when Kennedy died
Tiger Nuts, sherbet dips
Collecting cards from PG Tips

Penny bangers and two-penny chews
Elvis Presley in GI Blues
Wearing painful sensible shoes
Woodbines washed down with cream soda

Being scared of catching the pox
Hush Puppies and luminous socks
Chalk on the blackboard a horrible noise
What did you do with your Dinky Toys?

Swizzles refreshers and cola cubes
Remember when Zubes were good for your tubes
Girls in class developing boobs
And making masks for the smog
Double Your Money with Monica Rose
The very first record of Status Quo's
Radio Caroline, Tom Thumb,
Little Plum your redskin chum

Colonel Mustard, the Reverend Green
Whatever happened to Hope and Keen
Remember the ad for Ovaltine
Sheriff's badges and snake belts
Blind dates, roller skates
Bachelors Senior Service and Weights
Semolina they served at school
And clothes you lost at the swimming pool

It was always a sock you managed to lose
Even worse you lost one of your shoes
Going home and breaking the news
And getting a clip round the ear
Michael Miles, Provident cheques
Remember those National Health type specs?
The boys had brown the girls had pink

Remember those great big bottles of ink

Squints splints and Murraymints
Knackered lighters that needed flints
Waterloo Sunset by The Kinks
And going to work on an egg
Remember the horrible ad for Tunes?
Wearing flairs and pairs of loons
Five stones, we called them gobs
Bootsie and Snudge and Saturday jobs

Third pint bottles of milk
I Spy books and Acker Bilk
Thinking your hair was as smooth as silk
When you covered it over with Brylcreem

Acknowledgements

I've written a few books in my time and I've never really understood the Acknowledgements pages at the back of a book. I perfectly understand you should make reference to other books or authors you have quoted from but just listing names always seemed a bit of a worthless exercise.

Having said that, I have to admit that I have changed my opinion upon the completion of this particular book. As we have made our way through our lives we have all obviously met people who have been influences, good or bad. Our lives have been moulded around the places we have been and the people we met along the way. Had we not met anyone and been influenced by them we'd all be living in monasteries in Thailand.

So, against my earlier judgement I am delighted to give mention to those I personally met along the way plus those I never met but who were a great influence to me. It's quite remarkable how many names you need to mention when you're writing the story of your life. It runs into hundreds. The sad thing when you reach my age is that so many of them have passed on, yet I suppose that is why they need to be mentioned. They are the memories, the once upon a times, that built my personality. Yes, they are mentioned here in despatches just like war heroes.

Their listing also helps you to recall the various anecdotes and facts that you have read about within these pages. So, the following names are more than a list, they are reminders of those who contributed to my life well-lived. I have to say here that some were influences whom I never met, but they are listed just the same. My life wouldn't have taken the twists and turns it did without those I have mentioned. Most were friends and some were rather nasty so and so's who made me turn away and re-direct my life. The famous and the not so famous mingle together here but I stress that none of them are more important than any other. In some way, in some shape or form, they contributed to the life I have lived and for that, I thank them all most sincerely. I hope you enjoyed my life as much as I have. It really has been a life well lived. I wish you well and hope your life has and is a life well lived too.

Everything ends
Like a story or a song
Day turns to night
Until the next one comes along
So becomes tomorrow
More songs and stories to be told
Everything ends
But memories we hold

Everything ends
People come and go
Actors in the play of life
Support acts of your show
Few are with you always
They leave memories behind
Everything ends
But names will spring to mind

I thank them all

Steve Adams – Before he was Cat Stevens and later Yusef
Damian Aked – Folksinger from Rochester Folk Club
Phil Allen – Capital Radio presenter who stood in for me when Polly was born
Andy Aliffe – Producer of my final BBC Radio 2 programmes
Norman Armour – Blaney Crescent resident and Vicarage School footballer
Jamie Armstrong – Estate agent
Michael Aspel – Fellow Capital Radio presenter
Cliff Aungier – Friend and member of Blue Moon All-Stars football team
John Banks – Friendly bank manager who gave me an overdraft against the odds
Barrie Barlow – Jethro Tull drummer
Jenny Beeching – East Ham folk club resident
Martin Beak – Friend of my brother who gave me my first football boots
Kevin Bearman – Vicarage School football team
Ralph Bernard – Documentary compiler with whom I won radio awards
George Best – After-dinner speech
Len Bishop – My angry boss at Chappell's Music
Marc Bolan – My first support act by default
Jim Bowen – One of the nice ones who inspired my 200 Remembers
Max Boyce – Welsh folk comedian
Bernard Braden – Co-presenter of my first BBC Radio 2 series

Paul Brady – Friend and fellow performer at my Trafalgar Square performance for Shelter
Bobby Bragg – TV warm -up act and close friend
Geoff Bright – Vicarage School football team who played wearing glasses
Elkie Brooks – I was her support act for 4 years
Roger Brooks – Member of Blue Moon All-Stars football team
Joe Brown – Friend and fellow musician from Plaistow
Ken Brown – Co-organiser of Ilford Folk Club
Kenny Brown – Browns Stores, East Ham where I worked when Kennedy was shot
Bill Bryson – For whom I composed music for his audio book The Road To Little Dribbling
Dave Bubb – Tour manager and studio assistant
Carlene Carter – Appeared on my Capital Radio programme
Martin Carthy – Folk singer supreme
Dave Cartwright – Fellow songwriter on Transatlantic Records
Tony Catchpole – Blaney Crescent resident
Harry Cater – My uncle who allowed me to play his piano when I was 3 years old
John Cater – My cousin who I watched West Ham with along with my dad
Margaret Cater – My cousin
May Cater – My Auntie May
Brian Clough – A cigarette card I swapped regularly
Marc Cohn – Guest on my LWT TV show
Richard Cole – Blaney Crescent neighbour and friend of Jazz Summers
Jess Conrad – goalkeeper in celebrity football team who knocked me out

Billy Connolly - Inspiration
Mick Cook – Taught me my first chords on the guitar
John Cooper – Fellow West Ham supporter
Elvis Costello – Fellow folksinger back in the day
Roger Cross – East Ham Schools best footballer by a mile
Clem Curtis – Vocalist with The Foundations and my cruise companion many times
Helen Curtis - Friend
Nick Curtis – Friend with whom I founded New Forest Folk Festival
Jim Davidson – Got me my break into TV
Spencer Davis – Guest at my folk club
Jenny Dawson – Journalist on Stratford Express
Aiden Day – Capital Radio Programme Controller
Chris deBurgh – Fellow Supertramp support act
Susie Dent - Countdown
Ann Dex – Folk agent who sent me to Sweden
Princess Diana – A beautiful woman
Doris Digance – My Mum
Len Digance – My Dad
Rosie Digance – My youngest daughter and a very special lady
Donovan – My early inspiration
Wayne Dobson – Magician and 321 practical joker
Nick Drake – singer/songwriter and friend of John Martyn
Frank Duly – Blaney Crescent resident
Margaret Duly – Rhubarb thief
Blair Dunlop – Singer/songwriter and friend
Bob Dylan – Greatest inspiration who I never met
Dave Edmunds – Guest on my Capital Radio show
Ramblin' Jack Elliott – Carnaby Street Folk Club

Kenny Everett – Fellow presenter at Capital Radio
Ronald Fletcher – BBC Radio 2 actor who I wrote ditties for
Keith Fordyce – Presenter of Ready Steady Go
Alan Freeman – Fellow Capital Radio presenter
Dean Friedman – Close friend from New York
Sir David Frost – Neighbour in Hampshire
Tony Gale – Former West Ham footballer
Rory Gallagher – Guest on my Capital Radio show
Chris George – Member of Hunter Muskett
Gordon Giltrap – Les Cousins Folk Club, Soho
John Glascock – Member of Jethro Tull
Steve Goodman – singer-songwriter
Sally Grace – Co-presenter of BBC Radio 2 Stop The World, my first radio series
Sarah Greene – wife of Mike Smith
Tim Greenwood - Pisces
Lloyd Grossman – Through The Keyhole presenter who sat in my kitchen all day
Arlo Guthrie – Guest on my Capital Radio show
Rod Hamilton – Hammersmith Folk Club
Lucy Hampton – wife of tour manager Matt Hampton
Matt Hampton – My best tour manager
Peter Harbourne – Pilot when I flew to Falkland Islands in a Hercules
George Harrison – Baskerville Arms, Henley
Barbara Hayes – PA to Mr Bishop at Chappell's Music
Mike Heron – Incredible String Band member
George Hilsdon – Captain of Vicarage Lane School football team with the famous dad
Tim Hinkley – Elkie Brooks keyboard player

Terry Hiscock – Member of Hunter Muskett
Chas Hodges – Friend and half of Chas and Dave
Sue Holland – Early girlfriend and first vegetarian I knew
Tracey Hollis - PA
Roy Hudd – Friend and Music Hall genius
Lady Mavis Hunt – Governess of Falkland Islands
Sir Rex Hunt – Governor of Falkland Islands
Ashley Hutchings – Fairport Convention
Hamish Imlach – Scottish folk singer and friend of John Martyn
Colin Irwin – Friend who drove me to hospital after football injury
Rachel Ivey – merchandise seller
Bert Jansch – Friend and folk legend
Alf Jinks – Butcher my Mum worked for
Rita Jinks – Butcher my Mum worked for
Johnny Jones – Manager of Blue Moon All-Stars football team and organiser of Half Moon Putney folk club
Kenny Jones – drummer with my youth club band The Small Faces
Nic Jones – Fellow folk singer
Trevor Jordan – Elkie Brooks husband
Chris Kamara – Friend and football pundit
John Kirkpatrick – Friend and fellow folk musician
David Knopfler – Ilford Folk Club story
Mark Knopfler – Ilford Folk Club story
Les Lacey – Dad of my schoolfriend who took me fishing for the first time
John Lacey - Schoolfriend
Ronnie Lane – Small Faces member
Christine Lawrence – First girl I fell in love with

Bill Leader – Producer of Pisces album
Alvin Lee – Played on my Commercial Road album
Dave Lee – Close friend and wonderful comedian who I miss so much
Chris Leslie – Fairport Convention
Jon Lord – Played on my Commercial Road album
Adrian Love – Capital Radio presenter, my first programme as a radio producer
Georgia Rose Lucas – daughter of Sandy Denny
Jo Lustig - Manager
Nigel Lythgoe – LWT man who stopped my TV specials whom I hate to mention
Dougie MacLean – Friend and Scottish folksinger who wrote Caledonia
Laurie Mansfield – Signed me to International Artists
Johnny Marks – Chappell's Music
Steve Marriott – My first guitar story and leader of my youth club band The Small Faces
Alvin Martin – West Ham footballer
Steve Martin – Huge comedy influence whom I supported in America
John Martyn – Minard Road, Glasgow
Francis Matthews – Presenter of my second BBC Radio 2 series
Shelagh McDonald- Scottish folksinger
Cathy McGowan – Co-presenter of Ready Steady Go
Paul McNeill – Partner of Linda Peters
Ralph McTell – Close friend and inspiration
Margaret Meacher – My piano teacher
Spike Milligan – Paris Theatre, London whom I never met
Joni Mitchell – Guest on my Capital Radio show

Bob Monkhouse – Closest friend I made in the TV industry
Michael Moore – Darts player and fellow inventor of Mickey Marathon
Doug Morter – Close friend throughout my life since our schooldays in Plaistow
Drew Moyes – Glasgow Folk Centre
Liz Murray – Hatchet Pub landlady
Jimmy Nairn – P&O Cruises
Alan Nixon – My BBC Radio 2 producer of Animal Alphabet and other series
Phil Ochs – Inspiration whom I never met
Des O'Connor – Countdown presenter
John O'Connor – Pisces
Tom O'Connor – P&O Cruises
Roy Orbison – London Palladium encounter where I tuned his guitar
Peter Osgood – First after-dinner speech I wrote and the man who introduced me to George Best
Ian Paice – Fishing companion at Henley and Deep Purple drummer
Joe Pasquale – Friend and my support act through my TV days
Dave Peacock – Friend and half of Chas and Dave
Claire Peasie – Yorkshire Television
Dave Pegg – Fairport Convention
John Renbourn – Pentangle guitarist
Rachel Riley - Countdown
Ted Rodgers – 321 presenter
Brian Rust – Capital Radio presenter
Sally Sago – Cruise entertainment officer
Ric Sanders – Friend and Fairport Convention

Jo Sandilands – Boss at Capital Radio
Steve Scarsbrook – Tour bus driver
Phillip Schofield – Capital Radio presenter same time as me
Roger Scott – Capital Radio presenter
Martin Simpson – Fellow folk musician
Cathy Smith – Wife of cricketer Robin Smith
Mike Smith – Close friend and Capital Radio presenter
Robin Smith – Friend and England cricketer
Mr Snow – Blaney Crescent resident
Gillian Snow - Blaney Crescent resident
Keith Snow - Blaney Crescent resident
Phillip Snow - Blaney Crescent resident
Charles Sodeau – True Form shoe shop manager
Joe Stead – The Bus Folk Club
Jeff Stelling – Countdown presenter
Al Stewart – Friend and fellow folk musician
Percy Stitson – My schoolteacher
Bridget St John – Folk musician
Marian Stokes – Bluebell Folk Club
Rod Stokes – Bluebell Folk Club
Daisy Sullivan - Blaney Crescent resident
Danny Sullivan - Blaney Crescent resident
Kevin Sullivan - Blaney Crescent resident
Patsy Sullivan - Blaney Crescent resident
Redd Sullivan – Troubadour Coffee House
Jazz Summers – Manager and close friend
Billy Swann – Supported in Atlanta, Georgia
Bobby Tambling – After dinner speech
James Taylor – London Palladium
Livingston Taylor - Washington

Barbara Thompson – Bus Folk Club, Stratford
Linda Thompson – dear friend and top singer
Richard Thompson – Friend of many years
John Townsend – Battersea Folk Club
Roger Trevitt – Member of Hunter Muskett
Jethro Tull – Influential in so many ways
Dave VanDorn – Ilford Folk Club
Bob Voice – International Artists
Carol Vorderman – Great North Run
Rick Wakeman – Friend of many years
Johnnie Walker – Edinburgh Festival
Roy Walker – P&O Cruises
David Waters – Blackpool Folk Club
Linnie Watkins – The Hatchet, Sherfield English
Jack Westwood – Scots friend who took me to Minard Road
Alf White – The vet
Richard Whiteley – Countdown presenter
Debbie Whiteman – Ex wife
Ray Whiteman – Ex wife's previous husband
Martin Windsor - Troubadour
Colin Williams – Blaney Crescent resident
David Williams – Son in law
Dick Williams – Uncle Dick from Leytonstone
Ellie Williams – My granddaughter
Isabelle Williams – My eldest granddaughter
Keith Williams – Blaney Crescent resident
Polly Williams - Daughter
Winnie Williams – Auntie Winnie from Leytonstone
Christina Williamson – East Ham Folk Club
Robin Williamson – Incredible String Band

Jon Wyse – Wandsworth Folk Club

Printed in Great Britain
by Amazon

64718638R00183